THE MATERNAL FACE OF GOD

THE MATERNAL FACE OF GOD

The Feminine
and Its Religious Expressions

Leonardo Boff, O.F.M.

Translated by Robert R. Barr
and John W. Diercksmeier

COLLINS

Collins Religious Publications
8 Grafton Street, London W1X 3LA

Collins Dove
PO Box 316
Blackburn, Victoria 3130

Collins New Zealand
PO Box 1
Auckland

Originally published in Portuguese as *O rostro materno de Deus: Ensaio interdisciplinar sobre o feminino e suas formas religiosas* in 1979 by Editora Vozes Limitada, Petropolis, Brazil

First published in English in the United States of America by Harper & Row Publishers, Inc in 1987

This edition first published in Great Britain by Collins Religious Publications, London in 1989

ISBN 0 00 599197 8

Printed and bound in Great Britain by
William Collins Sons & Co Ltd, Glasgow

For my sister and brother, Maria Lina and Clodovis, of the Order of the Servants of Mary, that they may succeed in living the spirit of the Magnificat.

God is Father,
but, especially, Mother.

John Paul I

Contents

Introduction: Theology and the Feminine

SOCIAL AND RELIGIOUS IMPACT OF THE FEMININE

The male-female relationship is undergoing a shift in its center of gravity. Throughout our society, a patriarchal culture based on the predominance of male rationality is giving way to a more personal model centered on the individual and on personal equilibrium. This evolution brings a measure of relief to women, reduced for centuries now to sexual categories (single, married, widowed, available for marriage, and the like). Industrial society has, of course, exploited women's present strengths, but it has also encouraged the development of their further potential. Women have learned new skills. Demonstrating leadership and competence, they have entered areas heretofore regarded as the exclusive domain of men. Today there are few fields of endeavor in which women's contribution is not welcome.

Women's new involvement and activity has provoked widespread reflection. Meanwhile, the equalization process continues apace, threatening the foundations of a dying patriarchal culture. The critical, genuinely revolutionary challenges are manifold. We need only consider the mystique of rationality, regarded for the last four centuries as the key to understanding the world. Rationality implies objectivity. It stands in contrast to emotion, subjectivity, sentiment, and intuition, which are all seen as impediments to reliable analysis. The ideal is pure rationality, with a minimum of subjectivity. But in our culture, where rationality reigns supreme, the male is generally identified with rationality, the female with irrationality or emotion. Thus, the representation of rationality as the ideal implies a depreciation and devaluation of the feminine. After all, the irrational, the intuitive, and the emotional are of relatively little value in the present scheme.

This discrimination has long been traditional in Western theological thought as well. Saint Augustine argued, "It is the natural order among human beings that women be subject to men and children to their parents. For it is a matter of justice that the weaker reason be subject to the stronger."[1] Saint Thomas Aquinas agreed: "Woman is naturally subject to man, inasmuch as in man the discretion of reason predominates."[2]

We note that both of our theologians speak in terms of "nature," thus ontologizing and rendering immutable situations that are historical and changeable. The unfortunate result, with its legal repercussions even today, is that women are perceived as lacking in rationality, and placed on the same level as children and the mentally deficient.

Recent decades, however, have seen a devastating assault on rationality and its airs. The "nonrational" has come into its own. It has a value. It is not opposed to rationality, but is something different. Our culture is engaged in a tremendous reappraisal of the intuitive, of the feminine, of everything affecting or concerning subjectivity. We might well say that we are entering the age of Sophia, the feminine archetype with characteristics calculated to integrate masculine and feminine.

Due to the values incarnated in the feminine, due to the struggles of women to be recognized as persons and accepted as different without bias and without any toleration of the dominion of one person over another, and due to the new equality that women are achieving in social relationships, the question of the feminine has acquired great importance in our time. The feminine is becoming a focus of study and reflection in every area of anthropological, historical, sociological, psychological, and religious research. The vast majority of these discussions are oriented toward strengthening this emerging feminism. To be sure, there are still those who balk, stubbornly defending the patriarchy that yet rules society despite the multiple onslaughts of its adversaries.

Every indication exists that we are witnessing the emergence of one of the key archetypes of humanity's collective unconscious: the anima, in all of its multiple manifestations. A like event occurs only once every several thousand years. And when it occurs, the axis of history suffers a universal shock, as men and women once more produce a new self-interpretation and redefine their interpersonal relations. Within the institutional framework of the powers that be, the image of God flashes forth with a new face.

THE THEOLOGICAL FACE OF THE FEMININE

Theology is by definition a discourse directed and regulated by faith. Faith is a manner of living and thinking in which the entire world, and all human experience, is related to God. Faith sees, interprets, and lives all things in the supreme light of God.

Our subject, the feminine, has its theological facet. How does the feminine reveal God? And from the opposite direction, how is God revealed in the feminine? In others words: (1) How is the feminine our path to God? and (2) How is the feminine God's path to us? How can we know God through knowing the feminine, and how can God be present in feminine traits? Can we regard God as our Mother as well as our Father?

The tradition of our faith has concentrated its entire feminine content in Mary, the mother of Jesus. All of the numinous, luminous potential of the feminine is made concrete in her, so that we see her simply as "Our Lady," virgin, mother, wife, widow, queen, wisdom, God's tabernacle, and so on.[3] But the feminine has almost never been regarded as a way to God. In Christian culture as we have it, the proposition that God is our Mother goes against the grain. And yet, if we mean to take the emergence of the feminine in our culture as seriously as it deserves to be taken, we cannot evade this issue. Is it not a sign for Western culture that Pope John Paul I could state, in public audience, that while God is indeed our Father, God is our Mother even more? Theology, like any science or discipline, must examine the relevant themes of its time. True, by virtue of its own internal logic, its proper manner of threading its discourse, it is an autonomous science. But it depends for its subject matter on culture, society, and historical situations. These, after all, are what challenge it, thereby imposing a direction on its reflections.

Theology must be in a position to seize upon the analytical texts presented by other sciences and read them from its own perspective. In the area of the feminine as elsewhere, theology's consciousness will be either naive or critical. Theology betrays a naive consciousness when it examines its subject matter—here, the feminine—without benefit of an antecedent breach with the unspoken notions that hold our culture in their viselike grip: for example, when it accepts the prevailing ideology of women and the feminine, the patriarchal notion that wants to repress the feminine or relegate it to dependency on the masculine. From this inadequate point of departure, theological reflection may of course be epistemologically correct—in conformity with the grammar and syntax of its language—but its faulty social context or misguided cause will prevent it from being anything more than a conservative, or at best a progressive or "enlightened," thinking.

On the other hand, theology can profit from a critical consciousness, from submitting its subject matter to previous analysis at the hands of other sciences. Theological discourse is not immediate. It is mediated by the study of the human. It is not a "first word," but a "second word." It explores material already elaborated by the positive and human sciences. Only thus can theology avoid confusing and mystifying the reality under its consideration. Only thus, then, can it shed any light on the topic before us.

It will scarcely be indifferent to theology, however, which type of analytical text it takes up. Science does not produce homogeneous results. It has many methods of research, and many different interests moving it to engage in this research. The outcome is a variety of types of findings. In selecting the sort of text it means to read, theology will be guided by faith. Faith respects the autonomy of rationality. But it does not renounce its own identity. It imposes certain values, and chooses the methods that seem most likely to detect these values and to sweep aside what it regards as nonvalues and false positions.[4] For example, faith will direct theology to give preference to scientific texts that present women as persons, beings endowed with their own reflexive identity. It will prioritize texts that express the feminine as a structure at once autonomous and engaged in a reciprocity with the masculine. Conversely, it will ignore texts that insist on reaffirming traditional prejudices against women, as for example those that conceive woman as a mere appendage of man—Saint Thomas's *vir occasionatus*—or that present women as dependent and inferior. Theology's mandate requires its practitioner, the theologian, to accept the results and adopt the methods that are consonant with the intentions of faith—to accept, then, in the case of women, findings that are compatible with respect, liberation, a communion of brothers and sisters, everything opposite from discrimination and domination in any form.

Our first task, then, must be to appropriate available scientific findings on the subject of women and the feminine. We must have critical, analytical, authentically scientific and objective intermediate material with which to work. With this in hand, we can then undertake a theological reflection on the feminine element in men, in women, in Mary, and in God.

We shall attempt a recasting of the standard treatment of Mary by reflecting on the nature of the feminine.[5] We think that the feminine constitutes a sufficiently broad horizon within which to place the mystery of Mary, in whom we see the feminine as achieving its totality, including its final stage in God.

The task we set before ourselves is risky, and the theoretical and practical pitfalls numerous. Our reflections can constitute no more than literally an essay. We make no attempt to impose our position. We submit it to the better judgment of our critics and of the Church itself. The new knowledge that we use, and the change that society is undergoing where women are concerned, constitute an invitation to revitalize and recast traditional perspectives of faith on Mary. If theologians will not assume this task, who will?

At the same time, we are aware, and we acknowledge, that the individual who here writes on the subject of the feminine is a male religious. He knows he labors under an inherent limitation. It is not often that a male acknowledges that he writes as a male. Most theoretical works represent their author simply as a human being, thereby concealing the intrinsic limitations of the author's gender. A view of the feminine formulated by a male will forever be a male's view, not a female's—even though the feminine is not women's monopoly, but part and parcel of men's reality as well. We are probably not far from the day when women will develop a systematic Mariology in light of the feminine as realized both in themselves and, in its perfection, in the Mother of God and our Mother. Surely that image of Mary will be shaped very differently from the one we are about to sketch in the following pages. But until that day comes, we offer the best that we have.

I. THE PROBLEM: THE FEMININE AND MARIOLOGY

1. The Organizational Principle of Mariology

MARY IN THE EYES OF FAITH

Christian faith confers on Mary an unequaled, transcendent importance. Her eminent dignity is based on her privilege of being the Mother of God incarnate—not only in a physical, biological sense, but also, and especially, in the sense of her personal, free commitment, her acceptance of God's invitation. Her motherhood is virginal, perfect, and complete. But not even her virginity can be understood as a mere physical, biological fact. Rather, it is the expression of a freedom fully consecrated to God. But a virginity and motherhood that are the expressions of a total commitment to God presuppose an existence free from all contamination by the original and personal sin that traumatizes and splinters human existence, and free from this sin from the earliest beginnings of this privileged individual's existence. Thus, Mary comes to be venerated in a special way by virtue of her immaculate conception. Mary incarnates the new creation that God is forging from the old. She likewise embodies what the Church ought to be as a community of the redeemed. Only in Mary does the Church actualize its archetype and its utopia. Only in Mary is the Church completely Church. As the most eminent member of the Church, then, she occupies a corresponding place among the links of the salvific mediation binding all men and women: she is venerated as Mediatrix of All Graces, for in union with the Holy Spirit and her Son she is full of grace. Thus, Mary is associated with her Son, the Holy Spirit, and God himself in such wise that she is raised to the level of Co-Redemptrix. Finally, the perfection of her life is crowned in death, and she is taken up into heaven in body and soul, thereby anticipating the destiny of all the just and making concrete what must be the transformation of the entire universe in the Reign of God.

A SINGLE MEANING IN ALL OF THESE PRIVILEGES?

So far, we have simply presented the facts of faith about Mary. The people of God preserve her memory in worship and devotions profoundly rooted in their Catholicism. And yet, it is not only the memory of the great things God has done for her (Luke 1:49) that the faithful keep alive. They also attempt to translate the salvation accomplished in Mary by following and imitating her. Our Mother achieved her greatness by walking a narrow path of suffering, humility, and anonymity.

But then this same piety, in moments of reflection and light, asks itself: Are all of these Marian facts and events mere isolated phenomena? Or are they all linked, so that they form a single fabric? Do they perhaps contain a single meaning? Do they perhaps point to a single divine plan? If so, might it be possible to identify that meaning and outline that plan?

It is the task of the systematic reflection on faith—theology— to search out the unity that connects salvific events, however heterogeneous these events may appear. Faith is convinced that nothing happens by chance. After all, nothing escapes the dominion of God. In other words, God is not only absolute free will—which is why God's reasons need no defense—but also supreme wisdom and utmost rationality. And rationality presupposes oneness, unity, harmony, and meaning. God's ways are not our ways, granted, and Paul speaks of a logic of the cross (1 Cor. 1:18). But neither are God's ways simply meaningless. The human heart will never surrender to the non-sense of the arbitrary, nor will faith ever adore a mystery so dark as to be without any spark of light at all. No, all things are vehicles of a concrete Meaning—a meaning not always seen at first glance, to be sure, but a meaning accessible to devout reflection and human inquiry that has shed its possessiveness and self-seeking. As a discourse directed and regulated by faith, theology accepts the task of unveiling the structure of meaning underlying seemingly opaque facts. Theology puts on display the invisible, consistent reality whose visible expressions are historical events.

And so we must attempt to search out the primary, basic, radical notion proposed by the divine wisdom in Mary's regard. From what inner core do all Marian facts and events proceed and have their meaning? What does God seek to communicate to us through the Blessed Virgin Mary? What does God reveal to us about human beings and their destiny in the marvels worked in Mary? The answer, we think, reveals a new face of God.

If the fact that Mary was a woman has any importance, what face did God wish to show us through the element of the feminine? How does the feminine lead us to God? What is the ultimate meaning of the feminine for salvation, for humanity, for God? All of these questions are raised by an intelligent faith, a *fides quaerens intellectum*. We cannot afford to ignore them in our reflection.

Concretely, the fundamental mariological principle must reside in the feminine. In other words, with the feminine as our basic anthropological category, we shall be able to systematize all of the Marian facts and events that theological reason can detect, all about Mary that our faith confesses. We shall then attempt to ground our position in a new hypothesis, one that will seem strange in a context of the mariological tradition. Finally, we shall press our hypothesis into service as the prime axis of our meditation on Mary and her mystery.

Before addressing ourselves to the category of the feminine, however, it will be in order to survey the various mariological syntheses that are current in theology today.

THE UNIFYING CORE OF MARIOLOGY

A long, involved theological discussion on the unifying principle of God's secret plan for Mary, and through her for all of us, is still anything but moot.[1] Following are some of the mileposts along its route.

A *first approach*, out of a sacred, religious respect for mystery, simply refuses to inquire into God's secret plan for Mary. Who are we to seek to penetrate the thoughts of God? Theology, we are told, sometimes asks too many questions. In doing so it risks transforming itself into a refined way of profaning and desacralizing reflection upon God—a risk, we are warned, to which it has sometimes succumbed. Theology must never forget: it can only think *from* God. To enunciate propositions on the divinity in a prideful way, in a spirit of omnipotence, is really only atheism in disguise.

According to this first position, then, theology has the humble task of setting forth the salvific events as they occurred and as they were communicated by God. Thus, for example, this position asserts that Mary belongs to both Testaments, that she is the bridge between them; that as history developed, certain events occurred that reinforce and confirm her function in human salvation; and that these events make historical God's plan. This is the only way in which it falls to theology to consider the Immaculate Conception, Mary's perpetual virginity, her divine and human motherhood, her humble participation in Jesus' life, her death and assumption into heaven, and, finally, her mysterious presence among the people of God, whose veneration for her never ceases to grow.[2]

This approach has its value. Part of its utility consists in keeping theology aware of its limits, of the artificial nature of its constructs. There is no guarantee that our theological construct of reality coincides with God's plan. After all, Mary is essentially time-bound. She lived a pilgrim's life of faith and hope. She became the Mother of God. Through the cross, she became Co-Redemptrix of all humanity. She had to wait for glory. And this is all we know.

However, we do not do justice to these facts if we limit ourselves to naked observation of them. They cry out for reflection. They point to a meaning of some kind. And the intellect does not rest, nor will love keep quiet, until the thread that relates these facts has been identified. Theology is not content with raw knowing. It is driven to reflect on what it knows. It strives to transcend that historical positivism that is happy with simply stating and enumerating facts without shedding any further light upon them. Indeed, theology must be involved in the production of the light in which it reads the facts, for that light shines forth from knowledge and meaning itself.

A *second approach* argues that while it is perfectly legitimate to seek the unity of meaning of the Marian events, there is no need for a specific treatise on Mariology. Mary never lived in or for herself. Mary was a woman ever at the service of others—of God, of Christ, of redemption, of the Church, of the ultimate meaning of history. From this perspective Mary can never be the subject of a theological consideration of her own. Her place is in the other theological treatises. When we speak of God and God's plan, Mary is there, sharing the plan as it was before sin entered the scene, side by side with her incarnate Son as God's first love and first thought. When we speak of Christ, she is there as the mother of that Christ, Co-Redemptrix and Co-Mediatrix with her Son and Savior, in whom the work of human deliverance has been fully realized. When our discourse is on the Church, Mary is there as the prototype of what the Church must ever strive to be. When we speak of grace, she is there in fullness of grace, and as the full and perfect sacrament, after Christ, of the presence of God in the world. When we consider theological anthropology, Mary is there as the first new being of the creation renewed by God, recapitulating the eschatological history inaugurated by Christ. When we reflect on eschatology, she is there as the anticipation of the definitive reality of the Reign of God, when both matter and spirit will finally be transformed.

This is how Mary was thought of during the Middle Ages. The Second Vatican Council adopted the same approach.[3] In our own day, Latin American theology has consecrated this avenue. In all of its principal themes, theology must make some mention of our Lady as the creature who realized to a supereminent degree whatever values are being discussed or meditated.

This focus, too, has undeniable advantages. It respects the historical meaning of Mary's humble service. Mary is present everywhere, always discreetly but always completely.

However, this unsystematic approach to Mary on the part of theology runs the risk of omitting part of what faith confesses in her regard. Her theology can become impoverished, and fail to appreciate the wealth of revelation abiding in Mary. Mary does more than merely enter into and respond to any theological questions that might arise. She is a fundamental topic in her own right. She must be explored because in her, God is encountered to a depth surpassed only in Jesus Christ.

A *third avenue* at last makes bold to undertake a systematic reflection on Mary, and develop a positive mariological treatise. It establishes Mary's divine, free, personal motherhood as the unifying principle of all Marian facts and events.[4] Her divine and human motherhood, her concrete, free acceptance in faith of the divine invitation (she conceived because she believed), is indisputably the core of her mystery. All of her other mysteries and privileges revolve about this central point. Her virginity and motherhood are not simply independent realities, then. Her motherhood is repeatedly virginal: it is precisely as virgin that she is also mother. Her virginity is at the service of a motherhood that she fully embraces and totally directs toward the Messiah. Owing to her supreme dignity as Mother of God incarnate, Mary was immaculately conceived and is full of grace. Her motherhood gives her such a place in the life and lot of her Son that she shares to the highest degree the redemption he brought us: Mary is supereminently redeemed. From her physical motherhood likewise derives her spiritual motherhood of all of the brothers and sisters of her Son, and in virtue of this extended motherhood she participates actively in the deed of redemption in the form of a comeritorious mediation of every grace that is ever bestowed. Finally, as the mother who shares in the glory of her Son, she enters heaven with him, body and soul. Mary is the splendor of Christ.

We have struck an exceedingly rich vein. This is the classic mariological approach, the avenue selected by nearly all theologians of yesterday and today. But scarcely any of these thinkers ever reflect on Mary as a woman. It is precisely as a virgin mother that she is incorporated into the salvific process of all humanity. Salvation and God's liberating intervention in the world have feminine, maternal traits. God's purpose in associating Mary with God's plan is to place the feminine in a crucial role in the economy of the redemption and divinization of humanity.

A *fourth route* to a harmonization of the Marian mysteries in the light of a single systematizing principle takes as its point of departure Christ's central place in the eternal and universal plan of God. Mariology follows in the footsteps of Christology.[5] Christ, who is at once God and a human being, participates supremely in God and God's divine glory. Mary, in union with

Christ, is second only to Christ in this participation. This is because as mother of Christ she is associated with him in all fullness and intimacy. Now Christ's whole salvific reality will be Mary's, by participation and derivation. (Mary was not hypostatically assumed by the Word in history, as Jesus was.) Therefore, she is Co-Redemptrix, Co-Mediatrix, transfigured in heaven, and so on.

This structure is not without its grandeur. But it, too, sidesteps the crucial fact of the feminine, virginal, spousal, and maternal element in the divine deed of salvation.

A *fifth approach* situates Mary in the Church, as the prototype of that Church.[6] All the ideals of the Church are realized in Mary. The Church should be holy and immaculate: Mary is such, and to the ultimate degree. The Church is called to a life so intimately united with Christ as to constitute one body and one life with him: Mary was one body, one life, one love with Christ, and this to perfection. The Church is invited to share in the redemptive work of Christ as universal sacrament of salvation: Mary is our Co-Redemptrix par excellence, our total sacrament of salvation, in fullness of grace and in the materialization within her womb of the radical sacrament of salvation, Jesus. The Church must continually share in Jesus' lot of death and resurrection: Mary shared in the cross of her Son completely, and this is why she has already risen to everlasting glory. The Church is the sacrament of the Holy Spirit abiding within it: Mary actually became the Spirit's spouse.

As we see, the potential for a theology of the Church is actualized here through being made historical in Mary. However, despite the impact of a reciprocal relationship of *Virgo Maria* and *Virgo Ecclesia,* or *Mater Dei* and *Mater Ecclesia,* we cannot disregard the profound differences between the two analogues. The Church not only carries the risen Christ and his spirit in its womb—it can also offend Christ and his spirit, through sin and a hesitating conversion from sin, which was not the case with Mary. An exorbitant identification of Mary with the Church either idealizes and dehistoricizes the Church, or blurs Mary's crucial function in behalf of a Church at once sinful and saintly, thus falling short of an adequate account of her unique position in salvation history.

A *sixth avenue,* charged with interdisciplinary and ecumenical implications, places mariological reflection in the context of the Nicene Creed—the articles of faith common to all Christians, Catholic, Orthodox, and Protestant.[7] The Creed opens with the word *credo,* "I believe." Our backdrop is a horizon of faith, without which any credal concept loses its meaning. This sixth approach to a theology of Mary places the "I believe" on Mary's lips and in Mary's heart primordially and preeminently. Mary is the prototype of all believers. As she believed, so was it done unto her, and now she is God's Mother (Luke 1:28–38).

In light of the first article of the Creed—the assertion that there is but one God, the creator of heaven and earth—theology can reflect on Mary's place in God's salvific plan, and can address the matter of her predestination.

The second article—the confession of Jesus Christ as the one who for us and our salvation came down from heaven and by the action of the Holy Spirit and the Virgin Mary became a human being like ourselves—explicitly places Mary in a relationship of salvific instrumentality vis-à-vis all human beings, with the Holy Spirit and Christ the "only Son of God," of whom she is the mother.

The third article—Jesus' passion and resurrection—provides the context for a theological reflection on Mary's co-redemption, her communion with Jesus her Son, and her sharing in his lot (John 19:25–27).

In light of the fourth article of the Creed—"I believe in the Holy Spirit"—the theologian can underscore God's unfailing providence in Mary's regard. Mary was never abandoned by the Holy Spirit, but was associated forever after with the dynamics of redemption and union fostered in humanity by the Spirit down through the ages.

The fifth article, in which we profess our belief in the holy, catholic Church, gives an opportunity to present Mary as the prototype of this Church—redeemed humanity's new beginning and most excellent member.

The sixth article—the communion of saints—allows the theologian to speak of Mary in terms of her spiritual motherhood, her co-redemption, her mediation, and her intercession in a

Church considered as a communion rather than as an institution or a higher authority.

The seventh article—the forgiveness of sins—is the place to speak of Mary's immaculate conception—her preservation from all sin by virtue of the foreseen merits of Christ. This grace and privilege is not to be understood as separating Mary from the rest of us, say our theologians; but rather as the anticipation in Mary of the perfect work that God will accomplish in the rest of us only at history's end.

The eighth article of the Creed—by which we declare our belief in the general resurrection—can occasion a discussion of Mary's assumption, body and soul, into heaven, and her eschatological significance as the enthronement of creation in the definitive glory of God.

The ninth, and last, article of the Creed—"I believe in . . . life everlasting"—suggests a concomitant contemplation of Mary as Queen of the Universe, reigning jointly with her Son over a reconciled creation, not with the arrogant might of the rulers of this world, but in the service (see Luke 12:37) of the oneness and reconciliation of all.

This sixth approach responds to the interests of ecumenism, providing a common basis from which to dialogue, from which to integrate mutual perspectives. Theologically, however, it is not very sound. It attempts no organic comprehension of its object. Its structure, paralleling that of the creed, is didactic rather than organic. Furthermore, it fails to address the propositions of Mariology directly, and thereby fails to extract the specific demands of these propositions where a reflection of faith is concerned.

A *seventh, and last, avenue* of approach conceives of Mariology as a way to study salvation history.[8] Here salvation is understood as a historical process, ultimately initiated by God, in which the liberation of individuals is effected within a divine pedagogy of ever higher hopes, promises, and fulfillment of these hopes and promises. Vatican II conceived of Mary's mission in this way: she is a part of the divine economy of salvation.[9] The mystery of the Virgin Mary is presaged in the Old Testament in the prophecy of woman's victory over the serpent (Gen. 3:15); or of the virgin who will be with child and whose son will be named Emmanuel

(Isa. 7:14, Matt. 1:22–23); or when the poor and lowly are proclaimed the vessels of the messianic promises to be accomplished in them. In the fullness of time, God comes as close to humanity as possible, becoming one with us in our very flesh. But this incarnation is preceded by Mary's free acceptance. We can reflect on Mary's presence at Jesus' side in his childhood, in his public ministry, at the foot of the cross, in his resurrection, at the birth of the Church, at the coming of the Spirit, and throughout the history of faith. Thus, Mary's importance is always highlighted in connection with the redeeming and liberating deed of God in human history.

However, this outlook on salvation history is not without problems. Salvation history is not simply the history to which our Judeo-Christian Scriptures testify. Salvation history is all human history, including the history of the peoples outside the Judeo-Christian frame of reference. What might the place of Mary be against this vast and misty horizon? How do the great world religions enter into an understanding of Mary? How does psychosocial evolution, shot through with the Spirit, come into the picture? How do the Marian apparitions contribute to an understanding of the meaning of Mary for salvation history? These are the questions that challenge us, and they call for a systematic exposition of Mariology. Our systematization will be fruitful, however, only if we assume a universal category of salvation history such as the one we postulate here: the feminine.

As we may deduce from all that we have just stated, we have surely touched on a basic question. Method is not indifferent to the determination of concrete content. At base, what is the object of theological reflection with regard to Mary? The person of Mary? God's plan in history, as including Mary? The feminine as a way of God's self-revealing, with Mary as the full realization of the feminine? Surely this line of questioning will be sufficiently rich to sustain a systematic reflection almost entirely new to theology. Let us pursue it.

THE FEMININE AS THE BASIC MARIOLOGICAL PRINCIPLE

Each of the various principles that we have reviewed, by which theology systematically organizes the elements of its knowledge of the mystery of Mary, has a reasonable basis, as well as intrinsic limitations. No system is so perfect and harmonious as to be able to do justice to all the facts. Reason's finitude precludes the possibility of a perfect system. All syntheses are constructs. As such they only *tend* to capture the whole reality under consideration. They cannot actually achieve this objective. At the very least, a system necessarily contains one element that escapes systematization: its own presupposition. Its rock-bottom premise must remain outside the system. However rational a system may be, then, it will always begin with a free choice. Let us remember: "Reasons begin with reason, but there are no reasons for reason." Once the initial choice is made, reason necessarily takes action to construct the system of reality that will support that particular choice.

We choose the feminine as the nucleus from which to move out in an attempt to do justice to the Marian truths of faith. Now that we have made that choice, we can adduce justifying reasons—not with the intention of making the choice seem inevitable, however, but simply in an effort to supply the rational basis necessary for honest thought.

First, then, there is the extrinsic, raw fact that the feminine has never been invoked as the central focus of Mariology. We ought to have the experience of all of the richness such a focus could afford. As we shall see in the course of our study, the possibilities are endless.

Second, the feminine has finally come into its own as an object of anthropological and cultural reflection. It has become relevant for the ideology of the last few years, both theoretically and practically. A great deal of scholarly research is frankly oriented to the position that the feminine is a basic and real part of the human person. The fact that Mary is a woman, and that God wished to be the offspring of that woman, then, can scarcely be without relevance. Theology must investigate that relevance. Through its investigations, theology can collaborate in the effort on the part of so many other sciences to deepen the understanding of the feminine.

Third, we have a reason altogether internal to theology. It might be formulated as follows. It is not enough to "do Mariology"—to systematize the truths about Mary. It is crucial that

*Mario*logy be *theo*logy. When we speak of Mary, we must speak of God. We must ask: What is God's plan for Mary, for the feminine, for history? The question is genuine—and genuinely theological, inasmuch as it strives to discern the will of God as revealed in these realities. It is not, however, sufficiently radical. A question is radical when it strikes to the root. And it strikes to the root when it asks an ultimate question—a question beyond which there are no more questions. Our own question, then, will be radical, and hence genuinely *theo*logical, when it no longer has Mary, or humanity, or the feminine, or even Christ as its center, but God. Now one no longer asks what God wills for Mary. Now one asks what God wants, simply and absolutely, through Mary. Thus, the radical question is: What does Mary mean for God? What is God seeking to attain through the feminine? Could God have created the feminine as a means of total self-communication, and thus as a way of self-realization under this particular form? If we are right in regarding Mary as the supreme expression of the feminine, might we not say that God has been realized in a supreme way in Mary? In that case, through what divine Person is God realized in the feminine?

These are the questions that justify our choice of the feminine as the basic principle of Mariology. They unfold against a new horizon, and against this horizon not only shall we be able to know more about Mary, and know it more harmoniously, but we shall actually discover a new avenue of God's self-communication and self-realization.

Further, our exposition will attempt to set in relief the eschatological perspective—something very basic to a theological reflection that means to be radical. Eschatology is not just one more theological topic. First and foremost, it is a characteristic or facet of every theological topic. Every theological truth has an eschatological connotation. That is, it embraces not only a present and historical dimension, but a future, definitive dimension as well, a dimension of the Reign of God in its fullness. This is the very nature of eschatology—the study of something *already* present but *not yet* fully realized, something that is already concrete and real, but that will not be fully so until it reaches its final form in the definitive plenitude of God. For our part, then, we shall be considering the feminine not only as an analytical category, borrowed from anthropology (in its principal currents), but also, and primarily, as a theological category that will have to be properly constructed. And because our consideration of the feminine is theological, it will have to be eschatological. What is God definitively—eschatologically—doing by way of the feminine? This is the great question, and we shall have to answer it. In Mary we find the historical anticipation of the eschatological in its fullness.

We should not be accused of a kind of hubris in setting our sights too high. Pride and unbridled ambition are not in the quantity of questioning, but in the establishment of preposterous answers. There are no limits on asking. The faculty of inquiry is inhabited by a wild "demon"—the divine in us. Despotism always begins by prohibiting any questions. To forbid questions is to deprive the truth of its right to manifest itself. One who never asks questions is deprived of the warming, beneficent light of the encounter with supreme Truth. We admit that our response to our own tireless questioning will be but a stammering and a stuttering about the supreme Mystery that reveals itself in the traits of the feminine.

Actually, we are only adopting the attitude of our predecessors, the medieval Franciscans. My reverence for Christ and his mother, who is our Mother as well, they proclaimed, that I had rather say too much than too little in her praise.[10] We realize, of course, that we run the risk—a risk we accept—of finding ourselves in the framework of the old, notorious mariological maximalism. But the old maximalism is aesthetic and academic. We are maximalistic, to be sure—but not in a pietistic, *evasive spirit that would like to flood* (but thereby contaminate) that rigorous discourse of faith that is theology. We are maximalistic out of theology's legitimate, essential demand for radicalism. As the reader will note, throughout, we intend to carry our reflections on the eschatological dimension of the feminine, and on the particular and full realization of that dimension in Mary, to their ultimate consequences. In eschatology we must be maximalists. There is no other way to define the ultimate character of all that is—including, then, the feminine—in God.

II. ANALYSIS: THE FEMININE AND THE CONFLICT OF INTERPRETATIONS

2. Basic Epistemological Obstacles in the Area of the Feminine

We have selected the category of the feminine as our key to a radical understanding of the transcendent meaning of Mary. As this construct will have to meet rather rigorous demands in the service of our theological discourse, we now propose to define it more precisely and more adequately. To this end, we shall have to follow the twisting paths of the various disciplines, even as they lead us to conflicting interpretations, seeing that the feminine has lately become the object of such intense reflection at the hands of the various sciences.

Our approach to the feminine will pursue the following course: (1) a confrontation with the fundamental epistemological obstacles (this chapter); (2) an analytical approach (chapter 3); (3) a philosophical reflection (chapter 4); (4) a theological meditation (chapter 5).

Our interest is theological. But the theological face of the feminine is not self-evident. It is not a raw datum of experience. We must extract it from the texts of other disciplines, from the analyses of the sciences and philosophy. Hence it will be a construct. In order to have an analytically sound concept of the feminine, a concept with a critical content, one that can be used correctly in our own discourse, we shall have to engage in a preliminary study of other discourses upon the feminine. Otherwise, our use of the category of the feminine would be naive. If we made the mistake of thinking that the feminine were a raw datum of experience, our concept of it would inescapably be vitiated by the ideology of our culture.

EPISTEMOLOGICAL NOTE

First, let us quickly establish a *modus procedendi*. Since our preliminary approach to the feminine is to be an interdisciplinary one, we must clarify the grammar of our reflection. We shall have to take account of the interrelationships among the various orders of knowledge, as well as of the scope and the limits of each. We presuppose the received canon of hermeneutical procedures. Thus—in all brevity—we recognize that:

1. To Know Is to Represent the Real

We gain access to the real—here, to the feminine—not with a clear and unclouded vision, but with eyes inherited from our past and conditioned by our culture. Prior to any new knowledge we may hope to acquire, we are the creatures of certain fixed concepts and prejudices. This is why to know is always to interpret in light of—for or against—previous knowledge. Knowing is never a direct reading of the real. Cognition is never the reduplication of reality. This would be a most naive claim. Our representation of the feminine will take flesh within the material and theoretical conditioning of a particular time and place.

2. To Know Is to Construct an Object of Knowledge

Our second principle flows from the first. We cannot know what the feminine is in its objectivity. We can only know that which we are about to construct upon it. Accordingly, we must draw a distinction between the real object (the thing in itself, the feminine) and the object of our knowledge (the ideas and theories that we shall have regarding the feminine). Our cognition will always be through models, paradigms, formulae, mental constructs, and ideas by which we capture the real and become sensitized to the influence it exercises upon our intellectual capacity. To know, then, is to construct the very object of our knowledge.

3. Our Knowledge Is Always Only Approximative

If we never have direct access to the feminine, but always through some construct of the feminine, our knowledge will always be only an approximation of reality. Our cognition will never be absolute. The object in itself, the feminine in itself, will remain intangible. Each approach, each approximation formulates this object according to its own particular presuppositions, shaping it in light of the particular questions that guide the approach, molding it to suit the initial posture vis-à-vis its proposed object. The notion of the origin of knowledge in raw sense experience is a mythical one, and epistemologically naive. Our perceptions of a phenomenon are preorganized, already constituted. They merely reorganize themselves in light of our new experiences. From start to finish, our perceptions are limited by our constructs.

4. KNOWLEDGE IS ALWAYS HISTORICAL

Knowing is a vital act. It transpires in the framework of a particular time, place, and class interest. It is constructed with the instruments of knowledge appropriate to a particular phase of history. This is a further reason why our cognition of the feminine will be merely approximative, and why it must remain open to new possibilities springing from new questions, new interests, and new instruments of cognition.

5. KNOWLEDGE TENDS TO TRANSCEND IDEAS

Knowledge tends to transcend the idea, the theoretical construct, and arrive at the real itself, without, however, grasping it fully. It achieves this through experience and experimentation. All experience is oriented by theory; but then it goes beyond the theory, and allows new elements to emerge. Then these new elements reverse the flow, and call for a reformulation of the theoretical framework. All genuine cognition is achieved via this reciprocal movement of the rational toward the real and the real toward the rational. "The *one triumphs by assenting to the other:* empiricism needs to be understood; rationalism needs to be applied."[1] Cognition has the tendency to wrestle free of the mold imposed on it by its mediation, the idea, the theory. It cries out for an encounter with the real, via experimentation and experience. Experience is never pure and naked. It remains within its structural framework. But at the same time it is freed from this framework, whereupon it affords us a richer access to the real *through* new constructs.

6. IT IS IMPORTANT TO REFLECT ON WHAT WE KNOW

The sciences give us our ways of being. For example, they show us the feminine as a way of making the human being concrete. There is a time and moment for philosophical reason. What is a human being? How is the human mode of being related to being as such? What does the feminine reveal? These questions are the concern of philosophy, for philosophy attempts to "think through" the things we know.

7. THE MYSTERY OF GOD IS THE STARTING POINT

All knowledge may be conceived in terms of the absolute mystery called God. To cast knowledge in these terms is the task of theology. But theology presupposes the leap of faith. From a point of departure in faith, then, one must ask: What is the meaning of the feminine in light of God's revelation? How does the feminine reveal God, and how is God revealed in the feminine? Does the feminine have its ultimate ground and meaning in God?

We shall have to take all of these steps in the course of our investigation.

OBSTACLES TO A CORRECT UNDERSTANDING OF THE FEMININE

Few topics are so fraught with prejudice as is the feminine. Surely we will do well to regard with suspicion any current opinion on the subject. The great modern epistemologist Gaston Bachelard has shown us that the most difficult obstacles to overcome in terms of the (approximative) cognition of truth are precisely prejudices. In fact, Bachelard designates prejudices as "basic epistemological obstacles."[2] Science is born of the struggle against them. And so we must be aware of certain prejudices at work with regard to the feminine in order to avoid them as best we can.

SCIENTIFIC RATIONALISM

The first great epistemological obstacle is the very concept of modern scientific knowledge. Modernity is built upon the familiar premise that analytical reason can establish an objective understanding of human reality, and that this reality can therefore be translated into a conceptual structure. The rational mediation alone, we are led to believe, is capable of capturing the nature of being-man and being-woman. In the attempt, however, reason perpetrates a reduction of concrete experience that stands as ongoing evidence of the irreducibility, precisely, of the sexual relationship. This does not mean that our models are false. It does not mean that scientific falsifications are arbitrary, or, conversely, that every experiential boast is pure gold. But it does call our scientific assertions into question. It challenges us to ask ourselves in all honesty how far these assertions are faithful to the reality of the profound encounter of the sexes. Have our scientific propositions in this area been subjected to the cleansing crucible of experience? Reason's prideful drive to power requires us to vanquish false knowledge, to tear the mask from the face of merely seeming cognition. Neither the feminine nor the masculine is a rock-hard, eternal crystallization of being. Each is a web of relationships that outstrips the drive of the *logos* to tame all things. It is more of an eros, vanishing from our curious gaze in the bottomless depths of the human. It is as symbol rather than as concept that being-feminine can be seized by reason. Accordingly, we must blaze other trails to this human reality, different from the path followed by analytical instrumental rationality.[3]

SEXUAL ABSENTEEISM

Western tradition has come to define human persons as living beings endowed with reason—"rational animals." This definition-by-essence fails to take account of sexual differences. Gender is "ac-cidental"—incidental—to human nature as such, and, for that matter, ascribable not to our rationality, but to our animality. It is therefore not regarded as a datum of the human totality as such.

A like conceptualization leads to a monistic, undifferentiated representation of human reality. The Bible is careful to begin with sexual difference as the primary intrinsic determinant of the human individual (Gen. 1:27). But this has not affected subsequent reflection on and practice of the Judeo-Christian faith.

Even today this absenteeism on the part of sexual reality widely prevails in philosophy, hermeneutics, and the human sciences generally. Scientific or political practices are understood independently of the sexual identity of their agents. Psychology itself, so sensitive to sexual differences, seems to have paid less than adequate attention to sexual identity as a determinant of the human person. Even Freud, with his theory of a "penis envy" indicating a "state of impotency and infantile dependency" in women, really accomplished nothing but a reinforcement of the old antifeminist prejudices and male chauvinism of our culture.[4] One cannot help but suspect that this sexual monism may be rooted in a faulty anthropological premise—an oversimplified schematization of the structure of the human person. The same reduction occurs on the level of language, although current attempts are under way to rectify the situation: linguistically, the human race is identified with men, as if the male epitomized all of humanity and the female were either a corrupt derivation or, at best, some nice frosting on a magnificent human cake that could almost as well have been served up without it.

SEXUAL MONISM

Thus, the absence of the sexual cripples our understanding of the human person. Does its presence, then, guarantee an adequate theoretical conception? Scarcely. Women's subjection to men is age-old. The bulk of our cultural creations are sexist statements. From the Neolithic age, society has refused women the historical conditions necessary for autonomous fulfillment. Women have been made to depend on men in everything, especially in the area of family life. As housewives, women have worked without benefit of compensation. In their children they produce a new work force, which they do not own, in order to maintain the family members who work outside the home. Household activity has never figured in the calculus of economics or the scale of social values. Housework has been regarded as something of secondary importance, and accordingly has been categorized as "women's work." In time, the reality of this situation in the infrastructure penetrated the conceptual superstructure, yielding an understanding of woman as an appendage or lesser manifestation of man.

All this is changing today, but only on the level of theory. In its applications in history, in attitudes, in practice, sexual monism reigns unchallenged. The Church clings to an antifeminism now partially overcome in the larger society. Unconsciously, but with manifold consequences in terms of the conscious, the Church maintains a genuine political theology of the sexes, articulated in the following syllogism: God and Jesus Christ are masculine. But theirs is the right to control and command. Therefore, the male inherits the right to control and command.[5] In other words, in this view, in the male alone is human nature fully realized; in the female its realization is only a function of her relation to the male.

GENITAL DEFINITION OF THE SEXES

One of the most ghastly epistemological obstacles to a correct knowledge of the feminine is the reduction of the sexual to a genital or biological fact. But human sexuality is not only genital, not only located in the organs of reproduction and the erogenous zones. The human person is not naked *bios*. He or she is someone appropriately fulfilled either as a man or as a woman. Surely motherhood, for example, is a major biological event for a woman. But her personhood is not exhausted by that biological achievement. If, whether by her own decision or not, a woman does not become a mother, she is not thereby deprived of her capacity to conceive and engender life. She may well continue to do so in other dimensions of life, offering her care and protection in all her undertakings.[6] A woman's anatomical and psychological structures are "moments" in the overall project of being a woman. It is from the overall project that these structures draw their meaning. Thus, there is no validity in reductionisms that disfigure the integral image we must have of feminine reality if we hope to be faithful to its anthropological wealth. The reduction of sex to its genital aspect is one of the most pernicious vices of our unidimensional culture, which so readily transforms women into objects, instruments of pleasure of the male bed and board.[7]

ONTOLOGIZATION OF HISTORICAL MANIFESTATIONS

Another epistemological pitfall consists in regarding feminine reality from the viewpoint of a certain naive naturalism. Contingent historical realities, such as women's subjection to men, their dependency, their submission, and so on, are regarded as essential attributes of femininity. A simple product of history, the upshot of human practices and conflicts of interest, is attributed to the feminine as such. But the present cultural disadvantage of women is due not to some defect in the feminine, but to the unfair battle of the sexes. Men have subjugated women and exploited their forces for their own selfish benefit. This points to a theological problem. The human race is found to be in a decadent, unjust state. An appreciation of the historical nature of the present subjection of women frees the intellect to seek less asymmetrical solutions. The status quo is not necessary or preordained. It can be changed. An adequate grasp of this fact could also release women's repressed energies for their task as the principal agents of their own liberation.

POLARIZATION OF THE SEXES

Another pitfall to be avoided in an attempt to understand the feminine consists of a kind of sexual parallelism. Sexual dimorphism is obviously part and parcel of human nature. But the twin realities are not parallel, they are reciprocal. Man and woman are not side by side but face to face. They know themselves and each other to the extent that they arrive at a concretely reciprocal relationship. Ignorance of this fact constitutes a basic epistemological obstacle in the area of the feminine. Now the sexes are polarized, and to each is ascribed a series of irreducible characteristics.[8] Each roster is then systematized on the basis of various distinct criteria such as the biological, the psychological, or the metaphysical. There is a whole romantic, pseudoscientific literature purporting to establish these sexual symmetries. To the male fall rationality, objectivity, aggressiveness, the spirit of toil, creativity, exteriority, and the like. Emotionality, subjectivity, nurturance, submission, irrationality, and so on, are the exclusive characteristics of women. This repertoire of qualities and vices symmetrically distributed between two opposite poles vitiates our understanding of the sexes in its very root. Relationships between the sexes are mechanized and reified. It is absolutely necessary that we understand that the essential reciprocity between man and woman implies acceptance of the fact that each shares in the totality of human reality and all its qualities, albeit in different degrees. Feminine and masculine are not accidents of human nature. They are essential determinants of human nature. Each individual of the species is at once masculine and feminine. Male-female relationships are always personal, and therefore irreducible to any preestablished symmetry.

Exaltation of the Feminine: The Eternal Woman

There are two ways of refusing to accept woman. We may consider her infantile, and therefore rightly placed under male tutelage. Or we may exalt her to heights such that her status and role in this world lose their reality and specificity. As Balzac put it, "Woman is a slave to enthrone." And behold the Eternal Woman—that timeless, extrahistorical essence symbolized in so many absolutized feminine characteristics and preventing women from discovering their true calling and historical potential.[9] We are by no means denying the value of symbolic language. Indeed, we shall shortly lodge a strong apologia for it. But we must oppose *mordicus* the idealization of women by men. This is only a veiled form of discrimination and domination—even in the realm of the mariological. Theologians who, however unconsciously, toil in the service of male power interests, represent Mary only as the woman who knew how to say yes—"Fiat mihi . . ."—the woman who resigned herself to fulfilling the will of God, the woman who, in modesty and anonymity, remained hidden among her household chores. This is to ignore altogether the dimension to which Paul VI's encyclical *Marialis Cultus* directs our attention: "Mary was anything but passive, submissive, pious to the point of being out of contact with reality. No, here was a woman who did not hesitate to assert that God would come to the humble and the oppressed and cast down the mighty of this world from their thrones (Luke 1:51–53)."[10] Mary is a model not only for women, but for every one of our Lord's disciples, such was her commitment to liberation and to the realization of justice.[11]

In conclusion, we must avoid two basic obstacles, an old one and a new. The old one consists in speaking of the human person without speaking of sex. The new one consists in speaking of sex apart from any connection with the human person. No, we must speak of the sexual being, of the male or female person—of sex become human, of sex as something constituting the human person as such, not as something the individual has. We should speak of sex as an integral constituent of the human essence, whose role it is to place one person in encounter with another.

Conscious of these obstacles, we shall nevertheless attempt to outline certain basic theoretical perspectives on the feminine, in order to prepare the soil of our reflection for a theological consideration calculated to plumb the ultimate meaning of the feminine in God as anticipated in the history of Mary.

3. The Feminine: An Analytical Approach

We make no attempt in this chapter to rehearse the giant strides that have been taken in the interdisciplinary investigation of the feminine.[1] Even to summarize adequately the immense wealth of information available in this area would turn out to be an impossible task. The acknowledgment of this objective difficulty, however, scarcely exempts us from the duty of formulating certain propositions calculated to support a less nebulous understanding of the feminine sexual difference than the prescientific one we may currently entertain. Our understanding of the feminine sexual difference must be as immune as possible to the infection of ideological manipulation at the hands of prejudices still current in our society. It is in the area of sexual difference, more than elsewhere, that our knowledge of the feminine will be of a merely approximative, hypothetical nature.

In broad strokes, then: we can trace three general directions taken by current scientific analysis of the phenomenon of the feminine. The first maintains that sexual differences in personality, conditioning, function, and powers are culturally determined. According to this position—maintained by Mead, Brown, Williams, Sanday, de Beauvoir, and so on—a psychosexual neutrality prevails at birth. Neither physiology nor psychology, we are told, offer any justification for our political and economic division of the sexes. The sex factor is sufficiently malleable to be molded to either shape, simply through socialization. This position denies the existence of any a priori "masculine" or "feminine" characteristics. Male and female human beings can both be psychologically contoured—transformed into aggressive or dependent or passive individuals, and so on. These traits are not properly and basically "sexual" ones, then.

A second current asserts, on the contrary, that men and women are indeed endowed with their own respective innate sexual equipment, based on biological factors, and giving rise to distinct behavior and psychological characteristics in each sex. A great deal of importance is ascribed to education and socialization, to be sure, but in this view education and socialization must realize that they are dealing with realities sprung full-panoplied from antecedently given matrices. The principal sexual differentiations, among human beings as among the other higher mammals, emerge from biological factors of sexual difference and age.

A third position seeks to combine the first two in dialectical tension. Human beings are not only the highest species of mammals. They are also, and essentially, cultural beings, the forgers of history. We must therefore acknowledge a profound, complex interaction on the part of biological and sociocultural factors. This third position seeks to trace the social development of biological phenomena instead of maintaining the two factors in a causal parallelism. Surely, the causal relationships between socialization and biology are unclear. But this should scarcely provide a pretext for an arbitrary dichotomy, say the champions of the third view. This position transcends the twin determinisms of biology and culture: on the one hand, sexual differences are radically innate; on the other, they are also acquired. But it is important to establish a genuine dialectic here, say the proponents of this theory, lest we end with a feeble compromise between positions one and two. Sexual behavior arises and develops to the degree that a given organism, with such and such genetic characteristics, enters into interaction with an environment likewise endowed with such and such specific stimuli. Some behaviors succeed in establishing themselves in individuals—because that individual's genetic equipment and the responses of the environment are on the same wavelength. Other behaviors encounter more difficulty and are less likely to arise, owing to a relative lack of complementarity between genetic equipment and environment. Still other behaviors find no place to land at all.

Our position resembles this third view. The hypothesis that we shall maintain in the course of our reflections will be that the differences between the sexes are quantitative rather than qualitative. We shall assert at once a difference between the sexes and their fundamental reciprocity.

THE MALE-FEMALE DIFFERENCE

The human species exists in a basic dimorphism: that of man and woman. The fact is undeniable, and constitutes an indubitable enrichment of the human life project. But what is the basis of the male-female difference?

A first approach to this question will be on the biological level.[2] Here, if we consider the individual of the species, boundaries between male and female are fluctuating, and we shall see more on this in the course of our discussion. For the moment, then, we shall do better to examine the species as such.[3]

On the biological level, then, we have, first, the *genetic sexuality* of the individual of the species. The genetic sex springs from the feminine or masculine structure, as the case may be, of the nucleus of all of the cells of the human organism. Each of these nuclei contains twenty-two pairs of somatic chromosomes, plus two sex chromosomes. In each pair of chromosomes, one comes from the mother and one from the father. The chromosomal makeup of the female consists of twenty-two pairs of somatic chromosomes, plus a pair of sex chromosomes, each in the shape of an X. The chromosomal makeup of the male likewise consists of twenty-two pairs of somatic chromosomes, but when we come to his sex chromosomes, the twenty-third pair, one is in the form of a Y. The basic sex, then, is feminine, as determined by the XX sex chromosomes. The male sex, determined by an XY pair of sex chromosomes, owes its ultimate origin to the female: only the female has all four arms on each sex chromosome, while in the male one of the sex chromosomes is without one of its arms, hence its Y shape. Thus the "Adam principle"—the mythological origin of woman from man (which, as we have seen, arises in a sexist mentality) falls to pieces. (Of course, the more scientific "genetic primacy" of the female sex will be equally bereft of any implications for woman's superior personhood.)[4]

Besides the genetic, or cellular, sexuality of the human individual, there is also a *genital*, or gonadal, *sexuality*, manifesting itself in the genital organs belonging respectively to the male and the female. The genital sex directly determines the type of genital glands (ovaries in the female, testicles in the male) that an individual will have. The pregonad appears around the thirty-seventh day of embryonic life, and is already differentiated by the ninth week. As for the genitalia themselves, male and female both possess the same embryonic profile: the male Wolffian canal and the female Müller's canal are histologically (structurally) analogous. Originating in this embryonic bipotentiality, sexual development then charts a basic course for one sex rather than the other. The latter is not completely canceled, however, but merely remains in an atrophied state. Which sex will tip the balance in a given individual is determined by two basic factors, genetic and hormonal. As a rule, an individual's genital sex will be identical with his or her genetic sex, and inversions are extremely rare.

Finally, there is a *hormonal sexuality.* All of the genital glands, regulated by the sexually neutral hypophysis and the sexual hypothalamus (the nervous structure in the vicinity of the hypophysis), secrete both male hormones (androgens) and female hormones (estrogens). But they secrete them in different proportions, thus producing different secondary sex characteristics. Depending on which hormones are preponderant in the nervous structures of the hypothalamus, the hypophysis functions in a stable (male) or cyclical (female) rhythm, determining masculine or feminine behavior still further. Even the cerebrum is different in men and women.[5] And so we have a dimorphism both in physiological function and in behavior, the outgrowth of differences in the central nervous system between the two sexes.

Let us remember, however, that when one speaks of biological sexual determinants it is determinants of the species as such, rather than of individuals, that are meant.

Before we leave the biological level of sex determination, we should recall that human sexuality is ultimately rooted in the broader framework of all of the higher living creatures. Sexuality arises prior to the appearance of the human being and continues within that human being. It manifests itself as an instinct, a deep urge, an impulse toward the orgiastic and the Dionysiac, and its control through social rules is always problematic. Hegel's "law of light," here as in other areas, is constantly violated by the "law of darkness."

And so there is continuity between us and the other higher animals in the area of sexuality. But there is also breach. We are capable of overcoming life's determinisms. It is human beings' task to take a stand (through nature) against nature. We can regulate and redirect our vital impulses, thus placing them in the service of freedom. The "I" must appropriate its due—for only thus can it continue to become autonomous and free. It is in this struggle of the "I" that love is born as surrender and free gift to another. It is only through taming our nature along the course of our journey to freedom that sexuality can become the instrument of love—a love that will transform it into an expression of caring, a language of sharing and communion.

Despite the biological breach between the other primate species and *Homo sapiens,* we must acknowledge the undeniable importance of the biological factor in the determination of sexual differences in human behavior.[6] As we know, the sex hormones, specifically the prenatal androgens, actually effect a physiological differentiation between male and female in some parts of the central nervous system. Women who have suffered a fetal androgenization seem to resist a so-called female socialization, demonstrating instead certain interests and activity levels regarded as more typically male. Men with a history of a certain insensitivity to the prenatal androgens acquire frankly feminine behavioral traits, and resist "male" socialization. Androgens promote, and estrogens inhibit, aggressiveness. Men, who produce greater quantities of androgens, are much more strongly predisposed to aggression, exhibit a more developed musculature, and have a larger heart and lungs. The social outgrowth of this innate difference has assigned men tasks involving, for example, physical danger, territorial acquisition, domination, or power games, as transcultural studies have convincingly demonstrated. In parallel fashion, women's biological-hormonal structure has inclined them toward tasks involving the production, preservation, and nurturing of life. Women's parental influence is much more pervasive than men's. This difference has emerged in still other sociocultural differences in the male-female competition.

To be sure—let us repeat—this does not establish a crisp dichotomy between male and female behavior, but only a difference in the frequency and intensity with which behavior common to both sexes is practiced. Here the variable of the cultural environment must be taken carefully into account. One cannot properly speak of a fixed genetic programming peculiar to each sex. There are only different matrices, from which man and woman emerge to strike their respective syntheses with their sociohistorical environment. The environment and the congenital matrix together function as joint causes of male and female behavior respectively. But these twin causes, especially the environmental one, are susceptible to outside influences. For example, in a sociohistorical environment favoring unregulated competition, we can expect the male to dominate in nearly every area, and the woman to be repressed. Our highly competitive capitalistic society is structured in this way, and women are indeed repressed. In other societies, where competition is deemphasized and cooperation encouraged, conditions typically favor women's advancement. In an egalitarian environment, sexual roles are egalitarian as well, and a community of fellowship between the sexes is more practicable and likely. In an environment of personal and social equality, a less strictly sexual division of labor then favors a less starkly sexual differentiation between male and female. Again, transcultural research supports this hypothesis. Biological and cultural interaction are reciprocal once more.

Male-female differentiations appear on all levels of our analysis. Investigations in sexual phenomenology,[7] cultural anthropology, differential psychology,[8] as well as in other areas, have produced a great deal of data relevant for our considerations—too many even to list here. We shall have to content ourselves with an awareness of the reality and its problems. Phenomenologically, every human being is at once male and female in the sex of his or her body—which is never a thing, but a situation in the world, a confrontation with others. Being man and being woman are two mutually inclusive ways of being within reality, in a spirit of toil, aggressiveness, and transformation of the environment (the male within us), and in care, coexistence, and sympathy with reality (the female). All human differences carry with them an anthropological constant and a cultural development. The sexual human being is never isolated from a sociohistorical environment. Human nature is historical. History is natural to human beings. Consequently, any effort to dichotomize complex human reality is justified only as an imperative of analysis—never as a projection of anthropological truth. Human existence is a fabric of two forms of being, male and female. Man and woman, each in his or her own way, project existence. Each has his or her own way of organizing relationships and overcoming any breach between the individual and the existential or social.

MALE-FEMALE RECIPROCITY

We shall have failed to do justice to the man-woman relationship, however, if we merely acknowledge social differences. We must also consider the other side of the coin, perhaps an even more profound and genuine aspect of the human being as such than the one we have just explored. The male-female human relationship is characterized not only by differentiation, but by a radical reciprocity as well. Sexuality is not an object in itself, possessed by each individual in his or her own fashion. Sexuality is precisely the matrix of the face-to-face encounter of man and woman, in the immediate mediation of the body through which the world is given. Simone de Beauvoir has coined an expression that, understood in all its dialectical circularity, encompasses the whole truth of sexual reciprocity: "Woman becomes woman in the man's sight; and not only this, but man becomes man in woman's sight." Each of the two discovers the self thanks to the other, and has an experience as a sexual being on all levels on which human existence develops and is realized. Human beings do not *have* sex; they *are* sexual beings. As sexual beings they outstrip themselves, acquire a dimension of otherness, take on a reference to the other in their bodily determinants. This face-to-face encounter is an irreducible, basic fact, a fundamental anthropological structure that can only occur as encounter or rejection, love or hate.

Thus, man and woman *really* exist only in their reciprocal otherness. To insist on their mutual exclusivity, on the grounds of the differences just examined, is to lose sight of the sexes' genuine meaning and reality. "The encounter is primary, the encounter not of two neutral and disembodied consciousnesses, or of two temperaments, nor of two bodies or of two minds, but the human encounter of man and woman which occurs in a history and a culture, and which creates in turn the history and culture necessary for its occurrence."[9]

This two-way relationship between the sexes invalidates any sexual hierarchy pretending to a basis in nature. The relationship of the sexes is not one of authority and obedience, but of mutual responsibility. Note that we have not spoken of a complementarity, but of a reciprocity. Complementarity is a state of being in which each of two terms exists in and for itself, but incompletely: only in relationship are both parties fulfilled, only thus are they mutually complemented. The concept of complementarity fails to capture the dialogic structure of human existence, which never occurs apart from relationship and face-to-face encounter. Interpersonal reality is not a consequence of sexuality, not a secondary phenomenon. It is the very basis for the discovery of feminine and masculine. To understand man and woman as merely complementary would be to understand them as supplying some lack, some deficiency, in each other. The other would complement, make up for the deficiency in, my "I." But this would degrade genuine otherness. The concept of reciprocity has the advantage of connoting from the outset the mutual openness of the two terms involved.

At the same time, we also defend an element of complementarity between the sexes. And we maintain that this element, however inadequately it may represent the male-female relationship, points to a genuine problem. How, when all is said and done, does the female-male encounter occur in human beings?

We think we can formulate the answer as follows. Man and woman face each other in openness, experiencing the other at once as like but different, similar but strange, accepting the other as a person in his or her difference; whereupon a history unfolds that intertwines them and makes them responsible for one another. Their history will be one of encounters, of *yes*'s and *no*'s, of reticences and confidences, of rejection and self-bestowal, and of the common construction of the unforeseeable pathway of human life. Yet, despite the confrontations, the misunderstanding, the dialectic, the reservations—there will be the experience of something that has always been there, something not the object of free choice, and not the subjectivity of an I and a Thou, but something transpersonal, something that is the fundamental way of being human. Thus, a human being, who always exists either as man or woman, exists as one because of the other, with the other, against the other, in the other, and for the other.[10] When we come to the philosophical moment of our reflection, we shall attempt more adequately to identify the ontological fact implied in all of this. There is something created-and-not-created here, something binding man and woman together into one.

HISTORICAL FORMS OF MALE-FEMALE RECIPROCITY

As we have already stated, human sexuality always contains a sociocultural element. Reciprocity as the encounter of two "othernesses" has a historical, social dimension. Furthermore, we must recognize, the biological aspect of the human being, unlike that of animals, contains an excess of sexual energy. Not periodicity, or pattern of intervals, but an ongoing drive is the rule. This state of affairs emerges either in pansexualism or in displacement—the redirection of excess sexual energy toward ends not overtly sexual. But the solution in terms of displacement has given rise to the historical forms, institutions, and norms that we find ordering the relationships between men and women in our society. The artificiality of our sex-role differentiation is the result of our excess of sexual energy. Human beings are even capable of divorcing sexual pleasure from the other dimensions of the sexual relationship and using sexuality as an instrument of domination. In sex-role differentiation more than in any other area of anthropology, social and environmental factors come into play. Relationships between the sexes are never "natural," but always human—cultural, conflictive, and set within the framework of varying ways of distributing social roles and power. Here is the explanation for both the possibility and actuality of the "battle of the sexes," in all its manifestations, whether it be expressed in domination—patriarchalism or matriarchalism—or sublimated into higher forms of collaboration and community.[11]

For example, as Claude Lévi-Strauss has demonstrated, women are linked in a special way to the first moves from nature to culture.[12] The incest prohibition established a crucial positive link among human beings without which it would have been impossible to take the quantum leap from the sheer biological to a true cultural organization. Women, the social grouping's most precious possession, now suddenly constitute a complete two-way circuit.[13] They are the gift par excellence by which the interchange is effected that guarantees the existence of the group as a group: women have the function in the socially normative to be the efficacious sign, analogous to language, of socialization. But in the very act of serving these transindividual ends, they maintain their own value as persons. They are signs, but they are also producers of signs. Now the perception prevails that women are not only objects, but subjects as well, and indeed that they are diminished when they are converted into objects. This is the message of the many myths that proclaim that women will never be "swapped," or used as objects, in heaven. In heaven, the tenderness of a world of *interpersonal* harmony, which we never actually experience here below, will at last prevail.[14]

It is an undeniable datum of history that the last millennia have belonged to the man. It is difficult to ascertain what led men to subdue nature, and with nature, women. Worst of all, men subdued women's very hearts, making them accept and internalize their new role as pleasers of men. Simone de Beauvoir lodges the most radical criticism of this historicocultural development. Woman, she says, represents a special case in the dialectic of the master-slave relationship. In woman, the slave has actually been prevented from expressing herself in her own way.[15] Man has reduced woman to the mere incarnation of an "other" in whom to discover, confirm, and project his own "I." All forms of antifeminism, past and present, are based on this domination of women by men, as expressed on all social levels, including the religious and Christian.

Some investigators maintain the existence in history of the matriarchy—the social structure in which women are said to have exercised domination over men. Others say the patriarchy has always been the rule. In any event, the man-woman relationship as it has been made concrete in historical processes raises the question of whether it is even possible to construct social forms that would not fall into a negative dialectic. What is the organizing principle of history? The infrastructure? Values? Power interests? We have no wish to introduce irrelevant oversimplifications. We are only endeavoring to discern the determining factor. Discussion in this area goes beyond science, and enters the realm of philosophy, ultimately becoming theological. Why does history demonstrate such an incapacity to develop without a dark side—without its constant, heavy dose of social injustice and inequity? In the area of the sexual, history is the story of the subjugation of one sex by the other, to the deplorable impoverishment of both.

It is the task of our time to become aware of these distortions, and to inculcate practices calculated to enhance an appreciation of man-woman differences in order to embrace them, to see them as mutual gifts. Thus we may inaugurate a new age of less conflictive, more enriching sexual relationships.

4. The Feminine: A Philosophical Reflection

Philosophy is not a mere extension of scientific questioning. It is an order of investigation unto itself; an epistemological breach exists between it and science. Like poetry, philosophy springs from the wonder that something exists.[1] The existence of such an attitude and discipline as philosophy evinces the capacity of the human mind to rise above concrete determinations of reality, above beings, and question being itself. From a point of departure in *being*, philosophy contemplates the multiplicity of *beings*, as revelations and concealments of being. Thus, in the case of the man and woman, philosophy will ask how sexual bimorphism concretizes being as a manifestation of utmost reality. In developing this question, philosophy is altogether cognizant of the difference between its approach and that of the sciences. Philosophy surely recognizes the priceless value of scientific investigation, which deciphers the structure of beings—here, the masculine and the feminine—in order to systematize everything we can know of these beings analytically. To ignore science would be to contentedly wander in the fog of the illusion that "what meets the eye" is what is really and objectively there. Knowledge, the discourse of reality, would be confounded with ideology, the discourse of interests.

SCOPE OF PHILOSOPHICAL THOUGHT

But the human mind is not satisfied in the scientific endeavor alone. It breaks with the scientific order of questioning—*how* things are constructed, *how* they function, *how* we can change them—and raises an altogether new order of questions, bearing on the ultimate what and *why* of things. Philosophy and the philosophical attitude are obsessed with the fact that in what science tells us there always remains an unknown. In everything said, there is always the unsaid. In what is learned, there is always that of which we are ignorant. In other words, science fails to transfigure reality into a self-evidence. As we stated in the methodological discussion in Chapter 2, knowledge, especially scientific knowledge, is always representative, patterned, and approximative. Undeniably, knowledge reveals profound dimensions of the real. The male and female are a case in point. But it leaves other dimensions hidden. There are dimensions of reality that escape the scientific model of cognition. For example, we come to know the feminine to the extent that it answers the questions we ask about it. Yet, at the same time, we realize that the feminine itself is something much vaster and deeper than our questions about it. After all, our questioning is selective, and inquires only into dimensions that suit it, while ignoring dimensions in which our questions would have no meaning or have not yet occurred to us.

The anthropological sciences tell us of the male and the female human being as two distinct, related, modes of being human. But what is it to be human? This is the ultimate question the mind can pose in this area. This is the question, then, that philosophy asks. The mind is not satisfied with knowing something about man and woman. The mind seeks to know *what* it is to be human. Altogether understandably, this question transcends the domain of the analytical sciences. What it is to be human is scarcely the object of the experimental sciences. Scientific knowledge makes no attempt to represent what it is to be human. Science responds to any question about the human in terms of some concrete form of that human being, such as the male and female human being. But the human being as such does not exist in the flesh. A man or a woman does. No one has ever seen "the human being" walking along the street. The human being we see walking along the street is not *the* human being, but *a* particular, concrete male or female human being, a man or a woman. Nonetheless, we rightly say that man and woman are two different, but related, modes of self-realization as a human being. Thus, while there is such a thing as the human being, the human-being-as-such does not concretely exist. The human-being-as-such does not exist *as* a man or a woman exist. What is this *as*? This is the concern of philosophy as distinguished from science. What is "the human being's" concrete existence? And to ask this question is to touch upon the question: What *is* it to be human?

What is the human being? What is it to be human? How are we to conceive this being if, as we have just asserted, there is always a residual unknown in our knowledge of it—if darkness abides in the very light that gleams forth from its reality?

In terms of the reflections we have just entertained—our scientific analysis of man and woman—we simply do not know. Nor may the allegation of intellectual sloth be lodged against us, for we have pursued the scientific process right to the end. No, our nescience is simply proof that our access to the real by means of scientific instruments can never be a complete deciphering of the real. Science makes a dent in the real, surely. It develops the real under the formality of knowledge, and thereby in some measure reveals it. But it does not lock it up in its knowledge. Rather it respects the mystery that ever transcends the various cognitive approaches. What we know always ends in something we know not, something we can question, something still open. Man and woman are not exhausted in the knowledge we have of them. They continue to be food for thought. They demonstrate a living transcendence of all scientific data. They are always more than what we can say and systematize about them. In their limitation, they yet harbor a latent mystery, a mystery that constantly withdraws as human knowing approaches. Man and woman are host to a darkness that is out of range of the lamps of scientific knowledge. And yet, this darkness feeds knowledge. Mystery is not something "left over" after knowledge is constituted. Mystery is rather the very limitlessness of knowledge. Mystery is the everlasting challenge to know. "It is not knowledge that illuminates mystery, but mystery that illuminates knowledge. We know thanks to what we shall never know."[2]

By "human" we mean the unspoken, the mystery, of man and woman. The human is more than man and woman considered separately. The human being takes concrete form in men and women. The human being, then, is an identity occurring in difference.[3]

Philosophy as ontology is a reflection on that question that arises with the sciences but that cannot be adequately answered by those sciences. Ontology is concerned with the human rather than with the man and woman. That is, ontology is concerned with a mystery arising from man and woman that ever escapes the faculties of cognition, and that constitutes the unsaid of the anthropological sciences. Thus, ontology is a reflection (-*logia*, from *logos*) on the human considered precisely as being (*onto-*)—considered insofar as, in its concrete form in man and woman, it remains open, a question mark and a mystery.

Ontological reflection has no more data than those the sciences yield. Nor does it have access to any knowledge withheld from the sciences. It is simply the effort of thought to keep the mystery of man and woman alive in our awareness. It endeavors to forestall the scientific fossilization of man and woman. It seeks to remind scholars never to halt their study of the man and woman, as if man and woman could be shut up in the concatenation of a scientific system. It assumes the uncomfortable onus of functioning as a constant reminder that the most important thing about man and woman is invisible—that it is not what has been said, but what has been left unsaid, not what has been verified, but what remains to be verified, that ultimately matters. Ontological reflection consists in the attempt to think our knowledge through to the very end, inasmuch as what really counts is not just to know, but—it seems to us—to think about what we know.

In order to give a response, then, to our initial question—how we are to *understand* our scientific knowledge about man and woman—we may begin by saying that scientific knowledge informs us of the concrete *modes* in which the human is realized in the world—informs us about man and woman. It reveals the human to us in its modes, but it does not tell us definitively and totally what it is to be human. This question remains open. To reflect on it is the task of philosophy as ontology.

SEXUALITY AS AN ONTOLOGICAL STRUCTURE OF THE HUMAN BEING

To begin with an ontological understanding confirmed by scientific knowledge, we see that sexuality is not simply a marginal, genital quality of human beings. By the same token, sexuality not only has a biological dimension, but it penetrates all of the existential categories of the human person. Everything a human being does is marked by sexuality, for everything a human being does is done by a sexual being. Sex is not something the individual *possesses;* sex is the way in which that individual *is.* In other words, the human person is always man or woman. To be a man and to be a woman are two different ways of being in the world.[4]

All that the male undertakes, thinks, projects, and expresses signals his being-male and his virility. The parallel phenomenon occurs with the woman. The two can perform the same mechanical task, and in doing so make the same movements—but they will do so in different ways, for each is different from the other. And yet, although they are different, man and woman are related. They are found to be in a profound reciprocity and complementarity. The man is "for" the woman, and the woman is "for" the man.[5]

What does all this mean? Is the man taken alone, is the woman taken alone, incomplete, so that each stands in need of being completed by the other? Are they somehow like a lock and a key, which need each other in order to be complete, which are meaningless without each other? Our usual manner of speaking of women and men would seem to suggest such an understanding. But is the way of being human the same as the way of being a thing, like a lock or key? The human-being-who-is-spirit has a way of being all its own. It is impossible to reduce the human to other ways of being. And so the lock-and-key analogy fails.

An ontological reflection is attentive to this difference between being-human and being-thing. Perhaps we can spare ourselves the mistake of concocting illusory representations that ultimately lead to a falsification of the proper understanding of the man-woman reality and its reciprocal relationships. How, then, ought we to represent the man-woman reciprocity? Are they like a pair of terms facing each other in individual incompleteness, but complete as a pair? Or does each separate term somehow stand facing the pair as such, so that now two separate realities can open to each other on a deep level? Or is one within the other, so that a man carries woman within himself, and a woman carries man within herself? In this case, the man-woman relationship would be something quite different. Its dynamics would primarily move not from the outside in, but from the inside out. Then a woman would be in dialogue with, would embrace, would relate to the man within herself, and from this point of departure would dialogue with, embrace, and relate to the concrete, historical man she finds standing before her. And so it would go for a man. For every individual is at once man and woman.

Are we all hermaphrodites, then? No, because a man is not simultaneously male and female in the same way that a woman is. A man has woman within himself, but he *is* not woman. A woman has man within herself, but she *is* not man. In other words, to be a man and to be a woman are not simple, objective realities circumscribed physically, physiologically, and psychically. A man does not exhaust the entire potential of virility in making it concrete. Virility is found in a woman, as well. A woman does not exhaust the female in her concrete reality. Femininity is to be found in a man, as well. But virility and femininity are each manifested differently in a man and in a woman. In a man, virility predominates, and this is what makes him a man. In a woman, femininity prevails, and thus she is a woman.

Accordingly, instead of calling man and woman mutually incomplete, we prefer to call them relatively complete. Each has everything—but not in the same way, or to the same extent. Hence, neither is enough in himself or herself. Neither male nor female can take refuge in a particular concrete form. Each of the two is relatively complete, and hence, must submit to relationship, to reciprocity, to complementarity.

So what is it to be a man? What is it to be a woman? We may be helped in our understanding of the problem if we introduce another category—one to which we have already alluded in our reflection: that of masculinity and femininity. Male is not synonymous with man, since it may subsist apart from a man, and it does: in a woman. Female is not the same thing as woman, because there is femininity in a man. This observation would appear to be of profound importance. Serious consequences flow from it for the man-woman relationship. The identification of male with man and female with woman has occasioned incalculable discrimination, and an interpretation of the relationships and complementarity of man and woman in an outward, objective, all but reified sense.

In order to arrive at any understanding of what it is to be a man and what it is to be a woman, we must first explore what masculinity and femininity are. But first, inasmuch as masculinity and femininity are not entities in themselves but dimensions of being-human, traits of human personhood, we must consider the basic structure of the human being: personality, or personhood.

BASIC STRUCTURE OF THE HUMAN

The human is articulated in man and woman, and thus occurs within a profoundly dialectical structure. The human being as such occurs, on the one hand, as what the anthropological sciences say he and she is; on the other hand, the human being is something not yet described or investigated—what we might call an open possibility. The human being is at once be-ing and being-able-to-be. The human being is the known and the unknown, the deciphered and the mysterious, the clear, the studied, the thought, the word, the order, the system—but also the silence that wraps that word, the darkness emitting the light, the chaos from which the astounding may emerge, the mystery that can ever be sketched in outline, but that ever remains mystery. The human being is the difficult dialectical unity of the two dimensions that constitute the human being—in the form of man and woman.

The human being, then, is an identity realized in multiple differences. The human is essentially polar and multiple. The human is both self *and* psychological, sociological, historical, religious, cultural, internal, and external circumstances. To experience the human, on any level, is to experience a plurality sustained by a basic identity, inasmuch as all circumstances can bear upon the concrete reality of the human being without his or her being lost in them, without his or her being deprived of identity.

The human being never encounters himself or herself directly in perfect identification. Identification always comes by way of differentiation. Individuals come to know themselves through their self-image, or their idea of themselves. It is only through his or her efforts and accomplishments that the individual experiences the encounter with self. Human identity recedes with the subject's approach; and yet it reveals itself in all that it generates. The human being is engaged, then, in a joint life-project with his or her circumstances. The human being "co-thinks" with the thoughts she or he has, "co-acts" with his or her deeds. Hence, the human being occurs essentially as communion and community. Community is the vital sharing of identity-in-difference. The more the human being is able to embrace and share what is different, what is other, the more she or he exists in community and solidarity.

The basic structure of the human consists in an *and*. It consists in being a human being *and* nevertheless different from that with which he or she communes. It consists in being human as male *and* female, human being *and* world, human "I" *and* the "not-I" within, human "I" *and* thou, human being *and* society, human being *and* God, and so on and so on. In the dialogue with what she or he is not, the human being is built up and enriched. The capacity to accept, to bear with, and to commune with differences is the strength of the human personality, and constitutes the human personal identity. This task obliges the individual to be constantly open to the different and the new, to detach from self, to place herself or himself at risk. The basic human structure is dialectical, then, charged with tension, and always in danger of a self-closing, a retreat into his or her "home world," a rejection of differences. The human being's synthesis is never complete. He or she is always a world in the making. Construct the human, know the human, project the human as we will, we shall never exhaust the human's mysterious depth. The human being is ever the "known unknown."

MASCULINE AND FEMININE: DIFFERENT DIMENSIONS OF THE HUMAN

The foregoing reflections should be a help to us in our attempt to arrive at a better understanding of what the masculine and feminine elements are in the human being. They constitute the

poles of an existential dialectic, as we have seen. The feminine—
in every human being, man and woman—expresses the pole of darkness, mystery, depth, night, death, interiority, earth, feeling, re-
ceptivity, generative force, and the vitality of the human.

The masculine—in every human being, man and woman—is
an expression of the opposite pole: light, sun, time, impulse,
surging power, order, exteriority, objectivity, reason. Aggressiveness, transcendence, clarity, the thrust toward transformation, the capacity to impose order and project into the future,
belong to the masculine. Feminine traits, in both men and
women, include repose, immobility, immanence, a longing for
the past, and a certain darkness that challenges curiosity and
stimulates inquiry.

The feminine is the primordial source of life. The masculine
is that life in full bloom. The power of a vital fullness resides in
the feminine. The power of organization and domination surges
in the masculine. In the feminine is repose and preservation; in
the masculine, conquest and acquisition. Defensive struggle belongs to the feminine, offensive to the masculine.

But let us be very careful here. We are not saying that a man
actualizes all of the masculine, or that a woman actualizes all of
the feminine. A like identification—masculine with man and
feminine with woman—in the technical literature, as in psychology, anthropology, and the human sciences generally, has
always vitiated a lucid formulation of the problem, with serious
social consequences. The usurpation of the masculine by men
has resulted in the judgment (on the part of men) that the male
is the only vehicle of rationality, of the world, and of societal
presence—with women relegated to the realm of the private,
and to tasks of dependency often regarded as adventitious
ornamentation or satisfaction. The prime condition for more
human, more adequate relationships between men and wom-
en is necessarily the removal of this obstacle, which is cultural
(any "theological" considerations in its defense, such as emerge
in official church discussions on new ministries for women,
notwithstanding).

It is the task of each and every one of us, against the horizon
of our personal sexual and biological condition, to integrate our
masculinity and femininity into our life purpose. Individuation

proceeds by way of a dialogue between opaque, dark, passionate, shadowy, profound mystery and the clear, rational, objective, organized principle of order in human life. Each of us is all of this. It is all part of the dramatic world of human interiority. Each of us, then, is called to realize both our masculine and feminine humanity as best we possibly can.

We may encounter difficulty at either pole. Some of us overemphasize the masculine aspects of our personality, and become rationalistic, cold, and "objective"—light without heat. Others overdevelop the feminine, and become too exclusively irrational, passionate, and chaotic—heat without light. It is only in a combination of the two that life appears in all its harmony—not because tensions have been resolved, but because a synthesis of tensions affords us a deep sustenance and renewal. The dialogue of the two dimensions is part of every process of becoming a person. Without this dialogue, we have a "macho" man, or a "total woman," or an effeminate man, or a masculine woman. The masculine or the feminine within us is distorted into violence or fragility.

Male and female are not only biological properties, then, physiological characteristics of the sexes. They are profound ontological dimensions of each and every one of us.

As we have indicated, cultural manifestations of the masculine and the feminine vary enormously. Margaret Mead has demonstrated this beyond the shadow of a doubt.[6] Anthropological studies like those of Erich Neumann in depth psychology have shown the ambivalent nature of the masculine-feminine dimension.[7] Neumann makes use of the great myths. The feminine, incarnate in woman, is man's mother and lover, sister and daughter, slave and queen. She is holy and diabolical, angel and witch, maiden and prophetess, friend and enemy. Women are symbols of the day and the night, reality and the dream, heaven and earth. As Simone de Beauvoir put it so well: "Man searches for woman in nature, with all of its life-bearing forces, and all of its shadowy and destructive elements." The feminine can be the influx of the positive, benign forces that open paths to a man's undreamed-of horizons; or it can be the influx of negative forces that turn him into a slave.

Mythologies preserve the wisdom of deep human realities.

C

Thus, they are charged with the duality of masculine and feminine. The positive face of the Great Mother is represented by Isis, Demeter, and Mary. The negative face is represented by the Gorgon, Hecate, and Kali. The feminine that bestows, elevates, transforms, and introduces us to the vision of the unsuspected—initiates us into mystery—is represented by the Sky Venus, Sophia, and Mary. The feminine that seduces, imprisons, blinds, and maddens is portrayed by the Earth Venus, Circes, Astarte, and Lilith.

Women's growing awareness over the past decades of their situation of dependency in a preponderantly patriarchal civilization, along with the social transformation of relationships between the sexes, ought to be taken as the creakings of a new rotation of humanity's cultural axis. A new way of manifesting the feminine and the masculine is beginning to make its appearance. Now man and woman will be understood against the backdrop of a profound personal equality—an equality of origin and destiny, of task and commitment, in the building of a society of greater communion and less domination, of more democracy and less discrimination.

MYTH AS THE LANGUAGE OF THE MASCULINE AND FEMININE

It may seem strange for us to reject the dry, abstract language of ontology, and have recourse to the language of myth, in a section of an ontological study. But the ontology of masculine and feminine overflows the bounds of biological determinants, and is found in dimensions that only the figurative, representative language of myth can adquately translate. As Paul Ricoeur reflected: "At heart, sexuality continues to be all but impenetrable to reflection and inaccessible to human control. Perhaps it is this opacity that results in . . . its failure to be absorbed by either an ethic or a system. Only a symbolic representation can capture it, by virtue of the mythical that yet abides within us."[8]

The mythical within us is a remnant of humanity's historical past; but it is also a part of our psychic present. Primitive humanity, the humanity of the patriarchal or matriarchal eras, has left us more than the archeological grandeur of historical time.

It lives on in the psychic realities of our living, interior archeology today, as psychoanalysis has demonstrated. Personal fulfillment and human well-being depend very much on how we relate to those realities, on how our consciousness reacts to the contents of our subconscious—whether it accepts and integrates them, or resists and represses them.

The masculine-feminine universe lying deep in the human personality is inaccessible to discursive reason. It is, however, available to the wise exegesis of the ancient myths. In figurative, representative language, myths express the richness of the human mystery made specific in man and woman far better than does conceptual discourse, which always proceeds from definitions, limitations, and an epistemological reality-pruning.

This is why the polar unity of masculine and feminine in each of us, man or woman, is to be found in nearly all ancient religious mythologies and cosmogonies. Chinese thought represented the feminine and the masculine as a circle composed of two equal parts, one in light, the other in shadow: yin and yang. The Babylonian and Egyptian civilizations thought of all reality as hermaphroditic, and issuing from a single masculine-feminine principle (Ishtar). Chaos, earth, and night are functions of the feminine principle. Order, air, and day express the masculine principle. Plato's *Symposium* contains the following myth of the birth of man and woman. In the beginning, Zeus created only androgynous beings, each with two faces, four eyes, four ears, four hands, and two sexes. But because these beings sought to pit their strength against that of the gods, Zeus divided each in two, "as one divides a piece of fruit or an egg by means of a horsehair." In separation, male and female go in ceaseless quest of their lost primordial unity. Through eros, they seek to overcome their mutual imcompleteness. A Hebrew midrash tells us that originally man and woman had but one body with two faces. Then God separated them, presenting each with a separate set of ribs. But they strive with all their might to be one flesh again. In Genesis 1:27, humanity is represented as one, simultaneously man and woman. The notion of the plural, polar unity of each of us as masculine and feminine is as old as humanity itself. The studies of Carl Jung and his school on the psychology of the complexes confirm the truth of the ancient myths.

This truth, so graphically represented in the myths, astounds ontology. The individual is always both male *and* female. The individual is not of a piece, as the gods are. We are each of us a plural unity, an identity ever fulfilled in difference through a continual process that oscillates between identity and difference. The masculine and feminine in each man and woman actualize the dual unity of the human person.

What are the feminine and the masculine ultimately, radically? We do not know. We stand before a mystery. We only know what we have been shown by the cultural history of humanity. Human culture has always reflected the constant, immense reservoir of humanity's experience of good and evil in the personal and collective unconscious. Society today is no exception. But we do not think that these cultural forms ever exhaust the possibilities and virtualities of the masculine and feminine. History never repeats itself, never simply reconstructs the past. History is ever the creator and producer of the yet-to-be-experienced. Thus, the masculine and the feminine are open to the obscure dimensions of the future, whose realizations we may be able to foresee but never manipulate. We must prepare for the coming of the future, however, by a continual effort to anticipate it.

While we wait, we must not be utopians. We must cherish no visions of a total, complete reconciliation of the sexes.[9] History will continue to be the scene of their tension. History has already seen genuine wars of the sexes, and the scars they have left are deep. In light of this, the question arises: Why do the feminine and the masculine only occur in decadent realizations? True, the human being is intrinsically *fallible*, as Paul Ricoeur has shown in his excellent analysis.[10] We are the vessels of a congenital fragility that, if it does not *cause* our fall, at least renders that fall intelligible. The ultimate explanation for our perversion lies beyond the realm of philosophy. Perhaps it is a matter for theology, whose task is to tackle the problem of Meaning and to seek the most correct answer possible to this most metaphysical question of all. Be that as it may, philosophical reflection is altogether aware of the fact that the masculine and feminine, owing to the intrinsic reciprocity defining them, are enveloped in some mysterious, transcending reality that opens up the possibility of a face-to-face encounter and reciprocal communion.[11] What is this reality? This is the question that fires philosophical thought, today as yesterday and tomorrow. Masculinity and femininity represent an anthropological version of the basic question of all ontology: Why the one and the many? Why the internal differentiation of being? Why is there not only being, but beings? Why does humanity appear as man and woman?

Here the *logos* buries itself in its discursivity, and pure contemplation of reality-as-it-is emerges. And suddenly our why goes up in smoke. There is no need for an answer where there is no longer a question.

CONCLUSION: SIX BASIC PROPOSITIONS ON THE FEMININE

Having completed our analytic, philosophical incursion into the vast continent of the feminine, let us lay out some basic concepts for the enunciation of a correct grammar of discourse upon the human as feminine. Here, it seems to us, is what we must keep in mind:

1. *Difference:* The sexes are different. One is not the other. The human being is not a simple being. He or she is always concrete and comprehensible only in the difference between man and woman.
2. *Inclusiveness:* Notwithstanding their difference, masculine and feminine interpenetrate. Every human being is at once masculine and feminine, in a density and proportion peculiar to each individual.
3. *Reciprocity:* By virtue of their mutual inclusion, woman and man are not merely adjacent. They interface, in an existential vis-à-vis bearing upon all manifestations of life. Each discovers himself or herself in relation to the other. In light of the woman a man discovers himself as male. In light of the man a woman perceives herself as female. Reciprocity constitutes the basic experience of the human being as male and female.
4. *Historicity:* The face-to-face encounter of woman and man occurs in the most diverse ways. There is no preestablished mechanism. The correlates are constructed, dismantled, re-

built, and invented within a variety of historical conditionings. A difficult dialectic links the masculine and feminine, and it is often a negative one, manifested in a struggle between the sexes, with one pole exercising a despotism over the other. At this level, anatomical, psychological, economic, social, and cultural factors intervene. But there are also moments in which the dialectic emerges in more balanced, symmetrical relations, favoring a social intercourse that is more humanizing for both sexes.

5. *Historical originality:* Owing to their inclusive, reciprocal differences, both sexes can be described in terms of historical realizations of their major expressions—on the condition that they not be described exclusively in terms of those expressions, all of which pertain to a concrete masculine *and* feminine human nature. For example, where there is life, depth, interiority, mystery, religiosity, tenderness, and so on, there is the feminine, in both man and woman. Of course, these qualities will tend to manifest themselves more in woman.

6. *Unity in difference:* What we perceive, what we can analyze, is the male-female difference. But this difference yields to that profound unity that is the human person. All appearances to the contrary notwithstanding, the human being cannot be understood directly and immediately. There is no simple, direct concept of "the human being." We understand the human person obliquely, through the differences we perceive in him and her. Thus, the human person appears as a mysterious, disquieting depth, as a oneness in plurality and a plurality in oneness. Our perception of this complex reality permits us to fix limits to the discourse of reason, and to prepare for the discourse of pathos with its fabric of symbol and myth. There are many legitimate avenues, then, to the reality of the masculine-and-feminine human being.

5. The Feminine: A Theological Meditation

Having completed our philosophical reflection, we are now in a position to undertake a theological meditation. Indeed, it is only in theology that this writing can claim an audience.

SCOPE OF OUR THEOLOGICAL MEDITATION

It is the part of theology to radicalize a question, to exhaust its content. Theology goes in quest of the Meaning of meanings, the ultimate and unconditional Reality. Theology, as the etymology of the word suggests, undertakes a reflection in relation to God. Theology will investigate the feminine in two ways, then. It will ask: (1) To what extent is the feminine a path to God for humanity? (2) Conversely, to what extent is the feminine a path to humanity for God? In other words, how does the feminine reveal God, and how does God speak to us in the feminine?

First of all, of course, this question can be approached on a purely philosophical level. God is also the object of a philosophical reflection. Philosophy, too, in its highest expression, poses the problem of God—God as the supreme being upon which all other beings depend—and we have, for example, Aristotle's *theologikē epistēmē*. On this level, as we have seen, the feminine presents itself as a "perfection," a quality of the universe, and so as having its ultimate root in God, while God, conversely, must be reflected in the feminine. Thus, the feminine would have a divine depth, and God would have a feminine dimension. This proposition has a content even if we do not identify that content. Nor, indeed, have we any intention of entering into this philosophical question, inasmuch as it is not entirely new to Christian theological discourse.

Second, we could pose the theological problem of the feminine in terms of the existential leap of faith in a God incarnate in Jesus Christ (the Son) and spiritualized in the life of the just (in the Holy Spirit). Theological meditation is of a special epistemological nature. It has its own discourse, a different discourse from that of the sciences or philosophy. In light of the "theological difference," then, our basic question will be: How is the feminine, as seen by the sciences and philosophy, also a revelation of the Holy Trinity, Father, Son, and Holy Spirit? How is the Holy Trinity revealed in the feminine?

Theological discourse, whose intention is to be a rational grammar of the experience of faith, must therefore be enunciated on the level of faith—in our case, Christian faith. It will therefore seek to "read" the feminine from a point of departure in theological principles. These principles are indispensable. Only they can guarantee the theological character of a reading of reality. They will be developed from the fonts of the faith—Scripture and tradition. Hence, we must confront these sources. Scripture and tradition are the vehicles of God's official revelation.

Now, God's revelation will include material on the feminine, to be sure. Revelation will manifest the will of the Most High for this basic building block of personhood. But this revelation will not be simple or transparent. Revelation is historical, and uses the vehicle of the sociohistorical in order to communicate itself. Its form is influenced by the particulars of a place and time. It is important, then, always to discern, in the revelatory event, the transient historical fact from God's permanent communication. History and revelation are always intermingled. Hence, the necessity of a special discernment in order not to attribute to God what is human, or to humanity what is properly God's. No one is exempt from this effort at lucidity—neither the magisterium, nor the theologian, nor the individual believer who may wish to give reasons for his or her faith and hope.

We have a threefold task before us, then. First, we must see what Scripture has to say about the feminine and about women. Second, we must consider how tradition has received this biblical message. Finally, we must subject the findings of scientific exegesis and philosophy to a theological analysis.

SCRIPTURE AND CHRISTIAN TRADITION ON THE FEMININE

Judeo-Christianity is an eminently masculine religious expression. God is a Father, God has an eternal Son, that Son is born in time, of a virgin. In its institutional presentation, Judeo-Christianity is a religion of males. Theirs is the monopoly of the means of symbolic production. They are the ones who organize and preside over the Christian community. Women's place is marginal. Jesus Christ's masculinity has attained its divinization, while his feminine aspect, according to common tradition, has remained in its creaturely state.

This last statement should not shock us. The Judeo-Christian revelation was given in a patriarchal era, when the role of the feminine was secondary. Being historical, obeying the laws of incarnation, revelation accommodated its sociocultural matrix of male domination. The Old and New Testaments are books about men in a society of men. Women are merely "ancillary."[1]

The awareness of such a historical and ideological amalgam obliges us to undertake a hermeneutics of scriptural "depatriarchalization."[2] We shall have to maintain constant vigilance with respect to the infiltration of any masculinizing ideology into the religious expressions of the Bible and of tradition. Of course, we need not go overboard here: if it is true that the feminine constitutes a structural dimension of the human, then we shall be able to rely upon Scripture and tradition to include the feminine dimension in the content of revelation, despite ideology. Inevitably, the feminine will appear in the Christian Scriptures and in the witness of the history of faith. Our task is only to discover the inflation of the masculine in these fonts of our faith, and to underscore the feminine dimension there.

JUDAISM AND ANTIFEMINISM

The whole dialectic of the battle of the sexes and the marginalization of women is readily evident in what the Scriptures have to say about the feminine.[3] It is true that male-dominated ancient Judaism did tolerate a considerable female presence in the life of the people. The texts speak of the political importance of

Miriam. They highlight the role of the ancient prophetesses and antiheroines Delilah and Jezebel. The descriptions are moving and enchanting, as in the encounter of Abraham's servant with Rebecca (Gen. 24:15–67). The texts offer us a beautiful description of the figures of Anna, Sarah, and Ruth. And, of course, we must not forget that document of the ideal love between a man and a woman, the Song of Songs.

However, as the people of Israel settled down and began to build cities, the instruments of social power found their way more and more into the hands of men. Antifeminism became the rule, especially in the post-Exilic period. Sirach, so high in its praise of a "good wife" (Sir. 26:1–24), nevertheless betrays a blatant antifeminism: " . . . Worst of all evils is that of a woman" (25:12); "Better a man's harshness than a woman's indulgence . . . " (42:14); "With a dragon or a lion I would rather dwell than live with an evil woman" (25:15). Man's wickedness is because of woman, the writer explains: "In woman was sin's beginning, and because of her we all die" (25:23).

Again, we have the marked antifeminism of the Yahwistic account of the creation of Eve (Gen. 2:18–25) and the Fall (3:1–19). The Yahwistic account, which is a later one, dating from the tenth or eleventh century B.C., had the effect of reinforcing a masculinizing exegesis of even the Elohist version. In the latter, woman is formed from Adam's rib: "This one, at last, is bone of my bones and flesh of my flesh; This one shall be called 'woman' (*ishá*), for out of 'her man' (*ish*) this one has been taken" (Gen. 2:23). And the sacred text goes on: "That is why a man leaves his father and mother and clings to his wife, and the two of them become one body" (Gen. 2:24). The intent of the sacred writer is to demonstrate the unity of male and female, and so justify monogamy.[4] This doctrine should have been a discouragement to discrimination against women. But it encouraged it instead: the notion that Adam came first, and that woman was formed from Adam's rib, was interpreted in the later rabbinic theology as evidence of male superiority.

An antifeminist intent emerges much more clearly in the account of original sin: "The woman saw that the tree was good for food, pleasing to the eyes, and desirable for gaining wisdom. So she took some of its fruit and ate it; and she also gave some to her husband, who was with her, and he ate it. Then the eyes of both of them were opened, and they realized that they were naked . . . " (Gen. 3:6–7). The intent of the mythic account is to furnish an etiological demonstration of the fact that evil is humanity's, not God's. But in carrying out its intent, it adopts the antifeminism of the contemporary culture. Woman is the weaker sex. Therefore, it is she who falls, and seduces man.[5] Her primordial debility then serves as the ideological justification of her historical submission: "Your urge shall be for your husband, and he shall be your master" (Gen. 3:16). Later, we shall see how this text has been invoked to justify both discrimination against women and the notion that they are all seducers.

JESUS AND WOMEN'S LIBERATION

It is against this antifeminist backdrop that we must view Jesus' message of liberation. Women in Jesus' time suffered discrimination at the hands of both society and religion. First, they were not circumcised, and hence could not be a part of God's covenant. Next, they were subject to a series of rigid laws of "purification," by reason of their female biological condition. Finally, they had been personified in Eve, with all of the inferiority that that implied. Eventually, a male could actually write that he thanked God he had not been born a pagan, a woman, or one ignorant of the Torah.[6]

In an ideological context like this, Jesus must be considered a feminist.[7] He preached no explicit doctrine of women's liberation. However, his words and actions were feminist. And he laid down a general principle of liberation that had its repercussions for the contemporary subjection of women. The historical Jesus addresses his central message—the proclamation of the Reign of God—first and foremost to the poor, the marginalized, and the oppressed. But women more than anyone else were poor, marginalized, and oppressed. They understood him immediately. Flaunting all the rules of the time, a group of women followed him as his disciples (Luke 8:1–3, 23:49, 24:6–10). Jesus' ethical revolution consisted basically in a victory over the ethic of the law through an ethic of responsibility and love, expressed in a recognition of the person and a quest for community. Consistent with his project of liberation, Jesus breaks with many of the taboos of his time where women are concerned. He maintains a close friendship with Martha and Mary (Luke 10:38). In contravention of the ethos of his time, and to the wonderment of his disciples, he speaks publicly and alone with the Samaritan woman at Jacob's well (John 4:27). He defends the woman seized in the act of adultery, against current explicit, discriminatory legislation (John 7:53–8:10); he allows a known prostitute to touch and anoint his feet (Luke 7:36–50); he performs cures in favor of a great number of women, like the mother-in-law of Peter (Luke 4:38–39), the widow of Naim, whose son he raises from the dead (Luke 7:11–17), the daughter of Jairus (Matt. 9:18–19), the hunchback (Luke 13:10–17), the Syro-Phoenician pagan (Mark 7:24–30), and the woman who had suffered twelve years from a hemorrhage (Matt. 19:20–22).

Women figure often in his parables, especially very poor women: for example, the one who had lost the coin (Luke 15:8–10), or the one who went before the judge (Luke 18:1–8). While often severe with men, Jesus never discriminates against women.[8] In his criticism of the social practice of divorce and his defense of the marriage bond we have examples of his forthright, repeated interventions on behalf of women's dignity.

In sum, Jesus' attitudes and message signal a breach with prevailing mores, and constitute an immense novelty within the framework of the age. He regards women as individuals, daughters of God, addressees of the Good News, who, together with men, are invited to join the new community of the Reign of God. We must recognize, however, that Jesus only introduces a liberating principle. He testifies to it by his own practice, of course, but there are no immediate historical consequences. Any societal assimilation of the anthropological and ideological revolution inaugurated by Jesus has to await the transformation of economic, political, and cultural influences. As we know, the road from principle to historical reality is a rocky one. Social transformations are all intertwined. Each depends on modifications in other, more infrastructural, elements.[9] Until such modifications are forthcoming, then, any liberating principle continues to be but a seed, charged with potential life, encouraging criticism, and providing a reference point for ideals that will eventually bring about the required transformations. Only in the last two centuries has it become a historical possibility for women to begin to achieve actual, concrete, historical equality with men.

EQUALITY AND SUBJECTION: THE AMBIGUITY OF THE NEW TESTAMENT

Later Christianity failed to maintain the innovative breach inaugurated by Jesus Christ.[10] True, women initially carried on certain signal activities in the Christian community's proclamation and practice of faith.[11] Paul cites a great many women who had "worked hard" or "labored long" in the Lord's service (Rom. 16:12). Priscilla and Phoebe were deaconesses of the church of Cenchreae (Rom. 16:1). We know of Mary, Persis, Julia, Tryphaena, and Tryphosa. Acts speaks of Lydia, a dealer in "purple goods," wealthy and active in the community (Acts 16:14–15), as well as of Damaris, who had been converted in Athens (17:34). We hear of prophetesses, such as the four maiden daughters of Philip (Acts 21:9). We hear of women who made clothes for the poor (Acts 9:36–37). Paul mentions Evodia and Syntyche as having helped him in his struggle for the gospel (Phil. 4:2).

Despite this novelty—facilitated by the fact that discrimination against women in the Roman Empire was considerably less virulent than in Judaism—the New Testament reflects the attitude toward women of surrounding culture. For example, despite the understanding and tenderness he asks for women, Peter accepts the prevailing ideology that they constitute the "weaker sex" (1 Pet. 3:7), and demands their submission to their husbands (1 Pet. 3:1; Tim. 2:5; 1 Cor. 14:34; Eph. 5:22–24; Col. 3:18). The author of 1 Timothy states forcefully: "I do not permit a woman to act as a teacher, or in any way to have authority over a man; she must be quiet. For Adam was created first, Eve afterward; moreover, it was not Adam who was deceived but the woman. It was she who was led astray and fell into sin. She will be saved by childbearing . . ." (1 Tim. 2:12–15). The writer is, of course, referring to the sexist mythology of Genesis, which we have seen. This is the type of argument that was endlessly repeated in ecclesiastical circles, even to very recent times. Admittedly mythological texts are used in their literal sense to legitimate a situation of men's domination of women.

Owing to his influence on later history, Paul occupies a distin-

guished place in the area under consideration.[12] His writings
contain two elements in tension—one liberating, stemming from
Jesus, and one discriminatory, stemming from the surrounding
culture. In principle, Paul accepts the strange new notion, introduced by Jesus, of the equality of women. At the same time,
he fails to apply this novel notion to his culture, and continues
to think in terms of the subjection of women. His formulation
of the Christian message is clear and authentic: "There does not
exist among you . . . male or female. All are one in Christ Jesus"
(Gal. 3:28). It is in light of this equality that Paul can grant
women a parity with men in public worship, which was no easy
matter in those times. Because of this principle, he can say that
every man prays and prophesies and that every woman prays
and prophesies (1 Cor. 11:4–5). And yet, he seeks to maintain
tradition (1 Cor. 11:2) and restrict this same right of women,
under the pressure of traditional discrimination. He calls on
women to cover their heads in the assemblies (1 Cor. 11:4–5) as
a token of their subjection (1 Cor. 11:10). To justify this measure, the Apostle invokes an argument that we would regard as
ideological today. He seizes on the rabbinical teaching of the
Jewish philosopher Philo of Alexandria that there are discontin-
uous degrees of similarity to God. Thus Paul establishes the following degrees: God, Christ, man, woman. " . . . The head of
every man is Christ; the head of a woman is her husband; and
the head of Christ is the Father" (1 Cor. 11:3). "A man . . . is
the image of God and the reflection of his glory. Woman, in
turn, is the reflection of man's glory" (1 Cor. 11:7). And he goes
on to cite the ideology of the surrounding culture: "Man was
not made from woman but woman from man. Neither was man
created for woman but woman for man. For this reason a woman
ought to have a sign of submission on her head, because of the
angels" (1 Cor. 11:8–10). Then he remembers the evangelical
equality of the sexes, although this would seem to compromise
the force of his ideotheological source: "Yet, in the Lord, woman
is not independent of man nor man independent of woman. In
the same way that woman was made from man, so man is born
of woman, and all is from God" (1 Cor. 11:11–12). And the
balance is reestablished. But the ambiguity between the cultural
element and what Jesus has established remains intact.

In another important text, Paul demands that women keep silence in the assemblies, on grounds that it is not their place to speak, but to live their lives in submission (1 Cor. 14:34–35). Current exegesis inclines to the theory that this text is a later interpolation at the hands of certain Christian converts from Judaism. As to the argument itself, we have already considered it.[13] In any event, if our exegesis is to be consistent, we cannot justify discrimination against women in the name of Pauline revelation.

We find this same tension—between the Christian message of equality and the ideology of the surrounding culture—in the celebrated passage from Ephesians where Paul speaks of the relationship between a man and a woman in marriage (Eph. 5:21–33).[14] First some asymmetrical relationships are asserted: "Wives should be submissive to their husbands as if to the Lord because the husband is the head of his wife just as Christ is head of his body the church, as well as its savior. As the church submits to Christ, so wives should submit to their husbands in everything" (Eph. 5:22–24). The intent of this passage is to underscore the religiosacramental, or symbolic, significance of Christian marriage. Paul calls it a "great foreshadowing" (Eph. 5:32), or revelation of God's will. This will has reached its culmination in Jesus Christ, in whom God has shown love for all humanity. This divine love had been symbolized by marriage in the Jewish tradition, especially in the prophets. Paul stands in the same tradition. He takes Christian marriage as the lesser image of the greater archetype: God's love for humanity, or for that believing part of humanity that is the Church. In order to express this truth, however, Paul uses the cultural concept of Jewish marriage as understood and lived in his own time—as a relationship between husband and wife analogous to that between the head and the rest of the body. The head is master of the body, the member that gives the orders. Just so, the husband is "head" or commander of the woman, who is subject to him.

Paul takes *this* marriage, and erects it into an archetype of the relationship between Christ and the Church. Christ is the head, the master, of the Church, which is his body, just as the husband is the head of his wife. We must be careful to be faithful to the intent of this typology. Paul has no intention of defining the relationship between husband and wife here. On the contrary, he precisely *begins* with a (particular cultural) concept of this relationship—that of the subjection of the wife to her husband—without question or even purification. His intent is only to show the relationship between Christ and the Church. To this purpose, he uses the relationship between husband and wife, as culturally given, as a symbol. Just as the husband-wife relationship is one of inequality—*at that time*—so also is the relationship between Christ and his Church (of its very nature) one of inequality. Paul has no intention of canonizing the inequality of the marriage relationship, an inequality we today see as discriminatory. The marriage relationship is merely the symbol here. Paul simply takes it in its existing form and points out the similarity between it and the relationship between Christ and the Church. The latter relationship is of its very nature unequal because Christ is God and the Church consists of mere human beings. Christ is the savior himself, while the Church is merely the sacramental sign of salvation. The Apostle's comparison scarcely legitimates the inequality of relationships between men and women.

But then, after his reflection on the wife's subjection to her husband, stemming from his cultural milieu, Paul seems to recover the Christian message. He goes on to admonish the husband, "Each one should love his wife as he loves himself" (Eph. 5:33). After all, the two are one flesh (Eph. 5:25–33).

The ambivalence abides. Paul has managed to recover his balance, but his precarious compromise has been insufficient to prevent his texts—a reflection of the prevailing discriminatory culture—from being invoked as revelation and used to legitimate men's domination over women.

ANTIFEMINISM IN CHRISTIAN TRADITION

How has the tradition of faith received Jesus' message down through the centuries? Has it embraced equality for women, or is it fraught with all of the ambiguities we find in the New Testament?

Generally speaking, we may say that Christian tradition has preserved Paul's ambivalence.[15] In principle, there must be equality of the sexes. But in practice, women's subordination to men is maintained. Just as with slavery, Christianity was helpless to move from theory to practice. History is not made of voluntaristic acts, as we have seen. In order for an ideological revolution to be made historical, certain antecedent transformations must occur in the economic and sociopolitical infrastructure.

The gospel principle of male-female equality surrendered to certain de facto obstacles that seemed insurmountable, and above all inevitable, because they were seen as expressing the natural order of things as willed by God. Throughout the centuries, theologians and canonists busied themselves with absolutizing these obstacles, doubtless moved by the desire to explain the ambiguity (gospel novelty and historical subjection) and reduce the flagrant, scandalous contradiction between doctrine and practice.[16]

Thus, ideology enters the scene, and attempts to justify prevailing reality—an ideology resting on a male chauvinist, unilateral interpretation of the biblical texts, and sociohistorical traditions interpreted as natural law (although today we know very well that these traditions are merely historical).

It would be idealistic to expect of the Church what neither the Church nor anyone else had any notion of. What could have been expected, and what must now be expected, is that the Church live more prophetically its own truth, and in the name of that truth take a critical distance from surrounding culture. An outstanding specialist on feminism in the Church has said:

When Christians forget the spirit that ought to be guiding their lives, the Church has the tendency to be little more than a mirror of the prevailing culture, with the consequent reemergence of the old battle of the sexes. Women are seen as inferior creatures, threatening men's integrity. To eliminate them from ecclesiastical structures, then, seems ever so much easier than a burdensome search for understanding and cooperation in the service of God.[17]

We shall make no attempt to trace the Church's antifeminism here, not even in broad outline. Detailed documentation is abundantly available elsewhere. Let us, however, examine just one example of how biblical texts have been invoked to legitimate woman's de facto subjection to man. According to the account of Genesis 2:21–25, woman was formed from the rib of Adam. The first step, as we have seen, is to misinterpret this passage as teaching woman's dependence on man. Then Paul, in light of this declaration, says that as it is not man who comes from woman, but woman who comes from man, she must submit to him (1 Cor. 11:7–9). The third stage is to say that woman is not totally and adequately in the image and likeness of God—that this is man's prerogative; and this Paul suggests in 1 Corinthians 11:7. Finally, in the twelfth century, Gratian's *Decretum*[18]—the principal juridical source of canon law even today—citing phrases attributed to Augustine and Ambrose (really Ambrosiaster), draws legal conclusions from the latter misconception: "This image [of God] is in the male as a unique creation, the origin of the rest of human beings. He has received from God the power to govern in God's place, for he is made in the image of one God. For this reason woman is not made in the image of God."[19] Thus, once more, women's historical subjection to men is attributed to the notion that she was created from the rib of Adam that she might serve him. In the same vein, we have this celebrated passage from Augustine: "It pertains to the natural order among human beings that women be subject to men and children to their parents. It is a matter of justice that the weaker reason be submissive to the stronger."[20]

The canonization of antifeminism has had tremendous repercussions for the life of the Church. Even to our own day, it has reserved the things of faith, of community, and of ministerial ordination to the domain of the male. The declaration of the Congregation for the Doctrine of the Faith of October 15, 1976, on the question of the admission of women to the priesthood rests on the male chauvinist argumentation of centuries past as if nothing had happened in history since the canonical codification of the twelfth century.[21] According to the 1917 Code of Canon Law women are ecclesiastically classified with children and the mentally handicapped.

But besides this ideologization in the form of a biblical theology, we have another, this time of a biological order. In ancient times, it was believed that only the male principle was active in the generation of human life. Then this conceptualization was systematized during the age of High Scholasticism. In terms of this androcentrism, then, we have the following problem: If the offspring's whole being comes from the male, how does it happen that the offspring is sometimes female? The answer, regarded as a scientific one, was that females were a deviation, an aberration, a frustration of the only true and complete sex, the male. Thomas Aquinas, citing Aristotle, regards woman as a *mas occasionatus,* a deficient male destined merely to be the receptacle of the male generative force.[22] It is this biological deficiency that explains women's *imbecillitas naturae,* their fragile nature, and therefore their total dependence on men. "Woman needs man," says Aquinas, "not only to conceive, like the animals, but to be governed, inasmuch as the male is more perfect by virtue of his reason and stronger by virtue of his courage."[23] A like prejudice against women's capabilities leads, of course, to their being regarded as incapable for all practical purposes of discharging public responsibilities, civil or ecclesiastical.

Let us observe the ideological mechanism in operation here. It is not theoretical argumentation that results in the marginalization of women. It is women's concrete, historical marginalization that results in the argumentation. The argumentation only serves to explain the prevailing subjection of women, even in terms of the "natural." Thus, the historical die is cast. It is socialized by women themselves, since they must now accept their marginalization and subjection as natural and the "will of God." Even the great female figures of the Bible, and Mary in particular, have been interpreted in terms of this ideology. Mary is not presented as the liberating woman calling down the divine wrath on the rich on behalf of the poor, daring to raise her voice in denunciation of the conflicts of this world, but simply as the woman who lives totally in the shadow of the man Jesus, the model for women, in cooking and sewing, fetching water at the well, building the fire, buried in the anonymity of the family.[24]

Nature, however, is mightier than ideological superstructures. Strong, independent, decisive women have never been lacking in the history of the Church to show forth the feminine in its true qualities. Martyrs like Blandina, Agatha, Lucy, and Inez strengthened others in the faith. The English abbess Hilda (d. 680) presided over the Synod of Whitby, which accepted the Roman date for Easter, with all of the consequences that that entailed. We have Catherine of Siena, advisor to Popes Gregory XI and Urban VI in the fourteenth century. We have Teresa of Avila, the great mystic, theologian, and reformer of Spanish Catholicism in the sixteenth century. We have Joan of Arc, warrior and martyr for the truth, whose valor was too "manly" for the conventions of the time. We have Juana Angelica, the Brazilian abbess who stood like a rock against a troop of soldiers in defense of the right of sanctuary. These and countless other women, towers of strength, stand as rays of hope for the recovery of the feminine figure of liberation.

Even on the ideotheological level we have an acknowledgment of women's dignity, and we appreciate the abundant data here that lends support to our own personalistic, liberating reading of woman.[25] We have no intention of making a naive reading that would do no more than catalog the vices of the past. However noble the intent—to promote the equality of women, of course, not to sublimate their subjugation—intellectual honesty forbids us to pretend that our whole theological past has been a cipher. We must learn to appreciate the profound ambiguity of the fonts of our faith—Scripture and tradition—in this matter. As anyone can see, the texts come down not only on the side of domination, but also on that of liberation. Let us only declare the stance from which we mean to work: we take sides with the positive current of thought in Scripture and tradition, which elevates women to the same dignity men enjoy. In making this statement, we place ourselves in the most authentic tradition of the historical Jesus. We must acknowledge that there are discriminatory, antifeminist texts in the historical sources of revelation. But this is not part of revelation itself. This is due to the incarnation of revelation in a patriarchal age. These texts do not bind us theologically where their distorted aspect is concerned. After all, it is contrary to our faith to believe that God wills that human beings subjugate one another.

PRINCIPLES FOR A THEOLOGICAL ANTHROPOLOGY OF THE FEMININE

MALE AND FEMALE CREATED EQUAL

The first principle of Judeo-Christian anthropology is the one we have on the first page of the Bible, in the priestly account of the Creation written around the sixth to the fifth centuries

B.C. Quite out of harmony with the antifeminist spirit of his age, the sacred author of the first chapter of Genesis states forcefully: "God created man in his image; in the divine image he created him; male and female he created them" (Gen. 1:27). Here we have a crystal-clear indication of the fundamental equality of the sexes. Each is in the image of God, and equally so. This divine image is complete only as reflected in both sexes. Another vigorous affirmation of this view appears in a later chapter: "When God created man [humanity, Adam], he made him in the likeness of God; he created them male and female. When they were created, he blessed them and named them 'man' [Adam]" (Gen. 5:1–2). There is not the faintest suggestion here of woman's inferiority. She is the equal of the male in her dignity and rights in the sight of all of her fellow human beings. The historical Jesus never cites the Yahwistic account of the creation of woman from Adam's rib. In the dispute over the indissolubility of marriage (Matt. 19:3–6) he refers to the priestly account (Gen. 1:27), and takes no more from the Yahwistic version than the notion of the oneness of woman and man: " . . . And the two of them become one body" (Gen. 2:24). His intervention in behalf of the woman caught in the act of adultery (John 8:1–11, Luke 7:36–50) is the occasion of his attempt to establish male-female equality in the area of sin and sanction. Of course, the classic Christian formulation of the dignity of all persons is found in Paul: "There does not exist among you Jew or Greek, slave or freeman, male or female. All are one in Christ Jesus" (Gal. 3:28). Peter insists on the respect a husband owes his wife, who is "heir just as much as you to the gracious gift of life" (1 Pet. 3:7). The sacred writer employs the juridical expression of equality (*sugklēronomois*, "co-heirs") used in the estate law of the time.

At the same time, the scriptural texts declare that the sexual equality of our first creation has been historically compromised by sin. Sin, as Genesis 3:16–20 acknowledges, has affected both sexes from the beginning. It initiates relationships of independence. It calls for a principle of redemption.

MALE-FEMALE RECIPROCITY

The older of the creation accounts in Genesis, despite its male chauvinist spirit, clearly sketches not only the differences but also the reciprocity between man and woman (Gen. 2:21–24). When God presents to man the woman just created, man (Adam) says: "This one, at last, is bone of my bones and flesh of my flesh. . . . That is why a man leaves his father and mother and clings to his wife, and the two of them become one body" (Gen. 2:23–24). The expressions are different in the two accounts, but they amount to the same thing. Male and female exist for each other. They form a unity. When God decides to create woman, the decision is announced in a typically Hebrew idiom: "It is not good for the man to be alone. I will make a suitable partner for him" (Gen. 2:18). This means, "I shall give man someone to keep him company, someone similar to him." Woman was not created to be man's slave or servant, but his companion, someone of the same nature and dignity as he. The same reciprocity is celebrated in the Song of Songs, in its classic formulation: "My lover belongs to me and I to him" (Song of Songs 2:16, 6:3). Paul, momentarily free of the ambivalence that saturates his thinking, declares: "Woman is not independent of man nor man independent of woman" (1 Cor. 11:11); "Defer to one another out of reverence for Christ" (Gal. 5:21); and "A wife does not belong to herself but to her husband; equally, a husband does not belong to himself but to his wife" (1 Cor. 7:4).

The Feminine: Revelation of God

God is not revealed in biblical tradition in masculine language alone. The feminine, too, is a vehicle of God's revelation. God and Christ are personified in the feminine figure of Wisdom (Prov. 8:22–26, Sir. 24:9, 1 Cor. 24:30). The Wisdom exalted here is a hypostatization of God. But there is such an intimate correlation between woman and Wisdom (Prov. 31:10, 26, 30) that one may be symbolically substituted for the other (Prov. 19:14, 40:12; Wis. 3:12, 7:28).

God is likened to a woman who comforts (Isa. 66:13), the mother who cannot forget the child of her womb (Isa. 49:15; Ps. 25:6, 116:5). Jesus compares himself with the mother bird who seeks to gather her children to herself to protect them (Luke 13:34). At history's end God will perform the classic gesture of a loving mother in wiping the tears from our eyes, eyes so weary with weeping (Rev. 21:4). Every element of God's tenderness and *fetes equality of man & woman (which I feel with them) now ve no. 11/11 being the unexpected date of Angel embassie, bromistice —on day of peace & harmony & my no. 22 (11+11)*

THE FEMININE: A THEOLOGICAL MEDITATION / 77

caring, everything about God as ultimate refuge, everything about God's salvation, is presented in the tradition of feminine language. Here is how a great Russian mystic expressed it:

The most amazing thing we have still to discover is the fact that *man does not possess the paternal instinct to the same degree and intensity that woman possesses the maternal intinct.* . . . This means that, *in the human being, the religious principle is expressed by woman;* the specific sensitivity to the purely spiritual is in the anima, not the animus; and it is the female soul that is closest to the original sources of the Book of Genesis. All this is true to the point that even spiritual fatherhood employs images of motherhood: "I am in labor pains until Christ be formed in you" (Gal. 4:19).[26]

WOMAN IN THE NEW COVENANT: THE INITIATIVE OF FAITH

Women occupy a discrete, but most important, place in the Gospels. They appear at the beginning, in the middle, and at the end of Jesus' life. Thanks to Mary's *fiat,* a Savior comes into the world (Luke 1:38). When all the others have fled, Jesus' female disciples stay, at the foot of the cross (Matt. 27:56). Women are the first witnesses of the Resurrection (Matt. 28:19–20).

In John's Gospel, women perform an essential salvific function.[27] It is at the behest of his mother that Jesus works his first wonder at Cana in Galilee (John 2:11). The woman of Samaria brings the faith to her city (John 4:39–40). Martha and Mary impetrate the greatest of Jesus' public miracles, the raising of Lazarus (John 11:21–30). Mary Magdalene leads the apostles to faith in the Resurrection (John 20:1–18).[28] As we can see, women are the ones who take the initiative of faith, confirming what Athanasius of Sinai, and perhaps Irenaeus himself, said to the effect that in the religious sphere woman is the stronger sex.

THE FEMININE PRINCIPLE OF SALVATION

For Christian faith, not only does Mary, as virgin and mother, represent the fullness of the feminine in all of its various manifestations—wherever the mystery of life is involved—for she is the virgin mother of God in the flesh and she lives in intimate relationship with the Holy Spirit; but thanks to the mystery of the Incarnation—and we shall see this in more detail following—Mary and Jesus are actually bound together in an ontological relation. The flesh that Mary has bestowed on Jesus is the flesh of God. Accordingly, something of Mary's femininity has been hypostatically assumed by God.

In this sense, Mary's state of being Christ's and our Mother explicates something of Christ's redemption, an element which is not explicated itself in Christ's act of redemption and which cannot even be explicated in this act. This is the feminine and maternal quality of goodness. . . . This maternal quality of mildness, this particularly feminine tenderness, this *quid nesciam* which is the special mark of the mother cannot, however, be explicated as such in the man Jesus. It can only become explicit in a mother who is a woman. God chose Mary so that this maternal aspect of his love might be represented in her person.[29]

There is a feminine principle in our salvation, then, a feminine principle in the new being inaugurated by the incarnation of the eternal Son. But there is something even more profound: Mary maintains an ontological relation with the Holy Spirit, as we shall also see later on. To put it as Paul Evdokimov did: "The Virgin is the locus of the presence of the Holy Spirit and of the Child, the place of the presence of the Word. Both together render the Father's mysterious face human."[30]

WOMAN'S FULFILLMENT: NOT IN MAN, BUT IN GOD

These last observations lead us to discern something that we may not have noticed before—something that cuts across the whole of Scripture and Christian tradition. Women, like men, are called to become something beyond themselves. They are made to be totally God's. Their reciprocity and their unity in difference are cloaked in the vaster mystery of God, who can be recognized, served, and adored in life. We have in the apocryphal Gospel of the Egyptians, as well as in the pseudo-Clementine writings, a logion that, according to some scholars, actually goes back to Jesus. It is in the form of a response to Salome's question, "When shall I see the Reign of God?" Jesus replies: "When you have destroyed the garment of shame, and the two sexes are one—when male and female are male and female no longer—then you shall see the Reign of God."[31] In other words, when we have overcome this perversity of ours that is to our constant shame, when a perfect, harmonious, unperturbed oneness prevails between God and human beings and between women and men, when an intersexual discrimination in which one sex oppresses the other is banished for all time—then, and only then, the Reign of God, the absolute fulfillment of all things, and the harmony of order, will come. The Reign of God can only come, then, to the extent that human beings move outward from themselves, transcend the love of male and female, and attain to the love of an Absolute who reconciles both. After all, all things are God's and for God. Only then shall we have the end of the present, old order of things, and a new, universal beginning (Rev. 21:5). The ultimate destiny of woman and man is God. The plenitude of the human being, in his and her masculine and feminine differentiation, will be realized only in the bosom of God.

GOD IN THE FEMININE, THE FEMININE IN GOD

THE FEMININE: HUMAN PATH TO GOD

This will complete our brief survey of the fonts of faith in search of the word of God's revelation of the feminine. Now we must take up the feminine as it is presented in today's socioanalytic approaches and philosophical reflection, and make it the object of a theological investigation. Now, then, we shall be meditating on the feminine not as it is represented in the cultural context of the sacred fonts, but as it actually exists today.

First of all, we must recognize that positive theological principles are surprisingly and harmoniously compatible with the image of the feminine that we have indicated in our scientific and philosophical approaches. The religious reading of the feminine done in the past, even without benefit of the scientific or philosophical mediation, and despite all the shortcomings that we have observed, did reach the reality. The theology of the feminine did not become entirely mired in ideology. Faith saw the feminine as a path to God. After all, faith calls the feminine the image of God. In its contemplation of the meaning of the feminine (in male and female), the feminine's dimensions of life, depth, mystery, tenderness, interiority, and caring, faith finds God. Well did Paul say that the invisible becomes visible through a reverent consideration of the works of creation (Rom. 1:19–

20). But is not the feminine a consummate work of God's creation? Indeed, only the feminine and the masculine are revealed to be in the image and likeness of God.

In other words, horizontal, historical expressions of the feminine are incapable of containing or expressing its complete reality. This reality unfolds vertically, as well, opening out on an absolute called God. No one is sufficient unto, no one lives solely for, himself or herself. Surely man is open to woman and woman to man. Together they form a dual unity—which in turn is not sufficient unto itself. Even pleasure, eros, love, and fusion are "figurative": they prefigure, mediate, and participate in a fullness toward which both partners strive, but that is never totally attained. Female and male are radically personalized only when they are submerged together in a mystery that outstrips their love for one another. Then they open themselves vertically, as well, toward an absolute they dare call their God and Father. And they have the courage to welcome this God and Father into their lives.[32]

Analytically, we have seen that the human being is always male and female. Philosophically, we have concluded that feminine and masculine constitute ontological elements of every human existence. We are dealing with an utterly basic, primordial reality embracing male and female and constituting them in their reciprocity. With this observation we mean that anthropology cannot close up within itself, cannot be based on itself. It experiences a thrust toward the ultimate question: What, ultimately, is the human being, this thing expressed in masculine and feminine? Any attempt to arrive at an objective description of the differences between the two expressions trips up against an insuperable barrier—in that each of the poles under consideration is a constitutive reference to the other. This barrier poses a decisive, ultimate question about the mystery of human existence. It belongs to theology, then, to decipher this mystery, and theology does this in terms of the parousia of God within the anthropological.

For Christian faith, God is Trinity: Father-Son-Spirit. Is not the human person as male and female, then, a radical image of the Trinity? ("Let *us* make man in *our* image . . .": Gen. 1:26.) In the Trinity we find absolute Relationships that constitute Persons. The three Persons are not three terms in reciprocal relation. This would be tritheism. God would no longer be one. In preexisting the interplay of their relationships, the three terms would have their being at least to some extent independently of one another, and God would no longer be one. The correct understanding of the Trinity, as canonized in the councils of Nicaea, Chalcedon, and First Constantinople, proclaims the absolute precedence of the relations—which thereupon constitute the three terms Father, Son, and Holy Spirit.

Much the same thing occurs with the human being, as analytical and philosophical reflection demonstrate. Being male or being female is a reciprocity, a being-for-the-other, "a fundamental relationship that creates variable personal situations."[33] The basic problem of the Trinity is that of the relations of the divine Persons. But in the human being the same dialectic appears: the encounter of woman and man. Man is man only in woman's sight, and she is woman only in his—altogether analogously to what occurs in the Trinity. This reciprocity is the first and last element of being, in the human realm as in the divine. Just as the Son and the Holy Spirit constitute references to an unprincipiated Principle, an absolute Mystery, the Father, so also man and woman are constituted by reference to a dynamism that transcends them and constitutes the mystery of the human being. Does not the Son represent the masculine principle and the Holy Spirit the feminine? In theological tradition as in Christian piety, the Son is, of course, expressed in masculinity, for he has become flesh in a male. The Holy Spirit, however, is feminine—in Hebrew, "spirit," "breath" is *ruah*[34]—and is always associated with the mystery of life, grace, and generation, as in Mary's conception of Jesus Christ by the power of the Spirit.

THE FEMININE: GOD'S PATH TO THE HUMAN BEING

These considerations prepare us for another theological question. If we admit that the human person as masculine and feminine bears a genuine resemblance to God, then by the same token we shall have to admit that God is prototypically masculine and feminine. More specifically to our point, the feminine element in the human person would constitute the feminine in God.

May we then speak of a feminine in God? Is it legitimate to

invoke God as our Mother, as we have learned from our Lord to call him our Father?

This is a question that bears close examination, lest we introduce confusion into our faith. Were the response to be in the affirmative, however, we should surely be opening up vistas for theology and piety that would be possible only in our times, the age of women's liberating praxis and a new cultural consciousness of the equality and dignity of the feminine principle. In any event, we can scarcely afford to sidestep the question merely because it is controversial.

As we have seen, Holy Scripture and our tradition of faith ordinarily present God not as "she," but as "he." Christianity does not proclaim that God became a woman, but that he became a male. The eternal Word of God became a Jew of the male sex, Jesus of Nazareth, and through him salvation and God's ultimate revelation of the divine self have been bestowed on us. God has presented the divine self to us as Father, not as Mother. There is an eternal Son, not an eternal Daughter. Nearly all of Judeo-Christianity's key concepts, as we have observed, have a masculine background.

But theology's function as the rational discourse of faith consists in examining and becoming aware of the limits of these statements. Theology insists that God inhabits inaccessible light, and is therefore beyond sex. The theological tradition stemming from "Denis the Areopagite" never tires of proclaiming God as a supra-essential existence and super divine divinity.[35] When we call God pure spirit, what we are really seeking to express is that God is beyond any determination, including, of course, in the matter with which we are dealing, sexual determination. Therefore, when we profess that God is Father, Son, and Holy Spirit, we do not do so with any intent of connoting a sexual determination. The Persons are masculine, to be sure, but not in the genetic or genital sexual sense. All of our designations of God are analogical: they affirm at once a similarity and a dissimilarity. In all of our propositions about God, something is affirmed and something implicitly denied. God is Father, to be sure—but not simply in the sense in which we have an earthly experience of our fathers. The experience of God as Father is ambiguous, then. The *via affirmationis* needs the purification of the *via ne-*

gationis. Then, once the conceptual purity of the father image has been posited, we elevate it to its infinite dimension. Only now is a creaturely concept attributable to God—when it has been "processed" by the *via negationis* and the *via excellentiae.* But then we can say that the quality so processed is realized absolutely only in God—as, for example, the qualities of fatherhood and sonship are realized perfectly only in God as Father and Son. If we were to conceive of the feminine and the masculine or parenthood and filiation not only as objectivizations proper to each of the sexes but as ever-present dimensions of each and every human being, then it would be easier to comprehend that these positive dimensions can exist in terms of the absolute perfection of God as the source of all good and all perfection. The fact that the concept of God carries no sexist connotation in biblical Judaism is well established. The biblical culture always kept its distance from the religions that attributed sexual determinations to the gods. Yet, at the same time, Judaism asserted God's masculinity. It is easy to understand why, in the age of the patriarchs, when value was the monopoly of the masculine, the images applied to God were that of father and the like.[36] Not that they thereby become purely cultural attributes. No, they say something (analogously) true about God. But they also hide something. Perhaps the time has come, perhaps the historical conditions are at hand, for the discovery of the other face of God—the feminine, maternal face. Feminist movements, a new reflection of faith and practice attentive to the rotation of the axis of history, could be the vehicles for this divine revelation. A discovery of the feminine in God, the invocation of God as Mother, would not bind us to a conceptualization of God as sexual. We would only be acknowledging that the feminine and maternal qualities are realized in God absolutely. Before we examine this question, however, let us consider some historical testimonials to the feminine in God.[37] They will never be lacking, for, as we have seen, the feminine is part of the structure of the human spirit.

GOD THE MOTHER: SOME HISTORICAL TESTIMONIALS

A matriarchal culture—as we shall see in greater detail following—would be full of female, especially maternal, divinities.

The Hebrew culture is basically masculine, but even here, as we have seen, the Spirit is feminine. Jesus himself, in a passage from the apocryphal Gospel of the Hebrews, refers to the Holy Spirit as feminine: "Now my Mother the Holy Spirit took me by one hair of my head and bore me to great Mount Tabor."[38] In the canonical Gospels as well, Jesus' references to the Spirit have a maternal accent. The Spirit will not leave us orphans (John 14:18). The Spirit comforts (something typically maternal), exhorts, and nourishes (John 14:26). It is the spirit who, like the mother in the home, teaches us the name of God our Father (Rom. 8:15) and tells us how to petition God (Rom. 8:26).

History teaches us, and the psychology of religion demonstrates, that the divinity has always been culturally represented in both paternal and maternal symbolism. This symbolism is at the service of two types of religion. The one type is chthonic or telluric—oriented toward earth, life, generation, and the mysteries of death. This is the maternal religion. The other is uranic or celestial, and is oriented to the sky, infinity, and transcendence. This is the paternal type of religion. The former concentrates more on our origin, our original earthly paradise, and the primordial state of our reconciliation. The latter is turned rather toward the end of history, and seeks salvation and a future Reign of God. The one accents generation and conception; the other, birth. Judaism and Christianity are eminently uranic and masculine. The Kingdom is to come. It is a promise made to us for tomorrow.

Despite the predominance of the uranic, however, there also appear in the Scriptures, as we have seen, traces of telluric, maternal religion. God also appears as the comforting mother (Isa. 66:13) who lifts her baby to her face (Hos. 11:4), who cannot forget the fruit of her womb (Isa. 49:15; Ps. 25:6, 115:5). Jesus himself uses a language rich in feminine imagery when he says: "O Jerusalem, Jerusalem, you slay the prophets and stone those who are sent to you! How often have I wanted to gather your children together as a mother bird collects her young under her wings, and you refused me!" (Luke 13:34). And finally, in the Parousia, in the gesture so typical of a mother, God will wipe away every tear from our weary eyes (Rev. 21:4).

We have already spoken of the mysterious figure of Wisdom, the representation of God's goodness and tenderness toward the world. This image has a special importance in the Book of Job. In the first part of the story, God is a stern father, testing, punishing, and reprimanding his just son. Later, however, God becomes compassionate and sympathetic toward his son, taking the form of Wisdom. And beneath this feminine figure we discover a new face of the Old Testament God (Job 24, 38–42).

As André Manaranche says: "Despite all, when all hope is lost, what actually reappears is the motherly image of a oneness recovered at last: God is only father when he promises a mother's love."[39]

The maternal figure of God appears in the religious consciousness of Christianity, as well. Clement of Alexandria, reflecting on Mary's divine motherhood, states: "God is love, and we seek him precisely because of that love. In his ineffable majesty he is our Father; but in his love he has opened himself up to us and become our Mother. Yes, in his love our Father has become woman, and the greatest proof of this is his Son born of her."[40] In his eternal generation of the Son, then, the Father has become eternal Mother. After all, we say in the Creed: "I believe . . . in Jesus Christ, his only Son, our Lord, born of the Father before all ages." But is it not mothers who bear sons? We are reminded of the Song of Wisdom in the Book of Proverbs:

> The Lord begot me, the firstborn of his ways,
>   the forerunner of his prodigies of long ago;
> From of old I was poured forth,
>   at the first, before the earth.
> When there were no depths I was brought forth,
>   when there were no fountains or springs of water. . . .
>   (Prov. 8:22–23)

Or we recall the Psalm interpreted in Christian theological tradition as a paean of love addressed by the Father to his eternal Word:

> Yours is princely power in the day of your birth, in holy spendor;
>   before the daystar, like the dew, I have begotten you.
>   (Ps. 110:3)

This eternal generation, as the Creed explicitly insists, must not be interpreted as any sort of making or creation—*non factus nec creatus*—but as genuine generation—*genitus*—by the Father. We are to take this expression to the hilt, then. We are dealing with generation in the proper sense of the term. But in our experience it is the mother, the *genitrix*, who generates offspring, not the father. Would it not be altogether normal, then, to refer to the First Person of the Blessed Trinity as the eternal Mother, rather than the eternal Father? "Seeing that God is the most sublime source of all perfections in the created order, God must also be the source of motherhood, the supreme feminine perfection."[41]

According to Donald Nicholl, Saint Ephraim the Syrian (306–373) refers to the Holy Spirit as the Mother in God, the eternal feminine in God.[42]

Saint Anselm of Canterbury approaches Jesus as his mother: "And you, Jesus, good Lord, are you not also Mother? Would a mother not be one who, like a hen, gathers her young beneath her wings? In truth, Lord, you are my Mother!"[43]

In her *Revelations of Divine Love,* the great fourteenth-century English mystic Julian of Norwich writes: "God, Almighty, is our kindly Father; and God, All-Wisdom, is our kindly Mother; with the Love and the Goodness of the Holy Ghost: which is all one God, one Lord."[44] For Julian, the Trinity has three properties: fatherhood, motherhood, and the quality of ruler. She attributes motherhood to the Second Person, as our Mother in nature and grace: "The Second Person of the Trinity is our Mother in kind, in making of our Substance, in whom we are grounded and rooted. And he is our Mother in Mercy, in our Sensuality taking. And thus our Mother is to us in diverse manners working: in whom our parts are kept undisparted."[45]

The fifteenth-century Franciscan lay brother Nicholas von der Flüe, patron saint of Switzerland, recounts a vision in which the Holy Trinity appeared to him in the form of God the Father, God the Mother, and God the Son.[46]

Carlos, a schizophrenic in treatment at the psychiatric hospital directed by psychologist Nise de Silveira, has on various occasions drawn or painted a white goddess, with the inscription, "God My Mother."[47]

The definition of the dogma of the assumption of the Blessed Virgin Mary into heaven has led to a reflection on the ultimate meaning of Mary's divine maternity, as well as of her femininity in terms of the Holy Trinity. Thus, Victor White, the Dominican who was one of the first theologians to acknowledge the value of Carl Jung's analysis of the feminine, commenting on the dogma of our Lady's assumption, writes:

Perhaps this definition may lead the Church to a deeper consideration and an ultimate formulation of the mystery of God's motherhood: in her Assumption Mary returns to her source. Not she, but God is the ultimate prototype of motherhood and femininity, even materially. . . . Just as Christ, in ascending to heaven, carried us to the arms of God our eternal Father, may it not be that Mary, assumed into heaven, means to lead us to a deeper knowledge and love of God our eternal Mother?[48]

We find the feminine, maternal dimension of God in the Eastern Christian tradition as well, especially in Saint Gregory Palamas, and in modern times Vladimir Soloviev.[49] Carl Jung, in his research and speculations on the feminine—something we shall have to return to later—identifies the presence of a feminine principle, called the anima, in every male, and a masculine principle, the animus, in every female. In a context of the application of psychoanalytic theory to the Marian dogmas, this leads Jung to formulate the hypothesis of the divinization of the feminine in Mary. God the eternal Mother, the absolute Feminine, is totally historicized in the life of Mary.

The women's liberation movement has been the occasion of a frequent discussion over the past few years of the subject of God as Mother. The notion has been taken altogether seriously, and often almost as if it went without saying that God is indeed Mother as well as Father. A Yale theologian writes:

However, there is no longer any absolute need for limiting the image to that of masculine generativity, once it has become clear, as it has today, that the feminine principle of generativity is also active and self-contributing. In other words, there is no reason why the First Person of the Trinity cannot be called "Mother" as well as "Father"—no reason why creation cannot be imaged as issuing from the ultimate womb, from the ultimate maternal principle. Neither image, male or female, "says it all," since in the human analogy neither the male nor female principle can be the whole source of life. But both are appropriate, and perhaps only with both do we begin to restore to images the power they had in a simpler time.[50]

And this female theologian goes on to show that the feminine would be an apt category for expressing our understanding of the Son and Holy Spirit, as well.

There is also a keen awareness of the ecumenical importance of the theme of God as Mother, especially in dialogue with the religions of the matriarchal cultures.[51] In India, for example, the veneration of God as Mother (Shakti) is very much alive, both in the ancient traditions and in the modern version of Rama-krishna, who is quoted as saying to his wife, in order to justify his opposition to celibacy: "The Mother [God] has taught me that she dwells in every woman, and I have learned to look upon all women as if they were the divine Mother."[52] In a theologico-cultural atmosphere like ours today, it should have come as no surprise to hear Pope John Paul I declare to the faithful in a public audience: "God is Father, but above all, God is Mother."

THE ULTIMATE PRINCIPLE OF ALL FEMININITY: GOD OUR MOTHER

What is the theological value of all of these testimonials and arguments? Are they but an exception to the rule? Or are they the revelation of a great truth being manifested in the evening of the patriarchal age and inaugurating a new phase in our understanding of God? Can we carry femininity beyond its concretion in the male and apply it to God? Is it possible to speak theologically and properly of a feminine in God? If so, in what sense?

A basic theological principle states that all *pure* perfection reflects God, has its ultimate root in God, and can be predicated of God. All of the foregoing considerations have demonstrated that the masculine and the feminine are perfections of the first order. The masculine has served as the principal language of God's historical self-revelation in the Old and New Testaments. But the feminine is of the same dignity as the masculine, and has likewise served as a means of God's self-communication: we need only recall the basic text of Genesis 1:27, which so clearly states that the masculine *and* the feminine are images of God. In other words, whatever is concretely masculine and feminine finds its prototype and source in God. God-the-feminine serves as woman's supreme archetype. God-the-masculine serves as man's supreme archetype. The masculine and feminine in history have their ultimate origin in the mystery of God's own being. Just as all fatherhood in heaven and on earth comes from the eternal Father, as Saint Paul says (Eph. 3:15), so too all motherhood in heaven and on earth comes from the eternal Mother.

On the one hand, the historical feminine provides a route to the feminine in God. On the other, it signifies the created presence and likeness of that feminine. Thus, the feminine has an eternal dimension. In one historical concretion, this proposition is absolutely correct and true—in Jesus Christ, a male human being hypostatically assumed by the Second Person of the Most Holy Trinity. The modern understanding that every human being is at once anima and animus, albeit in different proportions depending on the sex of the individual, means that Jesus is masculine and feminine. He lives the masculine fully, since he is male. However, he integrates the feminine perfectly, too. But everything in Jesus is hypostatically assumed by the eternal Word. Therefore, in Jesus the feminine is God. In Jesus the feminine has been divinized. According to the christological principle of the *perichoresis* or *circumincessio, this* feminine, at any rate, is God.

Furthermore, a correct theological hermeneutics must depatriarchalize our representation of the Trinitarian mystery. Admittedly, Jesus revealed God as a Father, just as he came to us as the Son in the power of the Holy Spirit. However, we must understand what we ultimately imply when we speak of Father, Son, and Holy Spirit. By "Father" we express the reality of God as unprincipiated principle of all, the source and destiny of all things. By "Son" we denote that same divine reality as self-communicated in the form of Truth itself, as the infinite expression of the divine reality. The Holy Spirit is that divine reality, once more, producing a loving acceptance of its communication in the one who receives it. Thus, the Trinity consists in moments of God's one, single self-communication, moments of the unfathomable Mystery manifested as Light (knowledge) and self-communicated as Gift (love)—without losing its character as incomprehensible and impenetrable Mystery.

Now, if this is what is *thought* when we profess our faith in a triune God, then we can express it equally well using feminine terminology. Now the Most Holy Trinity will be Mother, Daughter, and Holy Spirit. Of course, we must intend to profess the same reality as is expressed in the traditional form, in traditional masculine language. We must intend to profess the same faith as that of our forebears in that faith.

But when we say that we find in God the ultimate source of feminine and masculine, what do feminine and masculine mean in God? Recalling the elements of our analytical and philosophical approaches to the masculine and the feminine, we can say that in our experience of the triune God in salvation history as the original, ultimate Source of reality, we discover a structure analogous to the structure we find in human beings. Here too, in God, is a plural unity, a plurality of modes of existing. The triune God, too, who exists in the likeness of human beings as they are in the likeness of God, is simultaneously constituted of identity and difference. God is mysterious, inaccessible depth, for God is feminine. At the same time, God is self-communication in truth and love, for God is also masculine. God is un-originated Origin (feminine), and at the same time a Giving, an extrojection (masculine).

Thus, the triune God—mysterious, and known as mysterious in the very knowledge, near and distant, fascinating and tremendous—can be experienced and invoked both as Mother and as Father. In using these expressions, whose roots are lost in the depths of the personal and collective unconscious, human beings will be expressing the Meaning of all meaning, final comfort, ultimate tenderness, and an intimacy that is never threatened.

WHAT IS THE ULTIMATE MEANING OF THE FEMININE?

It is the task of theological thinking to venture to explore ultimate questions. In the material at hand we must inquire into the ultimate meaning of the feminine.

What we have already said can afford a preliminary response. In the order of creation, the feminine finds its meaning in the revelation of the feminine of the very Godhead itself. After all, all that exists, in what and how it is, reveals God. All reality, then, but especially anything as personal as the feminine, has a sacramental dimension and function: to speak of God, to evoke God, to point to God.

But there is another answer. And it is a more profound one. It strikes to the heart of God's very being. God has created difference—here, the feminine—in order to communicate to that difference. The very existence of human beings as masculine and feminine finds its raison d'être in their potential to be receptacles of God. The mystery of Jesus Christ has a heuristic function, in the sense that in Jesus Christ we detect the ultimate will of God. Jesus the male reveals God's plan for the masculine explicitly. But he also reveals God's plan for the feminine (implicitly), since his reality, as the reality of a human being, contains both the masculine and the feminine. The male Jesus is thought of and loved by God in order to be able to be the magnificent vessel of God's personal self-communication to creation.[53] This is altogether in keeping with the design of the eternal Son himself to take flesh. Through the Incarnation, the Son is humanized. That is, he assumes the form taken by masculine and feminine in the male concretion. In turn, this male human being is divinized, and this involves the divinization of the masculine and feminine that enter into his constitution.

In virtue of the hypostatic union, we must regard the humanity of Jesus Christ as the humanity of God. But Jesus' humanity, being male, contains the masculine and the feminine in the proportion proper to a male. Thus, while the masculine acquires an ultimate, divine meaning in him directly, the feminine does so only implicitly, as the recessive component.

But if there has been a full and direct divinization of the masculine—in Jesus—can we not expect the feminine to be ordered to a full and direct divinization as well? Will not Jesus, God incarnate, be the paradigm of what all persons, male and female, are called to be? But this will mean that the ultimate end of the human being is not only resurrection in the blessedness of the Reign of God, but an even more sublime reality: to be one with God, in all creaturely finitude, to be sure, in a manner similar to that in which God and a human being subsist in one and the same Jesus of Nazareth, by the operation and grace of Mystery, answered this call within history. All other human beings, his sisters and brothers, will answer it when the Reign of God comes in its plenitude. Then God will be truly all in all (1 Cor. 15:28).

And God will be all in all men and women who will live under his Reign. Ineluctably, then, the feminine too is destined for hypostatic union with God.

As we know, it was the Second Person of the Blessed Trinity, the Son, who was united with the male Jesus of Nazareth. It was not the Father or the Holy Spirit. It was through the eternal Word that the masculine was divinized and eternalized. Indirectly, because the feminine is included in maleness, the feminine as well was this supremely full actualization. Now, then, we ask: which divine Person would be ordered to assume the feminine directly, and divinize it directly? This will not be faith, but theology, where hypothesis has always been legitimate. We think that it is the Holy Spirit to whom the feminine is appropriated. We hold this not only because in the Hebrew mentality the Holy Spirit is feminine, but because everything bound up with life, creativity, and generation is attributed to the Holy Spirit in the fonts of our faith. The Spirit hovered over the waters in the first creation. This suggests, in the Hebrew meaning of the expressions used, a bird, such as a dove, beating its wings. Theological research confirms our point.[54] The Holy Spirit would seem to have the mission in salvation history of hypostatically divinizing the feminine, directly and explicitly, and divinizing the masculine implicitly—just the converse of the divinization of the male human being Jesus by the eternal Word.

Can we identify that moment in history when this mission of the Spirit became concrete reality, as we can identify the mission of the Word in the direct divinization of the masculine? Or will the feminine be assumed and divinized by the Holy Spirit only at the end of history? Surely the Holy Spirit will divinize the feminine at the end of history, but we believe that we have been granted a concrete eschatological anticipation of this infinitely sweet event in the mystery of the Blessed Virgin Mary.

MARY, ESCHATOLOGICAL ANTICIPATION OF THE FEMININE IN ITS ABSOLUTE REALIZATION: A HYPOTHESIS

What we propose here is a theological hypothesis, a *theologoumenon*, not an official doctrine of Christianity, nor even part of

Christian theological tradition. We are aware of the novelty of this notion. The task of the "intelligence of the faith," the task of theology, is not exhausted in the explication of the content of oral and written tradition, or in a systematization of the pronouncements of the magisterium, or in an intelligent repetition of theological propositions consecrated by tradition. Theology also has the mission of shedding light on the examination of the truths of faith. True, this must be carried out with the reverence due Mystery—but never at the cost of the "intelligence" or understanding of the faith. Who despises understanding despises truth. But who despises truth hates the light. But the one who hates the light is far from God, because that one has abandoned the path that leads to God. Nothing that we are about to say enjoys any more authority than that granted theology by the Second Vatican Council. The task of theology, the Council declared, is to reflect on the mysteries of God and all that refers to God in the light of "analogy with things naturally known by reason, by comparing the mysteries among themselves, and in the light of the human being's last end."[55] Surely reason, in all reverence and respect, combining all of these elements, can manage to shed some light on God's plan for the feminine. Obviously, a theologian living in the community of faith submits his or her efforts to the better judgment of the *ecclesia docens*, the teaching Church.

We maintain the hypothesis that *the Virgin Mary, Mother of God and of all men and women, realizes the feminine absolutely and eschatologically, inasmuch as the Holy Spirit has made her his temple, sanctuary, and tabernacle*[56] *in so real and genuine a way that she is to be regarded as hypostatically united to the Third Person of the Blessed Trinity.*

SOME PRESUPPOSITIONS

Let us begin with some basic assertions in support of our hypothesis.

1. Human beings have the passive "obediential potency," the ontological potential, for a hypostatic union with a divine Person. We know this *a posteriori*, by faith, from its actual occurrence. The human being Jesus of Nazareth, from the

first moment of his conception, was assumed by the Second Person of the Divine Trinity in such a way that he is not only a human being, but God incarnate as well. If this were not a possibility, there would not have been an incarnation of God or a divinization of a concrete human nature. This possibility, to a subsequent realization, in any being of the same created nature as Jesus—that is, in all women and men.

2. If the Reign of God and happiness in heaven imply the absolute realization of all of the innate possibilities of human nature, then the possibility (obediential potency) of human beings to be united with a divine Person will be realized. Therefore, in eternity, all of the just, each in his or her own way and to a degree proper to each, will be hypostatically assumed by God, who will thus become "all in all" (1 Cor. 15:28). Thus, human beings will attain the supreme end for which they have been thought of, loved, and created by God: to be happy and to share in God's divine nature, allowing—because they are different from God—God to share in their human nature. God surrenders to human beings to the point of producing a unity without confusion and without change, without division but without separation, in a manner *similar* to what occurs in the incarnation of the eternal Son in Jesus Christ. What took place in Christ in time will take place in all of the just in eternity.

3. Human nature, assumed by the eternal Son, is simultaneously masculine and feminine (Gen. 1:27). Therefore, masculine and feminine have been divinized in Christ. Concretely, however, it is the masculine in the male Jesus Christ that is *directly and immediately* divinized, while the feminine is assumed and divinized only indirectly as a secondary component of the male.

4. Just as the masculine was divinized directly, so the feminine can be divinized—*directly and immediately*. Both are in the image of God (Gen. 1:27), and both have the same dignity and absolute destiny.

5. God *can* divinize the feminine, as the divine Persons are capable of hypostatically assuming a concrete human nature, and human nature has the obediential potency to be

so assumed; it is *fitting* that God divinize the feminine, because of the equal dignity of masculine and feminine, both of which have the same mission—that of being a sacrament of God within creation—as well as because the incarnation of the eternal Son occurred through Mary, who thus is the Mother of God; therefore, God *did* so assume the feminine, directly, and the masculine, indirectly, in Mary. *Potuit, decuit, ergo fecit!* God could, it was fitting that he should, and so he did.

6. We know only *a posteriori* that it was Mary, and no other woman, who was hypostatically assumed because her conception had been immaculate, she became the virgin Mother of God, she would be assumed body and soul into heaven, and she is Co-Redemptrix and Co-Mediatrix of salvation. It is she, then, who is prototype of the feminine in its absolute realization.

7. The divinizer of the *masculine* (with the feminine) is the Word. The divinizer of the *feminine* (with the masculine) is the Holy Spirit. The Christ-Adam and Mary-Eve parallels find their perfect symmetry here. Mary is not beneath Jesus, but beside him. Together they translate absolutely what it means to say that the human being is the image of God. The Son and the Holy Spirit together, in time, show the loving and mysterious face of the Father in the flesh.

If we are to be able to shed any more light on this most tender and touching event, we shall have to explore the relation obtaining between the Holy Spirit and Mary. Ever since the Second Vatican Council, with its canonization of a pneumatological principle for an understanding of the Church and of Mary to supplement the christological one, many scholars have undertaken detailed studies on this point.[57] We shall not have the space here to cover even the main lines of this research. We shall only cite the results of this research that have the most bearing on the matter at hand.

ANTECEDENTS THROUGHOUT CHRISTIAN HISTORY

Anticipations of our notion of a hypostatic bond between the Holy Spirit and Mary are to be found in the Greek Fathers, especially Cyril of Alexandria, who hold a kind of incarnation of the Holy Spirit, maintaining a *substantial* union of the Holy Spirit with the just. The idea came to have enormous influence on the great theologian Peteau in the eighteenth century, and in the nineteenth on Matthais Joseph Scheeben.[58] The latter spoke of an "incarnation of the Holy Spirit in the Church."[59] More recently, Heribert Mühlen has very capably defended the same hypothesis with the tools of history and theology. The Spirit, says Mühlen, forms a single *mystical person* with all of the just, especially the Christian community, "spiritualizing" its creature in as real a sense as the Incarnation made Jesus of Nazareth the Word.[60]

There is another approach, as well, to the *theologoumenon* that Mary's union with the divinity is of a hypostatic order. Mary as "Mother of the Church is the grace of the Holy Spirit," asserts the Pseudo-Philip of Harvengt.[61] Chardon and Gibieuf, of the French school, argue along these same lines.[62] Russian Orthodox theology like that of Paul Evdokimov and P. Bulgakov cites a hypostatic maternity of the Holy Spirit realized in Mary: "If woman is ontically bound to the Holy Spirit, the bond has universal value and meaning only if man, in turn, is ontically linked to Christ."[63] Or more concisely: " . . . Following the hypostatic distinction, the masculine is an ontic relation to the Word and the feminine is an ontic relation to the Holy Spirit. The 'uniduality' of the Son and the Spirit expresses the Father."[64] For Evdokimov, the *Theotokos,* the Mother of God, is the archetype of the feminine, in virtue of a "profound bond uniting the Holy Spirit, Wisdom, the Virgin, and the feminine."[65]

Father Maximilian Kolbe (1894–1941), a Conventual Franciscan and martyr of modern Poland, had a great devotion to the Immaculate Conception. Some of his expressions of the nature of the union between the Spirit and Mary are couched in terms of the greatest intimacy. Here is one of his formulae: "Filius incarnatus est: Jesus Christus. Spiritus Sanctus 'quasi' incarnatus est: Immaculata" ("The Son took flesh: Jesus Christ. The Holy Spirit 'as it were' took flesh: the Immaculate One").[66] For Kolbe, the Holy Spirit is the "uncreated Immaculate Conception," since the Spirit is the fruit of the love of the Father and the Son. Mary, then, is the "created Immaculate Conception."

Still others assert a mission proper to the Holy Spirit that would be parallel to that of the incarnate Word. Manteau-Bonamy, a well-known specialist in this area, holds: "The Spirit comes visibly in the shadow of the Shekinah. The Word assumes the conceived flesh; the spirit assumes the maternal potency of the Virgin that she may be in the act of conceiving. . . . It is the Virgin's fecundity that renders the presence of the Holy Spirit visible within her."[67] Thus, the visible and proper (not merely ascribed or appropriated) mission of the Holy Spirit takes a concrete form. The Spirit, too, now has a place to rest and to act: the virgin mother of Jesus Christ.

This time is more and more to the fore in recent mariological reflection and research, although most theologians exercise a certain reserve, and employ circumlocutions for expressions directly denoting incarnation and hypostatic union.

We are of the opinion that the word *incarnation* should not be used in this context, because it has become a technical christological term defining the hypostatic union of the Son with human nature. In the case of the Holy Spirit, we hold that a hypostatic union with human reality is not to be asserted, but that that union must be understood and expressed in some other way, since now one is speaking of another divine Person, with properties distinct from those of the eternal Son. The relationship of union between the Holy Spirit and the Blessed Virgin Mary, which is what Rahner calls a "quasi-formal self-communication," is realized in the creature with the notional characteristics of the Holy Spirit ("notional" denoting whatever is properly attributed to the divine Persons precisely in their distinction from one another). Without entering into a disquisition upon the reasons for so doing, I shall refer to the hypostatic union of the Holy Spirit with Mary as a "spiritualization,"[68] by analogy with Saint Athanasius's word "verbification" as the correlative of "incarnation."[69]

THE SPIRITUALIZATION OF MARY BY THE HOLY SPIRIT

We hold that Mary not only received the effects of the Holy Spirit's intervention in her life—as indeed anyone might, although it was surely to a special degree of intensity in her case—but that she specifically received the very person and godhead of the Third Person of the Holy Trinity. In saying this, we intend to assert that in its relationship with Mary the Holy Spirit exercises a proper, and not a merely appropriated, activity. Let us explain our terms.

A basic tenet of Trinitarian theology has it that "in God all is one, except as required by the opposition of the relations" that constitute the three divine Persons.[70] In other words, God's divine nature is utterly simple ("in God all is one"), so that any multiplicity is present only in what founds the distinction among the divine Persons. For the Father, this personal difference is the fact of being the origin-without-origin of the Godhead. For the Son, it is having his origin and generation in the Father. For the Spirit, it is to be "spirated" (literally, "breathed") by the Father and the Son ("Filioque") together.[71] Apart from these differences, the being and operation of God is properly attributed only to the three divine Persons precisely in their identity with one another, precisely by virtue of their adequate identity with the entire divine nature as such. If this were not the case, we should have three infinite beings, three almighty beings, and so on. Hence, we say that the Trinity as Unity created the world— the three Persons together precisely as one Nature, and not only the Father, or the Son, or the Holy Spirit precisely as a distinct Person. However, by virtue of a certain affinity between creation and generation, liturgical piety and the theological reflection on faith both "appropriate," merely attribute, the *creation* of the world to the *Father* in particular. Likewise, because the whole Trinity, as one God, saves human beings through the incarnation of only one Person, the eternal Son, liturgy and piety "appropriate" *salvation* to the *Second* Person in particular. Finally, the *sanctification* of humanity and the cosmos, which is actually "operated" or wrought by all three Persons of the Trinity conjointly in the oneness of their utterly simple nature, is "appropriated" to the Person of the *Holy Spirit*.

But theology also tells us of an activity genuinely proper to each of the three divine Persons. Only the Father begets or generates, and indeed without being begotten. Only the Son is begotten. Only the Holy Spirit is spirated, by the Father and the Son. Now, within the Trinitarian circle, the grammar of this discourse poses no great theoretical problem. The problem arises when we ask: Are there activities really proper to each of the divine Persons in their operation *ad extra*—operations proper to each of the divine persons that affect, for example, the redemption and divinization of hunanity?

At least with respect to the eternal Son, we can say with the absolute certitude of faith that there is a proper *operatio ad extra:* it the eternal Son, and no other divine Person, who communicates himself totally and absolutely to human nature, to the point of becoming incarnate in that nature. He alone receives this specific mission. "The word became flesh and made his dwelling among us, and we have seen his glory" (John 1:14). Here we certainly have a case of a proper *operatio ad extra,* that of the Son. As Karl Rahner says:

This axiom ["In God all things are one, except. . . . "] has absolute validity only with respect to the *suprema causa efficiens* (DS 3814). Non-appropriated relations of a concrete Person can occur when it is a matter not of efficient causality, but of a *quasi-formal self-communication* of God, entailing a proper relation of each of the divine Persons with the corresponding created reality.[72]

When we are speaking not simply of God's creation—which is the common *operatio* of the three divine Persons—but of the self-communication of one of the Persons, we are dealing with a really proper, and not merely appropriated, activity on the part of that Person. The really proper *operatio ad extra* of the eternal Son is the Incarnation. This is of faith, and thus beyond dispute.

Although the Latin theological tradition (unlike the Greek) has showed some resistance, today the opinion is more and more in favor that the Holy Spirit, as well, has a proper, and not merely appropriated, mission in history, and hence a proper *operatio ad extra.*[73] The biblical texts themselves suggest this. "Mary . . . was found with child through the power of the Holy Spirit" (Matt. 1:18). And again, "It is by the Holy Spirit that she has conceived this child" (Matt. 1:20). Luke is even more explicit: the angel speaks of a *coming* of the Holy Spirit. "The Holy Spirit will *come upon* you and the power of the most high will *overshadow* you; hence, the holy offspring to be born will be called Son of God" (Luke 1:35).[74] Then there is the descent of the Holy Spirit at Jesus' baptism; and again in his transfiguration on Mount Tabor; and finally on the first Pentecost. Our own interest, of course, lies in the meaning of the descent of the Holy Spirit upon Mary.

The Lukan text seeks to communicate a unique truth for salvation history based on two proper activities, one on the part of the Holy Spirit with regard to Mary, the other on the part of the eternal Son of God with regard to Jesus, the intention of both activities being the salvation of all human beings (Luke 1:32–33). The realism of the descent of the Holy Spirit need not be regarded as diluted through the evangelist's use of the literary device of expressing it in texts from and allusions to the Old Testament. A critical, but theologically naive, exegesis here could lose the revelatory content communicated in the text (Luke 1:35). The words, "The Holy Spirit will come upon you," are indeed an echo of Isaiah 32:15. " . . . The power of the Most High will overshadow you" alludes to the shadow of the cloud (Shekinah) that covered the tent in the desert (Exod. 40:34–45), or the temple of Solomon (1 Kings 9:10–11). But the strength of the Lukan text lies in the fact that the coming of the Holy Spirit is its main concern. Its primary interest is to establish that a descent of the Holy Spirit like that of the first morning of creation (Gen. 1:1) or at the first Pentecost (Acts 2:2), where the same terminology is used, is now accomplished in a personal coming of the Third Person of the Trinity upon Mary. Appearing since the days of the Old Testament as God's creative power, the divine, transforming presence in creation, and the power of the impossible (see Luke 1:37), the Holy Spirit is now linked with Mary.

Thus, we are dealing not with an anonymous, all-subjugating power, but with a divine Person who invites human persons to dialogue and cooperation rather than destroying them. This is what the Spirit does in inviting Mary to become the mother of the Savior. When she accepts, she is given the fullness of the Spirit's self-communication. The Spirit assumes her as the locus of the Spirit's presence and activity in the world. From the moment of her *fiat*, Mary is hypostatically assumed by the Third Person of the Trinity.

This literal "spiritualization" of Mary is not an end in itself. It occurs within the dynamics of the mystery of redemption and the divinization of humanity. It is ordered to the incarnation of the eternal Son, who in his own turn inaugurates the "verbification" of the world. Mary is raised to the level of God in order to be able to engender God. Only the divine can engender the divine. And so, after announcing that the Holy Spirit will descend on Mary and overshadow her, the angel adds: " . . . *Hence*, the holy offspring will be called Son of God" (Luke 1:35). Thus, Luke establishes a causal nexus between the divinization of Mary and the divinization of the fruit conceived in her womb. Mary is assumed by the Holy Spirit, and thus elevated to the level of God. Therefore, the fruit to be born of Mary will rightly be called God. As Henri Cazelles writes: "The descent of the Holy Spirit is not an invisible abstraction. . . . It causes Mary's maternity to be not only a human maternity but a divine one as well: the one engendered within her will be called Son of God."[75] This truth sheds light on the striking statements of tradition with regard to Mary. Now we understand better why Mary is not only the mother of Jesus but the Mother of God—not only the mother of God's flesh but the Mother of God-in-the-flesh. The Spirit, as Manteau-Bonamy tells us, assumes not only the maternal potency of the Virgin, that she may conceive, but her totality.[76] If the Holy Spirit had assumed only Mary's maternal potency, only one part and one function of Mary would have been assumed. But we know from our analytical and philosophical considerations that a woman's motherhood is not only her function, but her very person. She has a maternal spirit. Whether or not she becomes a mother, she will never lose her capacity for conception and engendering. Mary, in her totality, becomes the tabernacle and temple of the Holy Spirit. These expressions must be understood in a real, ontological sense, not only metaphorically or symbolically.

The Spirit, the eternal feminine, is united to the created feminine in order that the latter may be totally and fully what it can be—virgin and mother. Mary, as Christian piety has always intuited, is the eschatological realization of the feminine in all of its dimensions.

Mary was prepared for this culminating moment in the history of God and humanity. From the first moment of her conception her flesh was pure, immaculately conceived, without the least stain of sin. The Immaculate Conception was ordered to the divine spiritualization that came to pass at the time of the Annunciation, when the eternal Word took flesh and began to grow within her. From that moment forward, the process of Mary's spiritualization was under way. The Spirit began to assume in her everything that would ever happen in her life, to the very fullness of that life in the Assumption—the moment at the end and culmination of her life when she experienced the plenitude of divinization. Thus, the created feminine is eternally associated with the mystery of the Trinity, through Mary assumed by the Holy Spirit.

The mysterious reality of Mary's divinization has not gone unnoticed in the collective unconscious of the Church—the *sensus fidelium*. In his analysis of the elements of the unconscious and our interior archetypal archeology, Carl Jung has demonstrated an unconscious demand for the divinization of the feminine.[77] Simple folk, in the innocence of an unarticulated faith and far removed from the discourse of official orthodoxy, have always rendered Mary the homage of adoration. They relate to her as to someone by whom we find ourselves affected absolutely, as an ultimate source of comfort, grace, and salvation. In invoking Mary in this spirit, the faithful capture the eschatological truth in her regard, and acknowledge its anticipation in history.

As we see, the oft-reiterated complaint of both Protestant and Catholic theologians that Mary eventually usurped the place of the Holy Spirit in popular piety is not actually justified.[78] Expressions like "Mary molds Jesus within us," "Mary is our Advocate, Comfort of the afflicted, Mediatrix of all grace, Mother of Good Counsel"—or even "To Jesus through Mary"—as well as the chain of laudatory enunciations normally predicated of the Holy Spirit but used by the faithful in the Litany of Loreto, have sometimes struck theologians as exaggerated. But in the hypothesis we are defending, they only tell the whole truth about Mary. If Mary has been spiritualized by the Third Person of the Trinity, then everything that can be predicated of the Holy Spirit can be predicated of Mary and vice versa, by virtue of the general theological principle of the *perichoresis*.

Faith has no need to know all of its mediations, or be conscious of all of its theoretical implications, in order to maintain its truth and its certitude of that truth. The people of God have always intuited in Mary the personal presence of the Holy Spirit. In attributing to her all of the titles of greatness forged by their piety, the people have entered into a communion with that Holy Spirit who has spiritualized Mary.

With the understanding that we have just articulated, we deliver Mariology from the exacerbated Christocentrism that has characterized it in recent years (even in Vatican II). But we must admit that that Christocentrism has afforded us a holistic view of Mary's universal meaning for salvation history. The relation of Mary with the Holy Spirit has not been examined as it deserves, or allowed to bear fruit in systematic form. We now propose to embark upon that examination and systematization. The pneumatological dimension, in tandem with the christological, reestablishes the equilibrium of an adequate Marian reflection. At the same time, it does justice to Mary's eschatological actualization of the feminine that reigns through the Holy Spirit at the very heart of the Trinity.

We have not arrived at the point where we must apply the conclusions to which we have come to a view of Mary herself. As this view unfolds, we shall have to recast the main themes of classical Mariology. By ending our reflection on the feminine with its hypostatic relation to the Holy Spirit, we run the risk of mystifying it—magnifying it to the point where we lost sight of the historical concretion in which it has been realized. We therefore propose to contemplate Mary from within three different discourses, each of them having its own grammar and syntax: the historical, the theological, and the mythical. All three speak of the same reality: Mary. But they speak of her on three different levels. What history conceals, theology reveals. What theology reveals, myth exalts. Now, then, the theological task begins in earnest.

III. HISTORY: MIRIAM—MARY

6. Mary: The Historical Miriam of Nazareth

There is no biography of the maid of Nazareth called Miriam in Hebrew, and Maria in Greek and Latin.[1] We come up against the same problem in Mariology as in Christology. As happens with Jesus, our access to the historical Mary is hindered by the nature of the sources. These sources always theologize their history. The historical event is reported in the matrix of its interpretation by faith. As for the Marian apocrypha, they are plagued with pious legends and fantasies of all sorts, and have never been officially received by the Church.[2]

The New Testament contains little about Mary. She appears only eight times. Matthew's Gospel (chapters 1 and 2) speaks to us of Joseph's perplexity, the visit of the Magi, and the flight into Egypt. Mary is mentioned in Mark's Gospel twice, once on an occasion when Jesus seems to take a certain distance from her (Mark 3:21), and again when some individuals are astounded at his wisdom, and ask, "Is this not the son of Mary?" (Mark 6:3). The first two chapters of Luke recount the Annunciation, the birth of Jesus, the presentation in the temple, and the finding of the child Jesus in the temple. Mary appears twice in John's Gospel—on the occasion of the wedding feast of Cana (John 2:3), and at the foot of the cross (John 19:25–27). The Acts of the Apostles speak of her at Pentecost (Acts 1:14). Paul refers to her anonymously when he speaks of Jesus "born of a woman" (Gal 4:4).

We are struck by the fact that not a single New Testament passage focuses on Mary directly. Any reference to her is always in relation to her Son, Jesus, or to the Holy Spirit who comes upon her. She enters the story only because it is the story of Jesus, or because of the irruption of the Holy Spirit in the Annunciation or at Pentecost. Otherwise, we would know nothing of her at all. The New Testament does not idealize Mary. She is a poor and simple woman of Galilee, where her life is completely immersed in the social, political, and religious situation of her people.[3]

THE DEARTH OF INFORMATION IN THE SYNOPTICS

Let us examine the degree of historicity attaching to each of the eight references to Mary in the synoptic Gospels.[4] Except in the infancy narratives, the Gospels of Mark, Luke, and Matthew seem to enjoy a greater historical authenticity in Mary's regard than does the Gospel of John. Three scenes come under consideration.

JESUS' NEW FAMILY (MARK 3:31–35, MATT. 12:46–50, LUKE 8:19–21)

Jesus' relatives, his "mother and brothers," go in search of him. Mark 2:21 tells us the meaning of their search. They fear that Jesus has gone mad. Hearing of their arrival, Jesus asks: " 'Who are my mother and my brothers?' And gazing around him at those seated in the circle he continued, 'These are my mother and my brothers. Whoever does the will of God is brother and sister and mother to me' " (Mark 3:33–35).

First, the text permits us a glimpse of Mary's perplexity about her Son. He is a charismatic. In the minds of some in those days, just as today, this was a symptom of mental illness. True, Mary surmises what Jesus is undergoing—the clear experience of his messianic mission. But the other relatives miss this. Jesus' reaction could give the impression that he is cutting ties with his mother. This is not the case. What Jesus is doing is simply taking advantage of the reference to "mother and brothers" in the message that Mary and his other relatives have arrived on the scene, to point out that this circle of followers is the beginning of a new community, one in which all men and women will fulfill the plan of God. Now, of course, Mary more than anyone else enters into God's salvific design. Mary more than anyone else is open to complete cooperation with God. Her greatness lies less in her physical motherhood than in her total fulfillment of the plan that Jesus now proclaims. Thus, she is more profoundly Jesus' "mother" than any other person in the circle.

MARY THE UNPREPOSSESSING (MARK 6:3, MATT. 13:55; SEE JOHN 6:42)

Jesus causes astonishment with his wise words and creative actions. And so the question arises: Where did he get this? Who has been his instructor, that all these wonders pour from his hands? "Is this not the carpenter, the son of Mary . . . ?" (Mark 6:3). Mary is contrasted with Jesus. She is a simple, uneducated woman of a humble people. How could she have been the beginning of so much wisdom and so many signs? Here, at all events, we have a reliable historiographical datum about Mary: she was not regarded as a great woman of her time. She shared the general anonymity of the women of Judaism.

DIFFERENCE BETWEEN FLESH AND FAITH (LUKE 11:27–28)

Someone swept up in the enthusiasm of Jesus' auditors calls from the crowd, "Blest is the womb that bore you and the breasts that nursed you!" But Jesus responds, "Rather, blest are they who hear the word of God and keep it."

Again, Jesus is showing no disregard for Mary. He merely wishes to mark the difference between the carnal plane and the plane that really matters, that of faith. The privilege of sharing in Christ Jesus is not one of blood or race. It is an invitation extended to all, and is accepted when we accept a share in the life of faith and make an effort to embrace a new way of living. Here again, then, Mary is the very prototype of the sort of person Jesus is praising. Mary is the new human being par excellence. This is why she is so intimately associated with Jesus.

As we see from the synoptic texts, the historical figure of Mary is very much hidden. We hide genuine pearls in out-of-the-way places in the house.

THE INFANCY NARRATIVES: MORE THEOLOGY THAN HISTORY

Apart from these few texts, the synoptics favor us with a mention of Mary only in the infancy narratives of Luke and Matthew.

But these accounts represent a post-Resurrection theology, with Jesus' dignity in terms of his divine sonship and messiahship already well developed. Written between A.D. 60 and 80, the infancy narratives presuppose Mary's presence at the heart of the community, as we find intimated in Acts 1:14.[5] By the time they were written, Mary had communicated to the apostles both the mysteries of her life and the fruit of her reflection. Luke actually speaks of the secrets she had kept in her heart (Luke 2:19, 51). John, after Jesus' death and resurrection, has taken her into his home and associated her to his mission (John 19:27).

It is no easy task to distinguish historical event from theological reflection in the Gospels. The Christian community and its evangelists are theologians. Almost everything centers on Jesus. Mary appears as the fulfillment of the promises of the Old Testament. The elements of the infancy narratives regarded as historical are the following: our Lady's virginity and her betrothal to Joseph (Matt. 1:18–24), her virginal conception by the operation of the Holy Spirit (Matt. 1:18–20, Luke 1:35), the name "Jesus" decreed by the Most High (Matt. 1:21, Luke 1:31), and the fact of her Son's infancy in Nazareth (Matt. 2:23). These historical facts are interwoven with theological reflections on Old Testament texts.

Matthew, for example, recounts the origin of Jesus with special attention to the prophecy of Isaiah 7:14, "The virgin [ha almah] shall be with child, and bear a son, and shall name him Immanuel" (God-with-us). This prophetic text makes it possible to understand the mysterious conception of Jesus as a virginal one, without any carnal intervention (Matt. 1:18, 21). The word Immanuel—"God-with-us"—suggests something more than mere divine assistance. Mary's child is God in the flesh. What follows in Matthew's narrative centers on the figure of Joseph. Joseph is the witness of everything, the one who reflects, who acts, who confers legal status on Jesus' birth by giving him a name (Matt. 1:25). The intent of the recital of the visit of the Magi from the East is to attest to Christ's universality. The flight into Egypt and the massacre of the Holy Innocents is particularly appropriate to Matthew's theology, which presents Jesus to us as the new Moses.[6]

Luke gives a more detailed account, and takes Mary's viewpoint. She is the center of attention of his entire narrative.[7] Everything is built on Old Testament texts. Surely Mary had actually interpreted what was happening to her just as Luke now does. A religious person, especially a devout Jew, typically seeks to understand the events of current history in light of God's Word. The historical reality, it seems to us, is the following. Mary is betrothed to Joseph. She is still a virgin, as they are not yet living together. All this is in accordance with Jewish law. Then she is surprised to discover that she is with child. Now, like any Jewish mother, she has been looking for the coming of the Messiah. Oh, that one of her own offspring might be the Anointed of the Lord! Now the birth approaches, and Mary's puzzlement continues unabated. She has had no intercourse (Luke 1:34). She prays, she meditates on the Scriptures. Little by little the light dawns. She concludes that the Holy Spirit, the Source of all generation, has acted within her: the child she has conceived by the Holy Spirit will be the Son of God, the long-awaited Messiah.

This entire process of understanding, we say with all assurance, transpired with the assistance and illumination of God. In this understanding, the events would not have had a visibly miraculous, patently theophanic character. They would have been simple occurrences along the side roads of history. This is how God usually works to penetrate the course of events. The Lukan texts are at special pains to show Mary as a woman of faith. "Blest is she who trusted" (Luke 1:45). Mary has to discover the ways of God. Having found them, she accepts them with all her heart and soul (Luke 1:38).

These events are all narrated by Luke in Old Testament language. The Annunciation is all but identical to that of Zephaniah:

Annunciation of Zephaniah to Israel (Zeph 3:14–17)	**Annunciation of the Angel to Mary (Luke 1:28–33)**
Shout for joy,	Rejoice,
O daughter of Zion . . .	O highly favored daughter!
The King of Israel, the Lord	The Lord

Annunciation of Zephaniah to Israel (Zeph 3:14–17)	Annunciation of the Angel to Mary (Luke 1:28–33)
is in your midst . . .	is with you . . .
Fear not, O Zion . . .	Do not fear, Mary.
the Lord, your God,	You have found favor with God.
is in your midst,	You shall conceive and bear a son and give him the name
a mighty savior.	Jesus.

Now the Lukan account continues, employing a parallelism with the messianic prophecy of the Book of Samuel:

Nathan's Declaration to David (2 Sam. 7:12–16)	Gabriel's Annunciation to Mary (Luke 1:32–33)
I will raise up your heir after you, sprung from your loins, and I will make his kingdom firm . . .	Great will be his dignity
I will be a father to him, and he shall be a son to me . . .	and he will be called Son of the Most High.
Your house and your kingdom	He will rule over the house of Jacob
shall endure forever before me;	forever
your throne	and his reign
shall stand firm forever.	shall be without end.

The angel's final words seem also to allude to an Old Testament passage:

Exodus 40:35	Luke 1:35
The cloud	The power of the Most High
settled down upon the tent	will overshadow you;

Exodus 40:35	Luke 1:35
and the glory of the Lord	hence, the holy offspring to be born
filled the Dwelling.	will be called Son of God.

The account of Mary's visit to her cousin Elizabeth is constructed along lines exactly parallel to 2 Samuel 6:1–14, where we hear of the transfer of the Ark of the Covenant. In Luke's view, Mary is like the Ark of the Covenant, carrying the Holy Spirit, who is Jesus. This suggestion is of great value for the theological hypothesis we have proposed respecting the ontological relation of Mary to the Holy Spirit and to the Word whose mother she is.

2 Samuel 6:9–11	Luke 1:43–56
How can the ark of the Lord come to me? . . .	But who am I that the mother of my Lord should come to me? . . .
The ark of the Lord remained in the house of Obed-edom . . .	Mary remained with Elizabeth
for three months. . . .	about three months. . . .

Elizabeth's glorification of Mary is a copy of one addressed to Judith:

Judith 13:18–19	Luke 1:42
Blest are you, daughter,	Blest are you
above all the women on earth;	among women
and blessed	and blest
be the Lord God. . . .	is the fruit of your womb.

We shall examine the Magnificat in more detail later. There we shall see this same parallelism with Old Testament texts. In all of these instances we have a literary device that endows an event of apparently little meaning with a religious, transcendent meaning.

Luke concludes his account of Jesus' childhood with the episode of the pilgrimage to the temple in Jerusalem.[8] Here the evangelist develops a whole theology of the temple. The new, true Temple is Jesus himself, the Place where God dwells. At twelve years of age, Jesus has already begun to change the meaning of the temple. There is probably also a historical kernel in this account. Doubtless, the Holy Family did make a pilgrimage with their relatives to the most sacred place in Judaism. At one point, Jesus must have been lost in the caravan. His parents seek him anxiously. They find him in the temple. A tender, yet mysterious, dialogue ensues. "Son, why have you done this to us? You see that your father and I have been searching for you in sorrow." Jesus' response comes as a surprise. It is on a completely different level from that of the question. "Why did you search for me? Did you not know I had to be in my Father's house?" (Luke 2:48–49). We note the counterpoint between "father" and "Father." Luke makes it clear that Jesus is less concerned with bonds of flesh than with those of faith. Mary and Joseph are invited to transcend the carnal level—blood and family ties—and to place themselves on another level, one that can be reached only in faith, in service to the Father and to his plan for the Reign. However, the text comments, "But they did not grasp what he said to them" (Luke 2:50)—although it indicates that Mary's attitude of "keeping all these things in memory" (Luke 2:51) is all that Jesus requires of us. He asks only that we walk in faith. Mary's faith is the beginning of Jesus' new family, the messianic community.

THE GOSPEL OF JOHN: MARY'S SACRAMENTAL FUNCTION

In the Fourth Gospel, the figure of "the mother of Jesus" (John avoids the name "Mary") appears twice—at the wedding feast of Cana (John 2:1–11), and again on Calvary (John 19:25–27). Historically speaking, the Cana event probably occurred in Jesus' life before the years of his public ministry, in a context of social relationships among neighbors, family, and friends.[9] It is altogether possible that the wine did run out, that Mary intervened, engaging Jesus in dialogue, and that a prodigious sign was wrought. There can be no doubt that Jesus was a wonder-worker. In any case, whatever the event, John builds his theological reflection on it. One of the major tendencies of this evangelist is to contemplate an event on two different levels. One is material, carnal, factual, and informative. The other is symbolic, sacramental, spiritual, and performative. In the present chapter, where we are looking for information about the historical life of Mary, it is the former of the two levels that is of interest to us. The second is theology—an interpretation, however canonical, on the part of the evangelist. By having Jesus address his mother by the unusual appellation of "woman" (John 2:4), John relates Mary's function to that of Eve in Genesis 3:20. Mary is the new Eve, associated with the new Adam. Mary intercedes and achieves her end. She believes unreservedly in Jesus, and so realizes fully the basic relationship of the new community: faith. On the second, spiritual, level, for John the wedding has a symbolic, sacramental value in itself: it represents the eschatological marriage of God and humanity, and suggests the Eucharist as an anticipation of and preparation for that marriage.[10]

Prescinding from the theological reading, we may say that historically the wedding feast at Cana was an event in Mary's life that had little to distinguish it from a wedding in anyone else's life. Mary went to a wedding, shared the young couple's joy, would have been concerned about any embarrassment that might have arisen, and would have done everything she could to help if it did, to the point of having no qualms about asking Jesus to manifest his divine power. For the rest, as everywhere else in the New Testament, Mary does not take center stage. Others do.

Finally, John has Mary at the foot of the cross on Calvary.[11] His description is succinct, but of a moving human quality: "Seeing his mother there with the disciple whom he loved, Jesus said to his mother, 'Woman, there is your son.' In turn he said to the disciple, 'There is your mother.' And from that hour onward, the disciple took her into his care" (John 19:26–27). The historical basis of this scene is doubtful. Exegetes find two basic difficulties. First, the carefully contrived, artificial structure of the crucifixion account in John suggests that Mary's presence was probably part of the contrivance. Second, there is the absence of this vignette from the synoptic narratives. In any event, the theological style of the fourth evangelist calls for the revelation of a mystery in this scene. Again he has Jesus call his mother "woman." He makes the Apostle John, whose actual mother he also places here at the foot of the cross (John 19:25) Mary's son. Again we are presented with the antitype of Eve. In the person of John, all of Jesus' disciples become the children of Mary.

According to this theology, then, Mary undertook her universal motherhood in the supreme hour of the Redemption. This is the meaning of Jesus' words to John, "There is your mother." If we prefer to admit a historical basis for the scene of Jesus seeing his mother abandoned and entrusting her to the solicitude of the beloved disciple, we must also understand that this historical event occasioned the evangelist's reflection, and his discovery, in the material event, of a hidden, mysterious meaning for Mary's insertion into the process of the spiritual generation of all those redeemed by the blood of Jesus.[12]

MARY'S HISTORICAL TRAITS

As we have seen, Mary's historical outline is blurred by theological reflections on the interior greatness of this woman of the people, unknown to the mighty of her age, but very special in the compassionate sight of God. Nevertheless, the various texts and scenes that do betray something of the historical Mary would seem to tell us the following.

1. MARY IS THE VIRGIN BRIDE.

The texts take Mary's virginity for granted, to the point of building their theological reflection on it. As we shall see later on, virginity constituted a social value analogous to that of widowhood. At the same time, Mary was obviously betrothed to Joseph in accordance with Jewish custom.

2. MARY IS POOR.

A number of gospel scenes show us that Mary is a woman of the people, and that Mary and Joseph are a poor couple, for whom there is not a great deal of room in the world, pressing as their need may be (see Luke 2:7). The Greek terms (*tapeinōsis* in Luke 1:48, *tapeinos* in Luke 1:52) signify material indigence, the fruit of exploitation on the part of the rich, whom Old Testament legislation attempted to restrain in this respect (Exod. 22:20–24; Deut. 24:12–17; Lev. 19:20, 23:22). However, the word and concept were gradually acquiring a spiritual connotation at the time of Mary. God was seen as favoring the poor and oppressed, and determining that they would be the first to benefit from the reestablishment of justice in the coming Reign of God. Thus, the materially indigent come to stand for the pious, those who wait in hope for the coming of God's Reign. As we shall see when we consider the Magnificat, Mary marches with these hosts of the poor. She is totally open and available to God's mercy and liberating intervention.

3. MARY IS MOTHER.

We may call her the Virgin Mary, but the Gospels call her the "mother of Jesus." She has the same ties with her child as any mother has. But she is also able to let go and let him fulfill his mission. For Mary, ties of blood are less important than new ties springing from faith in Jesus' mission and her own. As Jesus' mother she is present in the crucial moments of his life—at his incarnation, his birth, his first visit to the temple, at the beginning of his public life at Cana, in the heyday of his popularity with the multitudes, at his execution, at his sending of the Holy Spirit at Pentecost to take his place and continue his work.

4. MARY HAS THE FULLNESS OF FAITH.

It is easy to imagine, in contemplating Mary, that all was easy and clear for her—that she knew that she was the Mother of God, that her Son Jesus was the Son of the Most High, or that she was the most highly blessed of all women. But the Gospels do not paint this idyllic picture. Instead, they present Mary as walking in the darkness of faith.[13] Her cousin Elizabeth says it outright: "Blest is she who trusted . . . " (Luke 1:45). She does not understand everything that is happening (Luke 2:50). She has to accept God's mysterious ways. But she trusts (Luke 1:38). Her faith grows as she reflects and meditates (Luke 1:29, 2:19). She reflects on what the angel's greeting might mean, overcomes her initial fright, and says, *"Fiat!"* The Annunciation illustrates the dynamics of Mary's faith. She is a virgin, but she discovers that she is with child. She is disturbed and afraid (Luke 1:29–30). She discovers the hand of God, the action of the Holy Spirit. She is conscious that what is growing within her womb is somehow divine. She does not doubt this interior illumination that has been granted her; she only asks how it will come about (Luke 1:34). She accepts unseen realities, and believes, because nothing is impossible for God (Luke 1:37). Is this not precisely faith as defined in the Letter to the Hebrews? "Faith is confident assurance concerning what we hope for, and conviction about things we do not see" (Heb. 11:1).

Without grasping the profound implications of what she was hearing from the angel, Mary believed. Surely she had a real awareness that her motherhood was somehow from the Holy Spirit. She realized, however vaguely, that the salvation of all men and women depended on the child that was beginning to grow in her womb. Then her life gradually clarified what she had confusedly seen. It is the part of faith to live in the twilight. Faith generates light as long as the individual accepts and surrenders to God's plan. This is our path, and it was Mary's narrow path. Faith is willing to live with perplexity, but it will brook no doubt. Mary never doubted. Zachary doubted when he heard that Elizabeth would conceive. "How am I to know this?" he demands (Luke 1:18). And he receives God's punishment: "You will be mute," the angel replies, "unable to speak—until these things take place, because you have not trusted my words" (Luke 1:20). But Mary believed, and is praised by Elizabeth for her belief: "Blest is she who trusted . . . " (Luke 1:45). It was in the strength of this faith that Mary was always available to others, that she was never centered on herself but was always at the service of her Son and her neighbor.

5. MARY IS THE VALIANT WOMAN.

Let us not imagine a Mary surrounded by ladies-in-waiting, dwelling in a palatial mansion, ringed round by celestial musicians, adorned with roses, and living in an idyllic paradise. Her life was like ours—opaque, difficult, and beset with the struggles of the day-in, day-out.

Her immaculate state did not, however, make it possible for her to escape from the fact that she was living in a sinful world which was predisposed to misunderstanding. She too was exposed to all those incalculable and irrational elements common to the human situation—the coming together of inexplicable circumstances, the machinations inherent in communal life, the senseless and harsh conflict of human passions—all of which can lead to the brutal oppression of a totally innocent person. Mary was no exception to this "normal" human situation by virtue of her immaculate state, but it did clearly bestow on her a special power which, though it did not diminish the pain of the situation in which she found herself, certainly enabled her to experience it, in her complete submission to God, in a totally different way.

We do well to envisage the family at Nazareth as people engaged in a struggle for their faith, bravely facing all life's difficulties in their complete surrender to God's supreme rule.[14]

This is the humble woman who was chosen by God to be the temple of the Holy Spirit and the mother of Jesus, our Savior and God incarnate. We celebrate all of the marvels wrought by the Almighty within her. Conceived without the original sin that traumatizes and alienates our existence, conceiving Jesus in a state of virginity that she maintained throughout her life, becoming the Mother of God, participating in virtue of this motherhood—silently and unassumingly—in the process of our salvation, and finally, assumed body and soul into heaven at the end of this earthly life, Mary is woman par excellence. These are not myths. There is every indication here that a concrete, historical personality was assumed by God, snatched from the depths of her anonymity to make broad the path for the definitive, total entry of God into the history of humanity.

E

To be sure, it can always be alleged that all of this is rather too like the ancient mythologies. Many today reduce Mariology to a chapter in the history of the archetype, a theme of mythical discourse. But we may also believe, word for word, everything that the basic texts and the community of faith have taught us. We believe not simply because there is a group who believe and we belong to that group, but because of the actual content of this Marian faith. This content speaks less of Mary than of Christ and the Holy Spirit. It is on their account that God works the marvels in Mary. We proclaim and believe in Jesus as our Savior, the immediacy of God in human flesh: but it is through Mary that these realities have been introduced into history. Mary never appears on her own account. She is always in a role of service to others. She visits Elizabeth. Together with Joseph she searches for her lost child, Jesus. She is the one to inform her Son that the wine has run out at Cana. Her presence is one of silence rather than of words. It is on account of others, and especially Christ, that we can speak of Mary.

A HISTORY THAT ANTICIPATES ESCHATOLOGY

We contemplate the divine events in the life of Mary in their eschatological meaning, as well. What do we mean by this? We mean that we must not consider the wonders of God in Mary's life simply as miraculous and astounding. They are intended to express God's ultimate design for humanity in general, and the feminine in particular, in that last, definitive plenitude of human destiny we call the eschaton.[15] This final situation, the state of our ultimate tomorrow, promised to all humanity, in which we shall be totally of and for God, has an anticipatory realization in history: it is already realized in Mary. In Mary, the feminine has been historicized eschatologically. In her, all of the positive dimensions of the feminine are present supereminently: Mary is virgin, mother, spouse, and so on, to the ultimate degree. Of course, when we say that the dynamics and impulses of the feminine blossom definitively and absolutely in Mary, we understand this as the work of God—as an ultimate expression beyond anything that history can achieve. In Mary, the history of the feminine has reached its culmination and terminus. This definitive, eschatological perfection characterizing the Blessed Virgin Mary, right during the course of our history, justifies the veneration and admiration that piety and thought have accorded her. Deprived of this eschatological understanding, such veneration would be a religious perversion, as well as utterly incompatible with and unjustified by history.

We know next to nothing about Mary and her manner of life. The little that the Scriptures tell us, however, manifests what is essential in her life, and in all human life. In Mary, we have the two principle structures of the human in all of their crystalline purity: acceptance, and gift; welcome, and surrender.

We see that human beings are, first of all, receptive beings. They do not bestow life upon themselves; they receive life. They do not create the world; they only transform it. Their eyes do not create light, nor do their lungs create air; their eyes capture light and their lungs are filled with an oxygen that was already there. Thus, the individual has the gratifying experience of the goodness and exuberance of a reality continuously and freely bestowed.

But human beings are also beings who give of themselves— and who, to the extent that they give of themselves, become more, grow. They are open not only to receiving, but to giving.

Mary is both. She is pure welcome, and complete surrender. She is totally available to the design of God. Her response is, "*Fiat!* Let it be done!" She does not always understand all that is happening in her Son's regard. But despite all, she accepts it, and stores it in her heart (Luke 2:51). At the same time, she takes the initiative. She surrenders to others, she gives herself to others, as in her visit to Elizabeth, or at the wedding feast of Cana. She is weak and simple, but she is full of messianic courage as well, and in her Magnificat celebrates the downfall of the mighty and the punishment of the wealthy (Luke 1:51–53). At the foot of the cross she is dignified and courageous (John 19:25–27).

These attitudes, which we know to be Mary's, are enough to show us that in her, the human is present completely and perfectly. She is not only the realization of the ideal woman. She is the realization of the ideal human being.

IV. THEOLOGY: MARY, OUR LADY OF FAITH

Introduction: The Divine Grammar

There is not only a Mariology "from below"—from the all-but-anonymous history of this woman of the people of God who is the servant of the Lord (Luke 1:38) and who confesses that the Lord has looked upon his servant in her lowliness (Luke 1:48). There is a Mariology "from above," as well, a Mariology emerging from theological reflection, the Mariology of a thinker who takes the viewpoint of God, and, perplexed, discovers Mary full of grace (Luke 1:30) and blessed among women (Luke 1:42). This Mariology is the deed of faith, of the religious enthusiasm of the contemplator of Mary in God's plan, of the piety that magnifies. This is textbook Mariology. This Mariology emerges from a concern with systematics and a core principle.

Textbook Mariology may answer our need for unity and simplicity, but it may sometimes deceive us, as well. God's logic is not deductive, as ours is. God's logic is disconcerting. We need only note the constancy of paradox in the Old and New Testaments to see that God must revel in it. We must be careful, then, that theological celebration respect the narrow path God has chosen to exalt Mary.

Our own exaltation of Mary must not fall into mythology, or succumb to the numinous world of archetypes, to the point of concealing the surprisingly unsurprising, the extraordinarily extraordinary life of Mary and her child, Jesus. The real greatness of the divine aggrandizement lies in its aggrandizement of the lowly. The wonder in the wonders wrought by God in Mary lies in their exaltation of the lowly and humble. God's glory has a different structure from human glory. The latter has need of boast, eloquence, exuberance, and luxury. The glory of God is made manifest in humility, revealed in insignificance, made concrete in the marginal. Indeed, this is precisely the condition imposed by God before God's glory will be communicated. It is not in spite of lowliness, but in it and through it that that glory is manifested. One who fails to grasp this divine grammar will comprehend nothing either of the incarnation of God in the world, or of the real meaning of Christian Mariology. What is worse, such a one will be in danger of reducing all Christology and Mariology to modifications of archaic mythologies. Historically, God did not choose for mother a Roman princess in Caesar's palace. God was not taken by the beauty of a Pallas Athena, but by the plain visage of a woman of the poor. The Holy Spirit chose a fragile woman of poverty to be the living royal temple of God. Mary did not give birth in a royal chamber, surrounded by ladies-in-waiting, but in a stable, surrounded by beasts. God did not choose what society and religion regard as great, royal, wealthy, and illustrious, but what they regard as insignificant, shameful, and marginal.

The Mariology of exaltation must know what it is exalting: these concrete, humble realities. It must extract the divine transparency that hides in the lowly, it must uncover the depth concealed in the humble. For this was the path the Most High chose to take to Mary and her child, Jesus. This was God's chosen path to a visitation of humanity.

A Mariology that fails to take Mary's history into account, a Mariology that is attentive only to its own discourse, loses its character as a discourse on salvation history. It will speak not of the historical Mary who was the Mother of God, the royal tabernacle of the Holy Spirit, but of a new Christian mythology of Mary, developed through fantasy. The criterion of all genuine Christian theology, that theology that will not allow itself to be transformed into pure mythological discourse, is its reference to the events wrought by God in history. It is the task of theology to understand the rationality that lies hidden in these events, and to discover their interconnections in God's plan, always keeping contact with them, always working in relation to them, the better to be able to love God.

Like Mariology, Christology and pneumatology find themselves limited by the theological atmosphere of their time. Not every age is ready for everything. There is the matter of growth. God's plan has matured in history and time. Luke's words about

Jesus are even more applicable to Mary: she too "progressed steadily in wisdom and age and grace before God and men" (Luke 2:52). She grew, from promise to fulfillment, from the dark of faith to the noonday blaze of the perfect knowledge of God's will, from her Immaculate Conception to the descent of the Holy Spirit upon her, from her virginal conception to the foot of the cross, where she contemplated in confusion God's chosen way to the liberation of the human race, from her tireless earthly pilgrimage to her full transfiguration in heaven. The Marian devotion is subject to the law of time. From its insignificant first beginnings, it grew little by little until its flowering in the third century, and its culmination in the great explicitness of our time with our understanding of Mary's unique relationship with the Third Person of the Most Holy Trinity. Mary incarnates, par excellence, God's time within human time. She is the link that joins the four periods of salvation history. Each stage passes to the next through the Woman. Mary belongs to the Old Testament in which she was born. She is a witness of the earthly life of Christ. She is present at the birth of the Church (Acts 1:14). And, body and soul in heaven, she inaugurates the age of totally redeemed, divinized humanity.

7. The Immaculate Conception: Culmination of Humanity

Humanity, as its geniuses and mystics testify, is searching for its perfect identity. It dreams of a future kingdom of peace, justice, harmony, and community, where the mechanisms of hatred, division, and destruction all about us are defeated for good and all. It seeks to heal the wound that pustulates in a constant disruption of human and social life. Until then, it must suffer the bitter experience of failure. It must learn to live with contradiction. But hope does not grow cold—the hope of a kingdom of a perfect, finally reconciled humanity.

Israel more than other peoples articulated this dimension of hope. The future holds the secret of a new humanity. And we are already headed in the right direction. The people of hope are God's beloved spouse (Hos. 2; Jer. 31:17–22; Isa. 54:4–8, 61:10). But they are a spouse who knows that she cannot live in fidelity. God's people are constantly falling into adultery (Hos. 2; Ezek. 16). But the day will come—When will it come?—when God will at last be able to say: "You are all-beautiful, my beloved, and there is no blemish in you" (Song of Songs 4:7).

In Mary conceived without sin, Christian faith sees the historicization of its hope, and the end of the search. At last God has raised up someone who can be the pure spouse of God's pure love. Mary is for us. Mary is the culmination of humanity, the coronation of Israel.

On December 8, 1854, Pope Pius XI defined it to be of faith that "in the first moment of her conception, by the grace and privilege of almighty God and in view of the merits of Jesus Christ, Savior of the human race, the Virgin Mary was preserved and exempted from all stain of original sin."[1] The papal bull *Ineffabilis Deus* further states that Mary was granted such perfection that nothing greater than she can be imagined except

God. No one else can ever hope to attain to her perfection.[2] Obviously, we are dealing with ultimate, definitive realities here. History has reached its terminus, and humanity may take its repose. For, in one of ourselves, we are transported to the fullness of history, the place of the realization of our utopia.

WHAT DOES IT MEAN TO BE FREE OF ORIGINAL SIN?

The solemn declaration of the extraordinary magisterium of the Church asserts that Mary was preserved and exempted from all stain of original sin.[3] By original sin we mean that original situation that engenders the incapacity for love, the shutting up of the human heart, and the impossibility of relating befittingly to the three great pillars of human existence, the world, others, and God. This perversion of the root of human life lies *ultimately* in the inhuman dimensions of human life, the dimensions of personal and social injustice, the dimensions of the historical wickedness of the manner of human sharing—in short, in our situation of original sin. We are all born into the sin of the world, united, by a tragic perversion of our original destiny, in our tragic lot as we are in solidarity with one another in our frugal victories. Yet, Mary is said to be exempt and free from every stain of original sin, by the redeeming deed of her Son, in such a manner that she actualizes that redemption in the sublimest way imaginable.

One might ask: How could Mary be redeemed before the birth of the Redeemer? To give a satisfactory answer to this question we must take God's perspective. The everlasting God, to whom past, present, and future are eternally present, foreseeing the liberating deed of Jesus Christ, delivered Mary from original sin in light of that foreseen universal redemption. Mary was never handicapped by the basic alienation that stigmatizes our own existence. She fulfills the human person that God always wanted—raised to heaven (we are bowed down by sin), open to others (we are closed in upon ourselves), and in communion with the world (we possess the earth selfishly). She is still a part of God's first plan. She belongs to the state logically preceding humanity's fall. Thus, Mary has no debt to pay by reason of a sinful situation. To be sure, she belongs to the history of humanity, she is born into this world of parents burdened with sin, but by a divine privilege she is uncontaminated. She takes no credit. This is God's free act, for God wishes for once to make concrete the new humanity, and to anticipate the ultimate blessedness of history when all of the just will stand before God immaculate and pure. Mary is already in our history, and at its very heart.

And so Mary is immaculate. She shows us, in the very course of our pilgrimage, what we shall be at that pilgrimage's end— each to our own particular degree—at the moment of humanity's consummation in God. Of course, to believe that Mary, by Mystery's design, is without sin is not to believe that her earthly life was a bed of roses. She partook of the blind, seemingly meaningless character of human existence. To say that she is immaculate does not mean that she did not suffer, that she was never troubled, or that she had no need for faith and hope. She was a daughter of earth, albeit blessed by heaven. She had human passions. Everything authentically human was present in her.

It belongs to the essence of the human condition to be open to various worlds, and to see oneself inhabited by these worlds. Each of us has a basic element of passion that bows us down to the earth; each of us has a dimension that opens us to the skies; and each of us has a dimension that folds us inward, toward our own heart. Each of these universes has its own impulses and tendencies, and they tug at each of us from every side. This is not human imperfection, however. This is human richness.

Concupiscence—the theological term for the plural dynamism of human existence—is, in its original sense as taught by the Franciscan theologians of the Middle Ages, neither sin nor the consequence of sin. It belongs to God's creation, and God's creation is good. Indeed, concupiscence is the condition for virtue and growth. The original human being, before the Fall, was granted the grace of integrity and "original justice." This being integrated the most disparate dynamics of personal life into a path directed toward God, open to others, and rooted in the world. Originally this being did justice to each of the dimensions that now tear us apart, without being sundered and without any dehumanizing restraint.

Then sin introduced disorder. Every passion was unleashed. Human beings were no longer capable of ruling themselves.

Concupiscence, as we have it *historically* through the ages—and only in this sense—owing to its disintegrating dynamics, is the consequence of sin and the occasion of sin. To say that Mary was preserved and exempted from all sin does not mean that Mary did not feel the different passions of life, with their specific demands, as does any normal human being. Unlike the rest of us, however, she succeeded in directing those passions toward a holy plan, and adapting everything to its proper place: she was wholly and completely the daughter of God, sister of us all, and free sovereign of the world. By the grace of God, her interior strength enabled her to order and direct everything within her toward the right measure of all her dimensions. The fountain that welled within her was pure as crystal, and rendered everything in her life pure as crystal as well—free from sin or any alienation and, moreover, full of grace and the divine life.

At long last, a creature has appeared in the universe who is pure goodness. Now the desert blooms, now the tree of life produces flowers that do not wither before summer. Now there is one whose life is openness itself, and that one has conceived a life more excellent still: Jesus Christ. Now for the first time it is possible to catch a brief glimpse, in this wounded creation, of a glance that does not lose the innocence of its brilliance, a deed unfraught with ambivalence, a gentleness, a beauty, a clemency without a threat held in reserve. Now humanity can begin again. Paradise is not altogether a thing of the past, gone forever, and the Reign is not everlastingly stuck in the future. Now there is a present that realizes the most ancestral dreams. Earth has wed heaven, flesh has reconciled with spirit, and men and women leap for joy before their great God.

WHAT DOES IT MEAN TO BE FULL OF GRACE?

To profess that Mary is full of grace is to admit that God—as goodness, gentleness, joy, righteousness, balance, transparency, freedom, and exuberance in all of life's dimensions—has given the divine self totally to this simple woman of the people. Grace is not something mysterious in the sense of being impalpable. Grace is the personal, living presence of God in life itself, dwelling there to make it more fully life, more open to heaven and earth alike. Mary's earthly life, then, was as difficult, troubled, monotonous, and painful as our own. These things belong to the very structure of a spirit immersed in flesh, a living transcendence existing within the narrow confines of an earthly immanence. The sinner suffers in these prison walls. We rebel, we shake our fist at the heavens, if indeed we do not curse life itself.

Mary, the immaculate one, suffered no less than the rest of us all of the spatial limitations and existential contradictions of this life. But she knew how to accept them all as manifestations of the structural mortality of life, and as an invitation to transcend them, mount beyond them, and desire God. Instead of diminishing her life, the human condition charged it with potential. The grace present within Mary integrated all things, making them all redound to growth in her life.

Undeniably, to be free from all the historical blemishes of our existence is a great privilege. But as one of the great theologians of our time has said, what has been true once will be true again.[4] We too shall live in a world of persons purified, a world in which we shall be totally for God, fully brothers and sisters, and completely free for the world. Mary anticipates the destiny of us all. Because of Mary, we have the certitude that God has not abandoned us to our disgrace. Mary is our new departure, our fresh start, provided only we are ready, for we are always surrounded by her love.

The immaculate conception of the Blessed Virgin Mary contains a secret meaning, then. It is not only a deed of the pure mercy of God, who has now begun to create a new humanity. The Immaculate Conception is the seed of still more excellent fruit to come. Here God has prepared a woman, made her totally pure and holy, that she may be God's own receptacle. Human beings are destined, have been created, to have the capacity to receive the gift of God's total, full self. As we saw in Part Two, Mary was prepared to be assumed by the Holy Spirit. In her, the feminine, charged with divinity, reaches its fullness. Still a virgin, she becomes a mother, and conceives God the Son. The secret, ultimate meaning of the Immaculate Conception lies not in Mary, but in God's wish to become incarnate. God determines to communicate the divine self totally. God prepares a living temple as dwelling place. God enters it, assumes it, and renders it divine. This preparation for the future spiritualization of humanity is the meaning and scope of the Immaculate Conception.

8. Mary's Perpetual Virginity: Seed of a Divinized Humanity

We have a special difficulty today with Mary's perpetual virginity.[1] The high value our culture ascribes to the exercise of one's sexuality makes it difficult for us to see the value of virginity.

CONFLICTING INTERPRETATIONS OF MARY'S VIRGINITY

Many Christians today think of Jesus' conception and birth somewhat as follows. Mary and Joseph lived in a deeply devout, pure home. Like the other fervent families of the time, they ardently awaited the coming of the Messiah. They prayed to Yahweh their God that one of their own offspring would be that chosen anointed one. And God indeed looked down with mercy upon the family of Joseph and heard their cry for redemption. The child of Mary and Joseph, engendered by their love, was hypostatically assumed by the eternal Son to become the Liberator of the world. In this representation, Mary is still pure, not in some biological sense, but in a personal, moral sense, as none of her activity compromised her relationship with God as the Absolute of her existence. Not even her love for Joseph competed with her love for God. Her Son was born of the purest love. He was offered to God before his very conception. And God, in a love that was purer still, accepted that child, that he might be the sacrament of the only-begotten Son of God in history. Virginity is a value, yes, but not so absolute a value that, in order to preserve it, God had to invent a supernatural way of conceiving Jesus—without male seed, through the activity and grace of the Holy Spirit. After all, marriage, too, has a sacred value, and is a sufficiently pure vehicle for the envelopment of God in human flesh.

Other Christians, conscious of the literary devices of the New Testament authors, hold that the picture of Mary as a virgin is simply a way of emphasizing the truth about Jesus. Christology, we are told, and not Mariology, is the focus of the gospel accounts (see, for example, Matt. 1:15–18, Luke 1:26–28). Accordingly, the account of Jesus' virginal conception in a biological sense is merely a literary device to convey the notion of a new beginning for humanity inaugurated by Jesus. Jesus does not prolong the history of humanity, reproducing its mechanisms of sin and grace. He establishes a new order, one of pure goodness, grace, and glory. He is the new Adam. He is the firstfruits of the new heavens and new earth. This new creation is not the work of human history. It is the exclusive product of God's free initiative. Jesus' virginal conception, we are told, is a model for the understanding and expression of this truth, which is the core of the gospel message. Only in relation to the uniqueness of Jesus did Mary's virginity begin to be spoken of—first her virginity *ante partum,* then *in partu,* then *post partum.*[2]

In commenting on these interpretations, we must admit that the incarnation of God would not in and of itself be bound to a virginal conception. God could just as easily have assumed someone engendered through human love to be the incarnation of the only-begotten Son. Would this incarnate God have been any less the Son of God, any less the Liberator, any less divine than is the one virginally born of Mary? Surely not.

However, this is *a priori. A posteriori,* let us ask: Does this explanation do justice to the testimony of our forebears in the faith? Is it only and solely the divinity and the uniqueness of Jesus, the human God, that the primitive Christian community sought to profess through its doctrine of the virgin birth? We think not. Further, Mary's relationship with the Holy Spirit would never have come to light—that relationship in light of which new theological perspectives are opened in terms of a self-communication of the Spirit analogous to that of the Son. Theology must reflect not on the product of our desires, but on the salvific facts as these are transmitted in the Gospels. There we are clearly told of the marriage of Mary and Joseph, their perplexity, and Mary's conception of Jesus by the coming of the Holy Spirit instead of by knowledge of man. If Joseph had been Jesus' actual father, he would have been accorded a role in salvation history, and accordingly a veneration, equal to that accorded Mary. But this is not what the fonts of divine revelation disclose. Joseph's role was a lateral, juridical one, distinct from the direct function of Mary as parent in the proper and true sense. When God determined to communicate the divine self substantially and absolutely, God's path to the world passed not by way of marriage, but by way of virginity. It was a path of love, but without the mediation of married love.

As for the second interpretation, we must indeed keep in mind that the intention of the accounts of Jesus' virginal conception in Luke and Matthew is christological. The evangelists' concern is surely with the unique relationship between Jesus (both his existence and his destiny) and God, and, to be sure, they seek to underscore the fact that in Jesus humanity has a new beginning. But is this all they wish to say? Do they simply mean that Jesus is the new Adam, the origin and head of the new humanity? Neither Luke nor Matthew speculate on Mary's virginity. They accept it as preestablished, as an indisputable datum, and they go on from there with a christological reflection. The texts of Matthew (Matt. 1:18) and Luke (Luke 1:35) referring to Jesus' virginal conception point directly to Jesus, admittedly, but they point obliquely to Mary as well. One cannot rigorously dismiss these texts as simple variations on a myth preexisting in the culture of the time. True, in Egyptian mythology the Pharaoh is the son of the god Amon-Ra and the virgin queen. In Greek mythology the gods have their sacred marriages (*hieros gamos*) with human daughters, either virgin or married, and thus produce divine or demigod offspring like Perseus or Hercules, or human beings, but illustrious ones, like Homer, Plato, Alexander the Great, or Augustus. But we must take into account the differences between the myths and the New Testament narrative. The latter, unlike the shameless myths, does not deal with sexual relations. The Holy Spirit does not appear as father, but as generative force (Luke 1:35). Jesus springs from the creative power of God and Mary's free acceptance, not from an activity linked in any way to the sexes.

Furthermore, as we have previously observed, to opt for a mythological interpretation is to leave unanswered the questions regarding the ultimate meaning of the feminine in God, and the meaning of the new humanity inaugurated in time and no longer the object of eschatological hope.

We shall have to have another interpretation—that of the great tradition that we espouse, the one that receives the testimony of our faith, reflected in the Gospels, as we see, and attempts to draw from this testimony the most magnificent possible consequences for our understanding of God's ultimate will for humanity and a world to come.

MARY'S VIRGINITY: ITS ORIGINAL MEANING

Let us attempt to recover the original meaning of Mary's virginity, so that we can accept the biological fact and go on from there. There is certainly a virginity and chastity that of itself has nothing Christian about it. In the Greco-Roman tradition, the vestal virgins were required to lead a life of perfect virginity in the service of the goddess Vesta for at least thirty years after their consecration. We have accounts in Greek mythology of virgins being offered in sacrifice to placate the anger of the gods— the classic example being that of Iphigenia, to whom Euripides devoted the seven tragedies we have and two others. Virginity, as we have already had occasion to observe, symbolizes freshness of life, stored energy, a pent-up vitality that, when coupled with innocence, has special salvific value. Here virginity has a cultic, ritual meaning. But this is not Christian virginity or chastity.

There are a virginity and a chastity that are lived as a moral virtue. Stoicism idealized a continence intended to be a complete control over the body and its demands so that the individual could be free to be elevated to the divine state. This can be a magnificent ideal, but it can also conceal an arrogant contempt for the bodily component of the human being.

Mary's virginity is of another inspiration. We must consider it in the context of the Old Testament world into which Mary was born. The Old Testament as a single literary unit accords virginity no special value. It is equivalent to sterility, and sterility was a mean, contemptible thing. When Jephthah's daughter learns that she is to be offered in sacrifice by her own father, she begs first to be allowed to go with her friends up to a high mountain, to mourn—but to bewail her virginity, not the fact that she is going to lose her life (Judges 11:37–40). Not to be a mother was not to be fulfilled as a woman. When Amos wishes to convey the depth of the misery of the chosen people he compares them to a virgin doomed to die without ever having borne a child (Amos 5:1–2; see Jer. 1:15, 2:13; Joel 1:8). There is no word in Hebrew to denote what we call a bachelor. That a man would remain unmarried and celibate was simply unthinkable. And so when Jeremiah embraces celibacy, it is understood as a radical, prophetic sign (Jer. 16:1–4). It represents and foretells the destruction and desolation of Israel. Why marry and procreate when we live on the threshold of the approaching apocalypse (Jer. 16:9)?

It is in the context of this attitude, then, that Mary's biological virginity must be regarded. Virginity holds no efficacy. And so Mary sings, "He has looked upon his humble servant" (Luke 1:48). Her virginity is an impoverishment, scorned by her world. Mary does not celebrate her virginity, this diminution in the eyes of her contemporaries. She exults in the marvelous deed of the Almighty within her (Luke 1:49). Her lowliness, her virginity, sums up the lowliness of the poor of Yahweh (the *anawim*). To be poor in the biblical sense is to live in pure readiness, in radical confidence in God, in confident humility before the Lord, and in a faith abandoned to the divine will. To be poor is the attitude of one who would be the servant of the Most High: "I am the servant of the Lord. Let it be done to me as you say" (Luke 1:38).[3]

And so, we see, Mary's virginity is not a technique for controlling the impulses of the body so as to be able to rise to divinity. We perceive no heroism required of Mary by her virginity. Mary's virginity is not a moral virtue, but, as Luke makes clear, a theological virtue. Mary lives by pure faith in God. Stripped of all self-assertiveness, she can surrender totally to the will of Mystery. Mary's virginity is not cultic, as it was with the vestal virgins. She has struck no bargain with God to gain God's good will. Divesting herself of all ambition, she becomes simply and solely the servant. She is nothing but her gift of herself.

Mary's biological virginity is part of the structure of the *kenosis*, the self-emptying, with all its attendant humiliations, that she shares with her Son. Her biological virginity is lowliness and deprivation, as far as others can see. It has value neither in society nor for religion. But Mary makes this situation of an apparently mean existential condition the path of humility, serene surrender, and boundless trust in God. She aspires to nothing. She is only completely available. It is this attitude that allows God to be born of her, first in her heart, and then in her most pure womb.

The New Testament will propose this attitude as the most fruitful one for receiving and living the Reign of God. Biological virginity, as we see, has no biblical value. Yet, it can serve as a buttress of humility and openness to God's will, and that is of inestimable value. In Meister Eckhart's expression, virginity allows God to be conceived in the heart. "Had Mary not first conceived God in her spirit," he says, "she would not have engendered him in her body."[4]

MARY'S VIRGINITY *ANTE PARTUM:* A NEW START FOR THE WORLD

The faith of the Church has always proclaimed, from the first evangelical testimonials (Matt. 1:18, Luke 1:35) to the present, that Jesus was born of a virgin. God wished to be born of a woman of a low, despised condition. This is God's way. The liturgical prayers and official doctrinal statements of the early Church bear witness to this faith, and it became part of all Christian creeds, right from the beginning of the second century. Then the doctrine became explicit in various councils: the First Council of Constantinople (A.D. 381; DS 150), the Council of Chalcedon (A.D. 451; DS 301), the Second Council of Constantinople (the fifth ecumenical council, A.D. 553; DS 427). Second Constantinople declares, invoking the fullness of its authority:

If anyone says that the holy, glorious, and ever virgin (*aei parthenos*) Mary is the mother of God only in an improper and untrue sense, or that she is such only by virtue of a relation consequent on having borne a mere human being, and not God the Incarnate Word who was born of her, let such a one be excluded from the community of faith.[5]

A synod of Italian and North African bishops, celebrated in Rome in the vicinity of the Basilica of Saint John Lateran in 649 under Pope Martin I, defines the meaning of "ever virgin":

If anyone does not properly and truly confess with the holy fathers that the holy and ever virgin and immaculate Mary was the mother of God, let such a one be excluded from the community of faith. In a special and true sense, in the fullness of time, without seed, and of the Holy Spirit, she conceived and gave birth incorruptibly (*incorruptibiliter*) to God the Word himself, to the One who was born of God the Father before all ages. After she gave birth, she then preserved this virginity, indissolubly and permanently.[6]

The Synod of Toledo, in Spain (A.D. 675; DS 533–36) and the Fourth Council of the Lateran (A.D. 1215; DS 801) confirmed these declarations. The classic formulation appeared on August 7, 1555, in a bull of Pope Paul IV (*Cum quorumdam hominum*) against an anti-Trinitarian Polish sect: " . . . Ever virgin, before giving birth, in giving birth, and after giving birth" (*ante partum, in partu,* et *post partum*).[7]

As we see, these statements are perfectly clear in themselves. At the same time, however, we must agree:

. . . We are not actually dealing with an absolute definition of the Church. The intent of the Church in these definitions did not bear directly and explicitly on Jesus' virgin birth as such. The actual profession of faith made here is simply in the unique, special nature of Jesus' origin. Neither, of course, is the declaration of Paul IV a definition. Nor again is that of the First Council of the Lateran, or of the Synod of Toledo. In other words we may say that these declarations of the Church, like the creeds of the primitive Church, profess the virgin birth without directly and immediately addressing a particular heresy contradicting it—whose condemnation would of course have been tantamount to an explicit demand for an absolute *assensus fidei*.[8]

The concern of the magisterium of the Church down through the ages has always been to underscore that Jesus' origin in the world owes nothing to male seed. Jesus is from God. It is secondary that Mary was a virgin in whom the Holy Spirit acted to engender the eternal Word in human form. Mary's greatness does not rest on her virginity, but in her being the *woman* chosen to receive the humanized Word in her womb. As a *woman*, she could have been a virgin, or she could have been married. The declaration and witness of our faith that as a matter of fact she was a virgin, and that she must be accepted and acknowledged as such, belongs to another level of reflection. It is on that secondary, reflective level that we are called upon to accept that the Word was conceived and engendered not by a married, childless woman, but by a virgin.

Intimately as it may belong to the permanent faith of the Church, the doctrine of Mary's perpetual virginity does not occupy a central place in the hierarchy of truths. The truths directly bearing on God and Christ, on the incarnate God and absolute Liberator of humankind, are more important than the Marian Truths. Today, then, when the latter are no longer accepted without question, so that they must be continually defended and justified, the need arises for a distinction between what belongs to the *essential* content of faith, and what belongs to a secondary level. A belief in Mary's virginity will have Christian—that is, salvific—meaning only for one who believes primarily in the incarnation of God in the human-and-divine reality of Jesus.

With these points established, we must now inquire into the revelatory intent of Mary's virginity *ante partum.* What *salvific* truth is revealed here? Let us abandon a raw theological positivism that would merely affirm the fact and ask the assent of faith. All truths, as Vatican II said so well, are for our salvation, and never simply for the satisfaction of our sophisticated minds. If God chose the path of virginity, and not that of biological sexuality, to enter the world, then there must be some reason why God did so, and we must try to find it.

First, we must concede that there are no compelling *a priori* reasons. *A priori*, God could have just as easily have had an earthly father. This earthly father would not have been in competition with the eternal Father in any way. God has no competitors. God is on an utterly other, altogether transcendent level of being.

Second, Jesus' virginal conception can have implied no negative evaluation of sex and sexuality. As we have seen, Judaism held prejudices against virginity, while exalting sexuality and motherhood.

Third, we must abandon for good and all the opinion of so many of the early Fathers that Jesus' virgin birth was a necessary condition for his exemption from the contamination of original sin. These theologians exaggerated the function of the biological factor in the transmission of original sin.

Finally, the reasons for Mary's virginity must be sought above and beyond Mariology. They must be sought in Christology and pneumatology. Virginity is presented in the fonts as a concretization of the truth that comes to us by and with Jesus. In Jesus Christ, especially after the Resurrection, the apostolic faith recognized the new Adam. At long last, a living being over whom death no longer had any dominion had entered the world. In him, life has all its fullness. A new world has dawned on the horizon of this old, mortal one—the desire of all the prophecies, the vision of all of the dreams of humankind. This *novum,* so intensely desired by all humanity, cannot spring from human effort. Everything we produce, regardless of the degree of self-denial and purity of intention with which we produce it, bears the stigma of its manifold imperfection. Persons may become better, but they cannot altogether exorcise from their lives the shadows that loom above those lives. And suddenly, here, in Jesus, all is fulfilled, and in what radiant splendor. Scarcely, then, is this Jesus the fruit of human striving. He is a pure gift of God. It is God who has taken the initiative and sown the seed of a new humanity. At long last, we are deliverd from sin and death. This is the truth manifested by Jesus' virginal conception. That conception is accomplished through the divine initiative and goodwill. Male sexuality contributes nothing. This is a new, absolute beginning, and its origin is "not by blood, nor by carnal desire, nor by man's willing it, but by God" (John 1:13). Jesus' virginal conception by the operation of the Holy Spirit makes concrete the gratuity of humanity's brand-new beginning.

Moreover, the new being inaugurated by Jesus is not a mere prolongation of the state in which humanity already finds itself. It is a breach, and a protest. It is a new, definitive creative intervention on the part of God. This breach is marked by the virginal conception. Anyone can be born of the loving encounter of two hearts. But those so born must inherit the history of sin in which those two hearts have loved. Now this circle is broken.

Jesus is born from on high. He springs from another history, one with its beginning in God and its terminus in the womb of the Virgin of Nazareth.

If Jesus' origins were altogether "from below," from within human history, he would be a vessel of the blemishes of that history, and would himself stand in need of deliverance. If he came only from on high, he would not belong to our history. He would touch humanity only tangentially. But he is the sacrament of encounter. He comes from below, from Mary, and he comes from above, from God. The virginal conception is the wonderful expression of this encounter. Mary belongs to humanity, and, even though she is preserved and exempt from all stain of sin, represents history before God. The generative force for this new beginning comes from above—from the creative, life-giving Spirit acting upon Mary. And the fruit of this loving encounter of heaven and earth is Jesus Christ, new Adam, head of the new humanity. Mary's biological virginity is at the service of the fulfillment of this divine plan, which only begins to be understandable to faith after its realization. Virginity in its sheer biological aspect is of no human or salvific value. To seek to reduce Mary's virginity to its mere biological meaning is the sign of an underdeveloped spirituality, a symptom of the lack of a religious sensitivity. The biological element is a bolster, an expression, a sign of another reality: the birth of a new humanity. Thus, Mary's virginity is not an end in itself. It is not in the service of its own exaltation. It is totally at the service of Christ and his universal significance.

How did the virginal conception take place? There is an external element to be considered here in terms of the juridical and social situation (single, engaged, and so on) in which Mary finds herself; and then there is the interior element of the specific form of the beginning of Jesus' existence in the virgin womb. With respect to the first element, we can offer certain plausible historical reflections. The second element, however, can only be viewed in terms of a series of various noncompelling hypotheses.

We read that Mary is "a virgin betrothed to a man named Joseph, of the house of David" (Luke 1:27) who is told "You shall conceive and bear a son . . . " (Luke 1:31). Startled, Mary wonders, "How can this be since I do not know man?" (Luke 1:34). How are we to understand this last expression? I believe that we must discard the traditional hypothesis according to which, even before the Annunciation, Mary and Joseph had decided to live a virginal marriage. Surely this would not have been impossible for divine grace. But to hypothesize it as the existential situation in which the virginal conception took place is just as surely to fail to take account of the negative value ascribed to virginity by the age. The hypothesis enjoying the greatest support of contemporary Mariologists holds that Mary did not intend a virginal marriage.[9] She was already legally married to Joseph—the meaning of betrothal in Jewish law—but they were forbidden to live together until the solemn reception of the bride into the bridegroom's home, which occurred only several months after the betrothal. Surely this is how we should understand the assertion that Mary is a "virgin betrothed to a man named Joseph" (Luke 1:27). During the period of her betrothal, before marital relations between herself and Joseph are permitted (see Matt. 1:18), she receives the invitation to be the mother of the Messiah. She asks how this is possible, since she is not living with Joseph. And she receives the explanation that this will happen through the Holy Spirit, without Joseph's intervention. The conception will be virginal.

Then Mary pronounces her *Fiat!* "Let it be done!" True, she does not comprehend all of the dimensions of her yes. But the important thing is there: she places herself at God's entire disposition. She foregoes the luxury of personal conjecture concerning the event. The name of the child that now begins to grow within her womb is Jesus, or "Yahweh has saved." At least Mary understands the boundless reality that name implies. Somehow, the seed of the liberation of all humankind will be found in her very own child. God's will is "divine," here, as always. It always respects the freedom of the other—the "otherness" of the other. The will of God is never the imposition of an overpowering will. It is always the proposal of a respectful love that asks the creaturely consent. Mary receives an invitation. And with Saint Bernard we can say: "All the universe is at your feet, anxiously awaiting your answer.... Speak, woman, the word heaven and earth await! ... Tell the angel, tell him now!

Rather, tell God, through the angel. . . . Behold, the desire of the nations is knocking at your door!"[10] Mary conceives Jesus first in her heart and mind. She believes. Then she speaks her yes and goes on to conceive him in her body. Her *fiat* links the history of redeemed humanity with the history of God incarnate in the world, and links them for good and all. No one can see what God sought to communicate to us, and then proceed to deny this link. To accept God incarnate, God in the flesh, and then to ignore that flesh, received from Mary, is to empty the Incarnation of its historical content and reduce it to mere phraseology. There is a material structure in the novel reality inaugurated with Jesus. The feminine has penetrated the divine reality forever. No one will ever be able to tear it away, for Mary has pronounced her decisive yes.

Joseph is aware of his bride's pregnancy. Because he is "just," a good person (Matt. 1:19), he decides to divorce her privately, and without public scandal. Mary has probably informed him of the divine origin of her pregnancy. Still, he plans to free her from her commitment—not out of a concern for mere legal justice, but out of a fear of God. His bride is wrapped in God's very mystery. Who can touch her or possess her now? She is all God's now. Joseph can adopt this attitude because he is radically good and just. Moses, too, would have liked to flee the bush aflame with God. But while Joseph is thinking all this he is favored with enlightenment from on high: "Have no fear about taking Mary as your wife" (Matt. 1:20). And so the wedding is celebrated. The marriage will be virginal, however, as both spouses are totally at the service of the Mystery Mary bears within her. Joseph will be the keeper of the Light that will dispel human shadows. He will guard the sacred lamp, Mary, and will watch over the Little Light, Jesus, the Light that is to shatter the power of darkness forever. Mary and Joseph live in celibacy for the sake of the Messiah and his Reign. They live by anticipation the religious mission undertaken by so many others of the Christian era.

We have seen the christological reasons for Mary's virginity. Now let us consider it in a pneumatological perspective. The Holy Spirit, too, has a historical mission of divinization in salvation history—that of divinizing the feminine. The reasons of appropriateness that call for the assumption of human nature in its male concretion are valid for the Holy Spirit and Mary, as well. The condition of virginity, with all of its maternal potentiality, must also be assumed. All that is in woman, then, is assumed—virginity and maternity together—as the fundamental determinants of womanhood. Virginity is appropriated by the Holy Spirit not as something apart, not as an entity or value in itself, but as an anthropological reality whose destiny is fully attained through motherhood.

With reference to the question of how the conception took place on a biological level, we know nothing with any degree of certitude. Faith guarantees that it was not *ex semine Joseph*[11] that Jesus was conceived, but declares him to be *conceptum ex Spiritu Sancto*. Whether God created a spermatozoon out of nothing, or acted directly upon the ovum to fertilize it without sperm, is a matter of sheer hypothesis, as no evidence exists either way. Speculation here can degenerate into an unseemly curiosity. What we can say, leaving all such details aside, is that Jesus, God become a human being, was conceived humanly-and-divinely. He is human, but he is not only human—he is also God. We were all conceived humanly. Jesus was conceived humanly-and-divinely.

MARY'S VIRGINITY *IN PARTU:* A BIRTH IN ACCORDANCE WITH JESUS' HUMAN-AND-DIVINE NATURE

Since as early as the second century A.D., especially in liturgical and apocryphal texts, Mary has been regarded as maintaining her virginity not only before the birth of Jesus, but during the process of that birth as well. The Synod of Milan in A.D. 390, held under Saint Ambrose, proclaimed this virginity *in partu* against a certain Jovinian, who had taught that, while Mary conceived as a virgin, she did not give birth as a virgin: "Virgo concepit, sed non virgo generavit."[12] Ambrose's doctrine is implicit in the declaration of the fifth ecumenical council, Second Constantinople (A.D. 553), as well, where Mary was proclaimed "ever virgin" (*aei parthenos*). Earlier, Saint Leo the Great's celebrated dogmatic Letter to Flavian, which was read in the assembly of the ecumenical council of Chalcedon (A.D. 451), made the same declaration. Tertullian, Origen, and Saint Jerome denied the virginity *in partu,* fearing the infiltration of a Docetism that would deny Jesus' true humanity. Sacred Scripture contains no formal testimony either way. Mary's virginity *in partu* is regarded as of faith not in virtue of any direct and formal definition by a pope or council, but because of the constant tradition of the Church, up to and including the declarations of the Second Vatican Council.[13] We do not know with any certitude what this *de fide* pronouncement means. As Michael Schmaus admits, "There has never been an obligatory and concrete determination of the meaning of this virginity."[14] Theological tradition holds that Mary suffered no pain, and that her hymen remained inviolate during the birth of the child Jesus. We are wont to hear a comparison with the passage of the risen Jesus from his tomb, or his bodily appearance in the disciples' midst through closed doors. But this is tantamount to saying that Mary conceived, and carried Jesus in her womb for nine months, and then at the end of that time did not actually give birth. Yet, the New Testament very clearly states: "She gave birth to her first-born son and wrapped him in swaddling clothes . . . " (Luke 2:7). There is the very real danger here of a heretical misunderstanding and misstatement that would deny Jesus' true humanity. Faith in Mary's virginity *in partu* was actually first professed in certain Gnostic writings of uncertain origin such as the Odes of Solomon, the apocryphal Gospel of Thomas, and the Ascension of Isaiah. Only later was it embraced by serious theologians like Ambrose and Augustine. Despite its problems, however, this profession of faith contains a truth that our skeptical ears need to hear again today.

Let us state once more that we are not dealing with a core truth of our faith precisely in speaking of Mary's virginity before Jesus' birth or, especially, of her virginity throughout the process of her childbirth. We are dealing with a secondary truth, whose existential acceptance may legitimately vary a great deal from person to person and even from generation to generation. This truth may be but a remote consequence of the facts of Christian faith about Jesus and his mother, then; but tradition has never lost sight of it, and we *must* continue to maintain it today.

Here is all we can say: The specific processes of the birth of

Jesus escape our knowledge. But it was a genuine birth, and it was unlike other births only in that it did not involve a previous sexual relationship. Jesus' birth corresponded to the nature of the one being born—someone both human and divine. There was a *true* birth, just as there was a *complete* motherhood. This is enough for faith. This is all we know, and all we need to know.

As to particulars like the alleged absence of pain or the physical integrity of the hymen, we have to say that all such considerations have been speculative in the past and continue to be so in the present. And this is how they should be regarded. They do not pertain to faith, but to historical representations of the faith. Mary was exempt from concupiscence as concupiscence is actually found in our present sinful human condition. The dynamic of our passions—which is what is meant by concupiscence—keeps us prisoner. We are not able fully to integrate this dynamic into a mission of freedom oriented toward God. We fail to allow God to assume pain, life's privations, our mortality, all the negatives that flesh is heir to. They disturb us, and move us to cling selfishly to existence and this world. Mary was not exempt from what belongs essentially to the creaturely status of human life. She was sensitive, she could suffer, she was capable of all genuinely human feelings. Indeed, because she was woman more fully than any other woman has ever been woman, it may well be that she lived all of these limiting dimensions with an intensity we could never suspect. After all, we venerate her as "Our Lady of Sorrows." But there was a basic difference between Mary's sorrow and ours. Mary embraced her sorrow, and integrated it into God. What we live in a disintegrating, threatening, merely passive way, Mary actualized in an integrating way, and it became an opportunity for growth, a grace-filled encounter with God. The sometimes-so-painful biological processes of motherhood, then—conception, pregnancy, and childbirth— were experienced by her in her profoundly human pregnancy, and yet were overcome by the grace of her divine motherhood in the process of their full assumption by God. Thus, Mary was genuinely free not from pain itself, but from the *way* we have pain, the *way* we experience the breach to which we are still subject, incapable as we are of integrating our negativity with God in a personal way.

MARY'S VIRGINITY *POST PARTUM:* TOTAL DEDICATION TO CHRIST AND THE SPIRIT

Mary's virginity after the birth of her firstborn son (Luke 1:7; see Matt. 1:25) is likewise of Christian faith. Modern Protestants, unlike their forebears, tend to deny this article of faith on the basis of gospel texts that speak of Jesus' "brothers" (Mark 3:31, John 2:12, Acts 1:14, 1 Cor. 9:5, Gal. 1:19). But in biblical Greek the word for "brother" does not necessarily denote a sibling. It can mean a cousin (Gen. 13:8, 14:14). An expert on the subject comes to the following conclusion:

The so-called brothers and sisters of Jesus were his cousins. In the case of Simon and Jude the kinship was through their father, Cleopas, who was Saint Joseph's brother and a descendant of David, as was Joseph himself. The name of their mother is unknown. The mother of James and John, likewise styled "brothers" of Jesus, was a certain Mary, but not the mother of Jesus. She and her husband were relatives of Jesus' family, although we do not know in what degree. There are indications that the father of James (and John) belonged to the priestly or Levitical class, and was perhaps a brother of Mary the mother of Jesus. We may assume that Saint Joseph died quite early and that after his death Mary and Jesus went to live with close relatives. The children of the family or families with which they lived grew up with the child Jesus, and so were regarded as Jesus' brothers and sisters.

Moreover, Aramaic has no concise expression for "cousin." The early Church adopts the expression "brothers," and it passed into early Christian Greek. And of course by calling them his "brothers" the Church honored Jesus' relatives, who enjoyed a good reputation in the communities of the faithful. Finally, it also made it easier to distinguish these persons from others who bore the same name.[15]

The meaning of Mary's continued virginity after the birth of Jesus is not to be sought in any sort of prejudice against a married, sexual life. Mary and Joseph simply placed themselves entirely at the service of Jesus' salvific meaning and the veneration of the Holy Spirit dwelling in Mary, although they continued to live together. Here was a couple engulfed in a mystery even greater than that of the loving encounter of man and wife. Perplexed and ecstatic, they contemplated Jesus, born of the operation of the Holy Spirit. We need not imagine that, merely because they had freely renounced sexual love in its genital expression, Mary and Joseph did not have a relationship of deep tenderness, friendship, and mutual, loving understanding. These are the traits pertaining to family life as such, and they constitute the legacy of virtues lived by Mary and Joseph in their marriage. This was the healthy religious environment in which the child Jesus grew and matured, acquiring the profound humanness and psychological equilibrium that he would one day reveal in his public life.

Mary's perpetual virginity, far from diminishing her femininity, elevates and transfigures her in the fecundity of her motherhood.

ANTHROPOLOGICAL AND THEOLOGICAL MEANING OF VIRGINITY

Why did God wish to be born of a virgin? We have cited the *a posteriori* christological reasons. God wished to give humanity a new beginning. On the one hand, through Mary, Jesus is of earth; on the other, he irrupts from heaven, Seed and Origin of a humanity at last delivered from sin and death and introduced into full union with God.

Beyond this basic christological reason, however, there is another, anthropological one.[16] No revealed truth has been communicated to us solely for our knowledge or religious curiosity. All of the truths of faith, besides deciphering certain dimensions of the mystery of God, also help us decipher certain dimensions of our own mystery. Through her virginity, Mary demonstrated an existence totally centered on service to the Messiah and totally open to the will of God. She not only lived this attitude in her mind, she symbolized it in her body, as well, in the corporeal virginity that was not a value in itself but that made concrete her openness to her motherhood. Thanks to this attitude of hers, Mary was able to open a new chapter in history. Throughout history, millions of people would consecrate their lives, in purity and virginity, in a renunciation of marriage and family—the most excellent values of creation—to place themselves at the disposal of the ultimate will of God, which is to live with and for God. Christian virginity does not mean only keeping oneself for God. Before all else, Christian celibacy is a mission to others, in the name of God. Hence its maternal character. It engenders works of care and service, for it is shaped by love. In imitation of Mary, generous souls will always hear this call, however many others will fail to grasp the value of their consecration. As Karl Rahner says, if a star shines in the dark of night and I do not see it, it is not the fault of the star. There is something wrong with my eyesight. My lack of sensitivity betrays the darkness that wraps my heart.

Mary is also our model for the basic attitude that we all ought to have before God, the only attitude worthy of a creature: openness and total acceptance. We may conquer earth and sky, accumulate all possible knowledge of reality, penetrate the bottomless depths of our interiority, and enrich ourselves with the totality of humanity's hard-earned experience—and yet be nothing in the eyes of the Absolute but wretched beggars with empty hands and vacant hearts, bereft of the one thing that can ever really satisfy us: God. We have an ontological virginity that can only be espoused by God. Everyone, including married couples, should live this radical openness. After all, it allows God to penetrate the human heart. This virginal attitude—no longer having anything to do with physical virginity—entails the relativization of all of the things of this world. Weighty matters though they may be, they can never constitute ultimate, definitive realities. When all is said and done, human beings have been created for God. This alone is our ultimate destiny. Intermediate goals and purposes to be realized in history are not excluded. But the ultimate goal "puts them in their place," confers on them their proper state of being, and always orders them to something higher. Intermediate life purposes are a door leading to other doors, a light calling for more light, until the day we arrive at the definitive reality in which the human being's insatiable searching comes to rest. To be virginal is to maintain oneself in the purity of this call, in a life of openness to the truly ultimate and decisive thing in human life: God.

A final question remains. In view of all of our considerations on Mary's virginity, what is its theological meaning? What does it mean to say that God was born of a virgin, that God received humanity from a virgin? As we have said before, it is here that we touch on the root mystery of all of the mysterious elements of Mary's virginity: how it is that God finds a unique and proper realization in being born of a virgin.

The ultimate meaning of Mary's openness lies precisely in the fact that, in uttering her *fiat,* she allowed God in some wise to realize the divine self—to become something that God had never been. The Spirit spiritualizes Mary. Through the Virgin Mary, the divine nature makes concrete its own virginity—the divine virginity—in creation. Of a sudden, God makes manifest total availability and openness, allowing the divine self to be penetrated by that which is different from God, allowing the divine self to be permeated by creation. God is total communion. Therefore God is supreme openness. But openness is virginity. God is utterly radical virginity. Mary's virginity is the sign and sacrament of God's virginity. Thanks to Jesus' conception, divine virginity encounters human virginity, Mary becomes the instrument of the revelation and historicization of the virginity of God. Grace, salvation, and the love of God have a virginal characteristic. Just as God's virginity is the source of the divine parenthood, so Mary's virginity is ordered to motherhood.

By virtue of the coming of the Holy Spirit on the Virgin Mary, her own created virginity is not the virginity of the Spirit itself. And thus, this profound dimension of to-be-woman is incorporated, for all time to come and for all eternity, into the reality of God in the Person of the Holy Spirit.

9. Mary's Human and Divine Motherhood

More important than Mary's virginity is her motherhood.[1] Virginity does not exist for its own self-important sake. Virginity is destined for motherhood. Here is the root of all of Mary's greatness. Mary is not only consecrated to God. She is possessed by God. She becomes the spouse of God. She is the mother of Jesus, who is God. Not without reason does the New Testament prefer the title "mother of Jesus" to that of "virgin" (which appears only twice, Luke 1:27 and Matthew 1:23, while "mother" appears twenty-five times).

Mary's motherhood is more than a part of her personal biography. It is not of interest to her alone. It is at the service of God's plan for salvation history, and therefore concerns all men and women. Just as Abraham served all humanity, so does Mary. Mary is not only the mother of Jesus. She is the mother of Jesus' brothers and sisters, as well. And Jesus' brothers and sisters are the whole human race.

We have asserted that Mary is at the service of God's plan for all humanity. What is this plan? Let us have the plain answer, without going into all of the metaphysical niceties. The plain answer is: God wills to be a human being, and wills human beings to become God. First, God wishes to communicate the divine self totally to someone different from that self. God wills to be realized by becoming other, by becoming a human being. But this is not all. God also wishes human beings to be realized absolutely. And what is the ultimate realization, the supreme actualization possible or conceivable for the human being? To become God. To be fully realized in a self-bestowal upon the utterly Other.

Now, in what manner does Mary contribute to this divine plan? What accrues to God's plan for Being by virtue of Mary's service? Human beings are male and female, feminine and masculine. In Jesus Christ, the male has realized his ultimate destiny inasmuch as the male human nature of Jesus (which includes the feminine) has been divinized. *A pari*, in Mary we are postulating the concretion of the ultimate vocation of woman, through a hypostatic assumption by the Holy Spirit from the moment of the Annunciation. The Spirit comes in a divine mission *ad extra* to assume her and make her the Mother of the Word Incarnate. Only the divine can engender the divine.

As we are beginning to discern, Mary is the *medium*, the means, the middle term, for the realization of the divine and human projects. She gives birth to a human being who is God—her divine motherhood. She gives birth to God who is truly a human being—her human motherhood. As mother, Mary stands at the intersection of the plans of God and the human being. The two enterprises cross paths in her. She has a meaning that transcends her, then—a universal meaning, affecting both the history of God and the history of humanity. Mary's greatness consists in her service to others, and her glory consists in her concealment so that others may appear in all their splendor.

There is genuine human motherhood in Mary: the fruit of her womb is a true human being, Jesus. There is also a real divine motherhood in her: the offspring she engenders is really God. Mary's human motherhood establishes a network of relationships with history and with humanity that deserves to be rendered explicit. Her divine motherhood inaugurates another network of relationships, this time with God and God's grace, which likewise ought to be articulated adequately. Mary is actually the pivotal point of all salvation history, then, both from the side of God and the side of humanity. On her that twofold history is supported and revolves. We cannot bypass Mary's *essential* meaning. Those who do so empty Christianity of its historicity. It is impossible to accept the incarnate God without accepting Mary, who gave God human flesh.

MARY'S HUMAN MOTHERHOOD

Mary is genuine mother, with everything human motherhood implies. Now, motherhood is a kind of generation. To be a mother is to be a progenitor—a *genitrix*. But generation posits two terms: the progenitor and the offspring. In human beings, the function of progenitor is usually divided between the sexes. Father and mother each contribute something to the generation of the child. In the case of Jesus, however, only Mary contributed. The Holy Spirit intervened in place of the male. For this case, then, we are interested only in the mother's contribution to the act of generation. With the discovery by K. E. Baer in 1826 of the female ovum, we began to be convinced, after millennia of tradition to the contrary, that the female plays an active role in generation. She is not, as had been believed, merely the passive seedbed ready for the male's active sowing. Through her and in her the human ovum is produced. The ovum, or egg cell, is itself an active, highly determined element, which in turn determines the newly engendered being. Gestation, nutrition, the development of the embryo and fetus, and childbirth all belong to motherhood. There is a biological, physical dimension in all of this that is spontaneous, that escapes awareness, that has its own rhythms ebbing and flowing independently of any conscious intervention. But we are dealing with human, not brute, maternity, and so there will be typically human characteristics present as well. The human mother is not a procreating machine. In her these biophysical processes find a human environment, impregnated with spirituality, emotions, and conscious, free participation. Profound relationships, whose depth and intensity escape the masculine *logos,* begin to be woven between mother and child. Death itself cannot sever the ties that arise in this manner. Beyond its biophysical aspect, true motherhood includes a dimension of freedom and consent. The mother maintains with the fruit of her womb a relationship of love, acceptance, and tender care. In this rich, intense relationship the specifically human, undetermined aspect of motherhood emerges. Now the complex ties between mother and child, which reach far into the depths of the unconscious, become conscious, are spiritualized, ennobled, and sealed in permanence.

Of course, we find all of these dimensions in Mary, the mother of Jesus. First of all, her motherhood was not simply fated to be. Mary's *fiat* in response to the invitation of the Most High sprang from a radical freedom in which she surrendered to the loving will of God with a total consent of her will. An act of freedom, and not of coercion or violence, stands at the beginning of the new history of God-with-us. The basic characteristic of the new being is always freedom, love, and surrender to the other. When this fails to appear in us, we have returned to the old being: evidently, God has not yet been born in the human heart. In Mary, motherhood arose from consent. God wanted it this way. God did not want this action to be an invasion on the part of God's omnipotence, in contempt for human liberty. God preferred that this deed spring precisely from the exercise of this freedom. Indeed, "God has need of woman in the very act in which he does without man."[2]

Mary consented because she believed (Luke 1:44). Believing, she conceived. She began to be mother, engendering Jesus. The chain of processes that constitute motherhood—ovulation, fertility, gestation, childbirth—were under way. From Mary, Jesus received his genetic code—his biological heritage. He received his personality from her, as well—his psychological personhood. In Mary's case, we had a virginal conception by the operation of the Holy Spirit, so that the determination that comes from the side of the male was omitted. Accordingly, the biological relationship between Mary and Jesus was far more profound, genetically, physiognomically, and psychologically, than that obtaining between other mothers and their offspring.

Although he was a male, Jesus received a fundamental determinant from his mother Mary biologically and psychologically. The feminine component in Jesus' concrete existence was much more salient than in that of most males conceived in the normal way. And inasmuch as Jesus was not only a human being but God as well, we suddenly surmise a reality that, doubtless, we should never have suspected: the divinization of the feminine. The feminine, too, was assumed by God in Jesus—converted into a vehicle of humanity's salvation and God's self-revelation. When the feminine passed from Mary to Jesus, it gained an eternal dimension.

Motherhood must have meant a very great deal to Mary. In her, femininity fairly exploded. Motherhood means more to a woman than fatherhood does to a man. It impregnates the most secret recesses of her being. As each child is born the mother is transformed and born again herself. And at the same time,

Mary, though she became a mother, remained a virgin. She rose above the scorn that virginity aroused in her culture, while simultaneously preserving all of the freshness, all of the feelings of integrity and fullness, that virginity encloses.

Motherhood is more than just a phase in a woman's life. Being a mother lasts a lifetime, just as does being someone's child. Caring for her child, bringing him or her up, and sharing in his or her lot are dimensions of all truly human motherhood. As Jesus grew and matured before the eyes of Joseph and, especially, Mary, as he learned from them to lisp his first words, what gladness! The day must have come when this child who was God could say, "Mama." And the mother could call him "my little boy." Here was an exchange of love and tenderness such as had never been before in the history of the world. Jesus learned to pray, to read the Scriptures, from Mary and Joseph. Later, the disciples would testify to the fact that he passed through this world doing good. Behind Jesus' profound human goodness, behind his extraordinary religious sensitivity, behind his existential wisdom, was the virtuous life of Mary, who knew how to communicate to her child her own reflection. Her intimacy with Jesus, her familiar converse with him as they prayed together, exchanged opinions and ideas, or shared their concerns about work and livelihood, are mysteries that can be preserved and grasped only by a mother's heart. All of this is the human richness of Mary as the mother of Jesus.

Every human being who is ever born is linked to all humanity, because all are bearers of the same human nature. Jesus is the brother of all men and women. He lived on our planet, breathed the same air as we, drank our water, contemplated the sun we see, grew up under the same stars. He received our earthly existence in all its bodily and spiritual dimensions. He forms with us, before God, the one, single humanity. And it was Mary who gave him all of this. She engendered Jesus for us, for all of us, and forever. If he is to be considered the human being par excellence—*Ecce Homo!*—then what dignity envelops this woman, virgin and mother! And if we further profess this human being to be God, then surely we must also repeat, with the inspired author, "Blest are you among women" (Luke 1:42), or with the heavenly messenger, "Rejoice, O highly favored daughter!"

(Luke 1:28)—"Hail, Mary, full of grace," as we say in her special prayer. For she was the mother of Jesus our God. Mary was the means by whom God was incarnate, by whom God took flesh and became one of us, a human being. The eternal Son did not come down from heaven in a ready-made, living body snatched from nothingness by God. God willed to take a flesh received from us human beings, that God might truly be our brother in the flesh. Mary participated in this divine operation. Because of her, God is linked to all of humanity by an umbilical cord.

MARY'S DIVINE MOTHERHOOD

Precisely as divine, Mary's motherhood is stretched between two poles. The first is the coming of the Holy Spirit upon her at the moment of the Annunciation. The Spirit dwelt within her, assumed her, and lifted her to the level of divinity. Therefore, whatever she would bear would be holy, and the Son of God, as we read in Luke (1:35). The other pole is the fact that Jesus is true God. Mary's divine motherhood is founded on her human motherhood. She engendered a human being who is also God. Accordingly, Christian faith has always proclaimed Mary to be the Mother of God. The person whose flesh was de facto conceived *in* the womb of the Virgin Mary, as well as *from* her womb, is directly and properly, really and truly, and not figuratively or metaphorically, the Second Person of the Blessed Trinity. Jesus is and has always been true human being and true God. At no moment was Jesus ever merely a human being. Mary did not engender a human being who thereupon was united with the Second Person of the Trinity. She engendered someone who, from the first moment of his conception, was God in person. Mary is the Mother of God incarnate.

RESPONSE TO SOME OBJECTIONS

Our last assertion is the unshakable conviction of the Catholic Christian faith. The definition of the Ecumenical Council of Ephesus (A.D. 431) was solemn and binding. But in order to come to a correct understanding of Mary's divine motherhood, we must first respond to certain basic objections.

For example, it might be objected that to be mother means to give origin to someone by means of generation; but God has no origin; therefore Mary cannot have given origin to God by means of generation. We answer that Mary is not the Mother of God "reduplicatively"—the Mother of God *as God;* she is the Mother of God insofar as God is *incarnate.* God was conceived and engendered by her insofar as God took flesh. The person Mary conceived and engendered is truly God. As John Damascene taught, in the classic formulation: "The Blessed Virgin did not engender a bare human being, but true God; and God not bare, but incarnate."[3] A correct concept of the hypostatic union enables us to call Mary the true Mother of (the human being Jesus, who from the very beginning of his existence was also) God.

Another possible objection: Mary did not engender the whole Christ, since she did not engender the Second Person of the Most Holy Trinity, who is eternal and who preexists all creation, cosmic and human alike. She engendered only a part of Christ—his human nature, and surely not his divine nature. We answer: Mary was a mother in the genuine and proper sense in which any mother is the mother of her offspring. She gives them not only their bodies, with God giving them their soul and their personhood; she is the mother of the whole concrete person who subsists and is historically realized in each of these respective bodies. The ultimate *supposit* of any of the attributes or activities of a human being is not that being's human nature, but precisely his or her personhood. Let us explain. Ultimately, it is not my eye that sees, but I, the person, who see. When I shake the hand of someone I greet, I am not greeting the hand I am shaking, I am greeting the person whose hand I am shaking. If someone has received a wound in the face and I treat the wound, I am not ultimately treating the person's face, I am treating precisely the person. It is the same with Mary's divine motherhood. Mary was not the mother only of Jesus' body, or only of his human nature. She was the mother of *someone,* the mother of the person Jesus, who was an incarnate, humanized divine Person, who subsisted and existed in the historical human nature of the Jesus of Nazareth who was engendered *in* and *from* her virginal womb.

Mary's divine motherhood was the consequence of her human, physical motherhood by which the eternal Son became a human being, entered the stream of life, and put down his roots in the history of humanity. This motherhood assumed its true dimension when it became the object of a consent. Mary conceived in belief, as tradition tirelessly reminds us. She allowed the Spirit to cause to spring forth in her womb a new life, the life of Jesus. While she did not understand all of its implications, certainly the Virgin Mary surmised in this event the realization of a messianic deed that would affect the whole of humanity. She perceived that she was entering into a direct relationship with God and with the destiny of the whole human race.

VARIOUS RELATIONSHIPS IMPLIED BY MARY'S MOTHERHOOD

Through her motherhood, Mary establishes a series of relationships that bear highlighting.[4] The first is a special relationship with the Blessed Trinity.

A Special Relationship with the Most Holy Trinity

Two divine missions are accomplished in the mystery of the Annunciation: that of the Holy Spirit in descending on Mary, and that of the Word, who, with Mary's consent, began to take form as a human being in her womb. In all of this, certain relationships are established whose term is the Holy Trinity. Not even the Father is excluded, as it is the Father who sends the Son and the Spirit, maintaining his mysterious presence in them. Mary's relationship with the Son and the Spirit is a *real* relation, and not merely a metaphorical one, or one in our own minds alone, for her person is objectively affected by the sending, the mission, of these two Persons. The relationship is also *permanent*, and not merely passing or transitory. Mary's relation to the eternal Son is permanent because the mother of an offspring is always the mother of that offspring no matter how much time may pass. Mary's relation to the Holy Spirit, her ontological bond with the Third Person of the Trinity, is likewise permanent, a definitive, once-and-for-all datum, positing her in a dimension that no one before her has ever occupied. Here theology borrows an expression from sacramentology to express a similar reality. Mary acquires an *indelible character* both in the incarnation of the eternal Son within her, and in the coming of the Holy Spirit upon her. The sacraments of baptism, confirmation, and order confer an indelible character upon the person who receives them, placing that person in a permanent, real, and special relation to the Church. Analogously, Mary acquires in the Incarnation an indelible character in the form of a permanent, real, and special relationship with the Son and the Holy Spirit, as well as, through them, with the Trinity as such. She alone bears the indelible character, the ontological reality, of being the Mother of God and living Temple of the Holy Spirit.

A Special Relationship with the Father

From all eternity, from the unfathomable reaches of his own substance, the Father engenders the Person of the Son, and together with the Son spirates the Holy Spirit. This intra-Trinitarian process is eternal and continuous. Now, the Son, whose generation is eternal, as we have said, knows another, temporal generation as well—that in Mary's womb. Mary is the link of the insertion of the eternal Son into human flesh and blood. The Holy Spirit, to begin once more with the intra-Trinitarian element, is the gift of the Father and the Son, and the link in the eternal bond between them. No intra-Trinitarian reality proceeds from the Holy Spirit. It is precisely the Spirit who closes the dynamic Trinitarian circle. But by virtue of the Spirit's full participation in the same divine nature that is possessed by the Father and the Son, the Spirit shares in the generative power of God *ad extra*—the divine generative power manifested not within the Trinity, but in creation. The culminating, properly notional and not merely attributed, deed of the Spirit, then, is to assume Mary, appropriate her female generative potential, and cause her to engender the eternal Son as her son Jesus. The entire generative force communicated to the Son by an intra-Trinitarian activity and to the Spirit for extra-Trinitarian purposes, proceeds from the Father. Mary participates in this force as well, and thus is inserted into the dynamics originating in the Father. She bears within herself the Spirit and the Son, and with them the unfathomable, infinitely profound Mystery of the Father himself.

A Special Relationship with the Son

Just as we have a double generation—one eternal, on the part of the Father, the other temporal, on the part of the Blessed

Virgin Mary—so, too, we have a double "filiation," or state of being-generated, in the Word. But the Person to whom this relationship attaches is the same in either case. At one pole, he proceeds from the Father; at the other, he proceeds from Mary. The presence and actuality of the latter, temporal, filiation is realized in a human nature taken from Mary's human nature. In Jesus, we find a great deal of what is in Mary. She is reproduced in Jesus. And yet, he who is so close to her, because he is the child of her womb, is ever so distant, as well, for he also abides in the bosom of the Father. On the one hand, Mary engenders the eternal Son in time. On the other, she is engendered in that Son in eternity. She has been created in the Son, with the Son, and for the Son. She is eternalized as the daughter of God in the eternal Son of God. Here we have relationships whose human and divine fabric escape the cold discourse of theology.

A Special Relationship with the Holy Spirit

With respect to salvation history, the Spirit is the generative force of the human reality of the eternal Son in the womb of the Virgin Mary (Luke 1:35). The Lukan text speaks to us with transparent clarity: the Spirit descends upon Mary and overshadows her. This is how biblical language expresses the special, proper mission to Mary undertaken by the Third Person of the Trinity. But this "coming upon" Mary of the Spirit means the assumption of Mary's human reality, as well, in an assumption as real and genuine as the eternal Son's assumption of the human reality of Jesus. When Luke says "overshadow," he is recalling for us the Shekinah, the real and mysterious presence of God in his temple. Now Mary is the temple, the sanctuary, the tabernacle, the abode—biblical expressions—of the Spirit. That is, she is the vessel of the indwelling of the Third Person, who has assumed her life. The Spirit in Mary raises her generative force to a divine level. The one to whom she gives birth, therefore, is holy, and the son of God. God the Mother engenders the humanity of the eternal Son.

The relationships of intimacy struck between Mary and the Spirit who surprises her and comes to dwell in her cannot be described by theology. We see the reality, but a deep and loving respect hushes our voices in the presence of Mystery.

What we can say is that, for the Virgin of Nazareth, all of these relationships with Mystery, however unaware of them she may have been in terms of our sophisticated concepts, opened the spillway of a serene, spontaneous, and enduring contemplation of a Mystery unveiled for her precisely without any sophisticated efforts on the part of the abstractive mind.

A Special Relationship with the Hypostatic Union

Through her motherhood, Mary genuinely bestows something on the eternal Son—the human nature engendered by her. But in the instant of its creation, this human nature is assumed by God. Of course, in taking on human nature, God also assumes the relationship of generation-filiation that characterizes that nature. Therefore, Mary, as mother of Jesus and Mother of God, is indissolubly associated with the hypostatic union. The real, permanent relation of generation-filiation is assumed by the eternal Word as its term. Engendered in time by Mary, then, the Second Person of the Trinity now enters into a bond with her that will be everlasting, to perdure for all time and all eternity. Thus, something of Mary, without its ceasing to be hers, is assumed by the Word precisely in the Word's divinity: her relation of generation-filiation as subject of that relation. Consequently, the feminine is eternalized, and receives, to the extent possible for a creature, a divine dimension. The nature engendered by the mother is not simply a human nature belonging to God. The hypostatic union of the eternal Son with human nature does not leave Mary untouched. Indirectly but truly, Mary enters the hypostatic union, by virtue of the fact that a relation that begins with her—her motherhood of the Word incarnate—enters the mystery of the Incarnation by co-assumption.

A Special Relationship with the New Humanity

By now it should be clear that neither Jesus nor Mary can be understood individualistically. Each of them is a new beginning for humanity. Mary enters into an intimate relationship with a redeemed humanity born of faith in this Jesus who is the new Adam and her Son. All who cling to Jesus Christ will form one body, to become sons and daughters in the Son. But as sons and daughters in the Son, they will share in the permanent relationship maintained by Jesus with his mother. Now, Mary engenders not only Jesus, but the Savior of the world. She becomes the mother of the one who will deliver his people from their sin (Luke 1:31, Matt. 1:21). Thus, Mary's bonds with the history that her Son will make down through the centuries are indissoluble. All people are included in this bond, co-engendered in the very movement initiated by Mary's *fiat*. Well does faith celebrate Mary as the Mother of all the faithful. Mary is the universal Mother of the redeemed. The Spirit who engendered in Mary the eternal Son continues to engender her other daughters and sons, Jesus' brothers and sisters, all down through history. Tradition understands Psalm 87 in an ecclesiological and mariological sense when this psalm sings of messianic times when all will belong to the people of God. The Jerusalem mentioned in this psalm is the Church, and symbolically the Virgin Mary.

> I tell of Egypt and Babylon
>   among those that know the Lord.
> Of Philistia, Tyre, Ethiopia:
>   "This man was born there."
> And of Zion they shall say:
>   "One and all were born in her;
> And he who has established her
>   is the Most High Lord."
> They shall note, when the peoples are enrolled:
>   "This man was born there."
> And all shall sing, in their festive dance:
>   "My home is within you."
>   (Ps. 87:4–7)

It would be difficult to express Mary's universal motherhood more profoundly and poetically than is done in the language of this psalm.

A Special Relationship with the Church

The Church is that portion of humanity that has explicitly accepted the gift of salvation in Jesus Christ: the *communitas fidelium*. Mary stands in a unique relationship with this humanity that has directed its life toward the following and discipleship of her Son in the power of the Spirit. Just as she engenders Christ, she continues to engender Christians. And they are engendered in the same power of the Spirit dwelling within her. That is why Mary is proclaimed Mother of the Church. But this is not all. The entire Church, the community of the faithful and the people of God *in via*, is invited to live divine grace more purely, and with a greater determination, and thus to actualize the new being inaugurated in the persons of Mary and Jesus. This is the basic calling of the Church. But it is lived as a tendency, a beginning. It is made concrete within a whole series of historical contradictions. It is completely fulfilled by Mary alone. In her God has shown historically what is desired of all, of the whole Church, and what will be lived in glory by the redeemed. Mary is not a static archetype, then. She is dynamic, she awakens new life, she helps build the new humanity. Ever the mother, she continues to engender new children for the human-and-divine history that began on earth and will culminate in heaven. She repeats her *fiat*. "Do whatever he tells you," she says (John 2:5).

The Spirit that is spiritualized in Mary continues spiritualizing the society of the redeemed. Once assumed in Mary, the Spirit has never left the world. The Spirit continues to assume all who are open to redeeming grace, and creates a mystical person in the corporate body of all the redeemed. The Spirit prolongs the generative power of God down through the centuries. Engendering Christ through and with Mary, the Spirit continues to engender Christians, as well, through the Church—the sisters and brothers of Jesus Christ.

THE HUMAN AND DIVINE HOLINESS OF MARY

The whole complex of relations involved in Mary's human and divine motherhood, relations that reach the Holy Trinity of God, relations of spiritualization, incarnation, humanity, and Church, make Mary a saint without equal, in the most rigorous theological meaning of the word. The word *saint*, or *holy*, did not originally denote a moral quality, or the result of a life of encounter with God. Originally, *holy* meant "sacred." It denoted all that belongs to God—anything to be found in the sphere of the divine. In this original, ontological sense, Mary is surely "all-holy," as the Eastern liturgies address her. She was chosen by God, without the possibility of her having merited it, for the realization of God's marvelous deeds, in and through her (Luke 1:49). The most marvelous of these deeds is that she is the locus of the realization of the two divine missions, that of the Spirit and that of the Son. She is the completely open receptacle of the Spirit and the Son, who can allow them to fulfill the eternal decree of the humanization of God and divinization of the human creature. The Spirit dwells and acts within her in such a manner as to cause a human and divine life to be generated in her without male participation.

In view of this deed to come, and in order to prepare her for it, God delivers Mary from all sin. This pure, holy new being is not the fruit of human history. She is the gift of God, who wished to pour forth upon the world a reflection of divine holiness. This root, radical holiness of Mary is in no way the fruit of her will, her virtues, her efforts. It is due to the exclusive initiative of God. Mary is holy because she would hold the Holy in her womb. This first, primordial sanctity of Mary is the product not of human willing, but of the gracious dispensation of God.

But Mary is also holy on a personal level, and this holiness is the result of her life of fidelity to God. Mary's personal sanctity is also a gift of God, but it is like a gift from a mighty victor to one of his warriors. Mary succeeds in accepting God's plan for her with all her heart and soul. She believes (Luke 1:44). She lives in faith, obedience, and humility (Luke 1:38, 1:45). She surrenders without reserve, demonstrating that she belongs totally to God (Luke 1:38). Acknowledging Mary's holiness, the angel calls her the "graced one," in the Greek of Luke (Luke 1:28). God bestows this sanctity upon Mary that she might be humanly prepared for the function she is to fulfill in salvation history. Before conceiving in her virginal womb, Mary has already conceived in her virgin heart. God has already been born in her soul. That is why she can conceive him in her body.

From Mary's divine and human holiness flows that eminent dignity of hers that places her above all other creatures, a dignity comparable only to that of Christ. Mary lives this dignity and sanctity in the obscurity of an ordinary life, in a tiny town of

Galilee and later in a small city on the shore of Lake Gennesaret, Capernaum.[5] The most precious treasures are hidden away in the dark depths of the earth or sea. God works in the same way. God hides greatness in the small, transparency in the opaque, and sublimity in the simple. Mary is the archetype of this truth.

10. Mary's Resurrection and Assumption

What was the last end of this so singular creature, the one called Mary? Faith has taken a special interest in this question, especially from the fifth and sixth centuries onward. Nor is it a frivolous, merely curious interest. It is an expression of love. What can have been the final outcome of her life who is venerated as the finest fruit of creation, the work of the Spirit, and the Mother of God? With consistent, intuitive logic, Christian believers have come to the following conclusion.

In Mary's case, "end" must mean something more than *terminus ad quem*. It must designate a pinnacle, a culmination. Mary's end must have been the perfection she reached in her final objective. It cannot have been circumscribed by the limits of death, then. Surely she burst this barrier. Surely she achieved the fullness of resurrected life. And so faith, after long centuries of reflection, has proclaimed the resurrection of the Blessed Virgin Mary from the dead and her bodily assumption into heaven.[1] On November 1, 1950, Pope Pius XII at last declared and defined *ex cathedra* as a dogma of faith (*de fide*) that "the immaculate Mother of God, the ever-virgin Mary, having completed the course of this earthly life, was assumed to the glory of heaven body and soul."[2]

If life is called to be life, and not death, then the mother of the Author of life, the temple into which the Principle of all generation entered, must share in the mystery of life more than any other being in the universe.

DEATH AS CULMINATION AND INTEGRATION

It is a matter of dispute whether or not Mary died. This is why the text of the infallible dogmatic definition cautiously states, " . . . having completed the course of this earthly life. . . . " For our part, we hold that Mary died. After all, only from death can there be true resurrection. Only the dead can be raised. Surely Mary died—after all, her life was fully human, and death is the natural outcome of life. Even had we not sinned, we should nevertheless die. Sin introduced not death, but the anguish, the fear of death. In the concrete, women and men live in a condition of sin. Hence, they have a fear of death, and are unable to integrate death into the structure of mortal life. That fear, and that inability to integrate death, is the consequence of sin. By virtue of this historical situation, Scripture can say that death, meaning death as concretely experienced by human beings, entered the world by sin. Mary, free and exempt from all sin, was able to integrate death into the God-created life to which it belongs. She did not regard death as meaningless fate, or simply as the loss of her life. She regarded it as an opportunity—a stepping-stone to a fuller life in God. Death furnishes us with the opportunity to perform a supreme act of love, and to surrender to a Greater that transcends us. And yet, this surrender fulfills us to the highest degree. In this sense, death is a good, and was perfectly assimilated by Mary. Without death, the grandeur she won us would be shrunken. Mary herself would be less, and a jewel would be missing from her crown of glory.

Moreover, Mary was completely associated with the lot of her Son. It was through his life and his death that Jesus liberated us. Through her own life and death, Mary participated in this universal messianic deed. For her, death was neither punishment nor anguish. It was the manner in which she offered her gift of self, offered her life in sacrifice.

One who has lived life like Mary's can scarcely be held by death. This mortal coil of ours hides a seed that death cannot crush. It can only liberate the hidden power of that seed. Death is its bountiful fertilizer, and in death the whole vitality of life bursts forth as if spring has come. This is resurrection. Resurrection is not something that occurs after death. It occurs within death itself. Hence, to say that Mary died is not to say that her earthly reality was given over to corruption. The life that is latent in mortal life erupts in death. Therefore, the Virgin Mother was raised at the moment of her death.

We must never misinterpret resurrection as the reanimation of a cadaver. If it were, it would be but the extension of the structure of mortality, of enclosure by space and time, of the need for sustenance and preservation. Resurrection is the materialization of another *form* of life, a life free of earthly bonds, a life that shares in the very life of God. And so resurrection must be defined in terms of glorification, the absolute realization of life, and the eschatologization of the possibilities inherent in earthly life. In resurrection we have the enthronement of life in its final, definitive form in the Reign of God. It is human life. Mary preserved her personal and corporeal identity. But now she lives the final, ultimate form of life, life as God has predestined it from all eternity.

Mary was assumed into heaven *body and soul*. This is not the dogmatizing of the anthropological dualism we have inherited from Greco-Roman culture, the separation of body and soul with which the Western world interprets the human phenomenon. This framework, which the occidental mentality will understand, is simply employed in the dogmatic definition to emphasize the comprehensive, altogether complete character of Mary's glorification in her assumption. It is not only Mary's soul—not only her interiority, her human transcendence—that shares the fullness of life in the Reign of God, but her corporality, as well—our earthly rootedness, our material, carnal bulk, our relationship with the cosmos and history. The whole woman is cloaked in this absolute realization and fulfillment.

We Christians emphasize Mary's personal glorification. This is our way of professing our faith in the absolute destiny to which our bodies are called. Our bodies are both strong and fragile, charged with vitality and contaminated with the virus of death. Some of us exalt them to the point of the worship of a false god. Others of us hate them to the point of wishing to destroy them, which is to destroy ourselves. Our bodies are where we feel the surging reality of love and the depths of suffering and pain. In resurrection and assumption, our bodies will be rescued from their ambivalence. They will be the object of blasphemy no longer, but of benediction. No longer will they be the wall that divides us from God, from others, and from the world. They will become the crystal-pure, wide-open door to communion.

They will be transfigured into the sacrament of the intimate and mighty encounter with the even more powerful reality of God. In her body and in her soul—that is, in the totality of her existence—Mary already lives and enjoys this ineffable human and divine realization.

While she lived in this world, Mary's body was the vehicle only of grace, love, understanding, and goodness. It was never the instrument of sin, of the human self-assertion that infringes on the autonomy of others and causes a rent with those others. This is why her body, unlike ours, was reassumed and glorified in its very materiality. Our bodies are also the medium of a lack of love, the medium of perdition. This is why their materiality abides in death: they have been the agent of death. In the resurrection, while preserving our bodily identity (our personal "I," with its permanent reference to the materiality of the world), we shall gain a new material expression as well. Mary had no need of a new material expression. In Mary, everything was always pure and holy. After all, she was the abode of the Spirit of God. Her resurrection merely assumed these realities, consummating them in their maximum fullness.

WHAT DOES MARY'S ASSUMPTION MEAN FOR HERSELF?

How can one describe Mary's risen body, enthroned in celestial glory? What does it mean for her to be filled with the Spirit and reigning beside her Son in glory? What transcendent meaning do we perceive in a feminine already introduced, in Mary, within the Divine Trinity?

Here we are daring to meddle in questions that vanish like smoke in the light of religious imagination. Paul, who acknowledges that he has caught a glimpse of the new heavens and the new earth, confesses: "Eye has not seen, ear has not heard, nor has it so much as dawned on man what God has prepared for those who love him" (1 Cor. 2:9). It were better, then, that reason fall silent, and allow fantasy to speak. But let us not forget the facts of the feminine. All that we ever experience on earth as good, loving, great, profound, caring, intimate, and true, will be fully realized in heaven. There the heart will come to rest in a secure, unthreatened Love, and life will drink at the eternal well-spring of Life. Mary enjoys this radical humanization of her femininity in a singular, utterly personal manner—she who was, and continues to be, the Mother of God and the living Temple of the Holy Spirit.

For Mary, the Assumption means her definitive encounter with her Son, who preceded her in glory. Mother and Son abide in a love and a union that is utterly beyond our imagining. No longer need she believe in his divinity despite appearances. Now she sees reality as it is—the truth of his divine filiation and her divine motherhood.

And so Mary finds herself in the company of the eternal, only-begotten Son of the Father. The relations that we have seen to be implied by her divine and human motherhood become transparent to her. She finds herself immersed in the Holy Trinity of God, through the Holy Spirit who fecundated and assumed her and the Son whom she engendered. She discovers, amidst ineffable light, the meaning of the eternal generation of that Son she engendered in time thereupon to be linked with him indissolubly throughout the centuries. Finally and utterly, she grasps what it means to be daughter in her Son, from whom all divine and human filiation proceeds. Now she experiences all that has ever escaped her consciousness in all of these respects, including her bonds with all humanity and her union with the Church.

Mary rejoices in the revelation of the final meaning of the femininity she had always actualized in herself but now discovers in its divine source. Mary's assumption signals the moment in which she as woman begins to live the plenitude of that ineffable hypostatic union with God the Holy Spirit that defines her ultimate situation. Mary on an eschatological level is supremely divinized—preserving her created nature and thus remaining utterly distinct from God in that nature, but indissolubly one with the Spirit. We have already examined all that this culminating event means: the definitive return of the feminine to God, and God's acquisition of that feminine for divine self-realization.

WHAT DOES MARY'S ASSUMPTION MEAN FOR US?

Mary's resurrection and assumption have always been the inspiration of a mystique of the person of the Virgin Mary in his-

tory and in the Church. Mariology is in constant danger of de-
generating into the empty memory of a long-ago past, made real
for faith alone by a relentless scholarly research into the sources
of that faith in Scripture and tradition. Our Lady can become
an idea, an abstract principle, a means for the construction of
our system of salvation history. Mary's resurrection and assumption corrects this potential deviation. Mary is still in the world,
still at the heart of the Church, with the living presence of someone alive. She may be invisible to the eyes of the body, but she
is not absent. She is present, in a real, however ineffable, way,
still active among us despite her phenomenological impercepti-
bility. The faithful achieve their relationship with her not only
through the memory of her person and her deeds, but by immediate contact with her living, risen person. Only the pure of
heart can comprehend how intimate, tender, maternal, and embracing our relationship with our Most Holy Mother, the Virgin
Mary, can be.

Mary eminently makes concrete our own destiny in glory, especially in the feminine dimension of our existence. As Vatican
II proclaimed " . . . The Mother of Jesus continues in this present world as the image and first flowering of the Church as she
is to be perfected in the world to come."[3] This means that Mary
now lives, body and soul, what we too shall live when we achieve
heaven. While we are still pilgrims on the earth, she functions
as the image of our objective. Moreover, she is the most precious
fruit (the firstfruits) of the human harvest, of which the whole
is called to transfiguration and resurrection in heaven. All who
are in the Lord (2 Cor. 5:6) have already been raised with him
(Col. 2:12, 3:1). Our union with the risen body of the Lord is
so radical and genuine that death can no longer sunder it. This
is why we believe that we shall rise from death. We shall arrive,
fully realized, body and soul, in heaven. Our Lady actualizes this
truth to a degree that is without equal, unique, and hers alone,
a degree like that of Christ's realization of the same truth. We,
in dependence on the risen Christ and Mary assumed, share in
their resurrection. As one theologian observed:

If Mary is the personal model of the glorious Church, then ideally the
one same state of the Church glorified will be verified in Mary and in
the elect. Mary's assumption looked at in this way represents in a most

clear fashion the actual state of the heavenly Church, whose "imper-sonation" she is. She is not the personification of a future state of this heavenly Church, but the personal expression of the present state of the collectivity, which is the heavenly Church.[4]

What has occurred with Mary in such a sublime and matchless way, comparable only to Christ's resurrection and ascension, will occur with everyone who dies in the Lord: resurrection and ex-altation to heaven. From there, from glory, she comes to us and abides with us, shining like a light to reveal the true path to be trod by men and women in their feminine dimension. Whilst we walk amid the trials and tribulations of the present, we lift our eyes to heaven and pray, "Hail, Mary, our life, our sweetness, and our hope! *Salve!*"

WHAT DOES MARY'S ASSUMPTION MEAN FOR GOD?

The assumption of the Blessed Virgin Mary into heaven not only affects herself and us, but God as well.[5] God is the principal pole of the relation that constitutes the Marian events and mys-teries. We have already seen the properly *theo*logical implications of Mariology, and we need only recall them here. Mary's as-sumption permits God a more profound relation with her. Mary in glory is the subject capable of receiving God's personal, ab-solute communication. Now, because this relation is eschatolog-ical, and hence in its absolute perfection, it must be a relation by which God fully realizes a oneness with Mary through the Holy Spirit, who made her a living temple at the time of the Annunciation. But let us note: even in the eschatological Reign of God, this hypostatic union of the Holy Spirit with Mary finds the fullness of its expression without confusion, though without division, and without the destruction of Mary's identity. God, as eternal life in the permanent process of self-realization, encoun-ters a new expression of divine reality in the feminine as made humanly concrete in its highest degree in and by Mary. Now self-realized in another, in Mary, God the Holy realizes that other, as well, to the highest degree of her capacity—that other whom God conceived in the divine eternal mind and loved in the divine eternal will in order to permit the arrival of the total Parousia in her.

From this moment forward, creature and Creator, the human feminine (accompanied by the masculine) and the Holy Spirit, configure an eschatological history, the history of the supreme synthesis, the history of the absolute return to unity, without confusion of substances, won back and finally lived in the Reign of God forever and ever. Now the feminine acquires its final dimension—its dimension of eternity.

A new history calls for a new language. This language does not as yet exist. Let our game of words, that old quackery of ours, fall silent. Its terms and concepts, drawn from the old world that passes away, can never be adequate to the new reality. Only pure thought, engendered by pure faith, will ever surmise the ineffable purity of the unfathomable mystery of the male and female human being. In heaven, once more, God has taken flesh, in Mary, to dwell again in the midst of redeemed humanity. And we, in faith, have seen her glory, the glory of the tabernacle ensouled by the Holy Spirit, Mary full of grace and glorified in heaven.

11. Mary's Universal Mediation: In Solidarity with the Human Race

We might have concluded our reflection on the maternal, feminine face of God with our consideration of the resurrection and assumption into heaven of the Blessed Virgin Mary. What more could be detected in the mystery of the Mother of God and our Mother? In her and in Christ her Son, we decipher the ultimate destiny to which we are called: to allow God to be realized, to become more, by becoming incarnate in the human masculine and feminine. However, these very considerations give us something else to think about. What is the theological meaning of Mary's solidarity with the destiny of all humanity? What is the meaning of her universal mediation of grace in light of this common destiny?[1]

Christian piety intuitively venerates Mary as the Mediatrix of All Graces, and our universal Advocate. Recent decades have seen an attempt by theology to clarify the ambiguities inherent in these expressions. A reflection on the faith has made a special effort to demonstrate the relationship between the unique mediation of Jesus Christ (1 Tim. 2:5) and the mediation of Mary and of other human beings. The difficulties here are not so much theological ones, or interfaith problems. They are primarily philosophical questions. They bear on a correct understanding of the mode of existence proper to human beings, and the kind of relationships human beings might establish, whether among themselves or between human beings and God. Once this philosophical question is clarified, many other difficulties vanish, especially those stemming from Lutheran theology. Then the legitimacy and value of theological expressions of Mary's solidarity with the human race or her universal mediation are more easily accepted. Her mediation is not exclusive; it is inclusive, as it simply reinforces and maximizes a structure that involves all women and men.

ANTHROPOLOGICAL AND ONTOLOGICAL FOUNDATION OF MARY'S MEDIATION

No human being is a windowless monad. Every man or woman sinks roots in our material, bodily infrastructure. We all extend into the social fabric. We all take on the whole historical load of the past. Human beings are not natural beings, in the sense of being purely biological. We are cultural beings, as well. That is, it is true that in some sense we come "prefabricated," like other animals, but in another sense we come labeled "Some Assembly Required." Human beings are never isolated individuals. We are persons. A person is the human being specifically in his or her capacity for unlimited communion, and for the production of symbols by which meaning is conferred on the world and on human action upon that world. On the specifically human level, to-be-human is always to be social. A human being is always *Homo socius*. In other words, "I" cannot be divorced from "we" in the concrete. This can be done in the abstract, and we do it, in order to be able to communicate verbally, in order to have a systematic language. But concretely, my "I" is always related to our "we," because my "I" is always incarnate in a body, in the world, in a social strata. It shares the lot of the surrounding reality. The irreducibility of the person as the mystery of this or that particular reflexive consciousness cannot be represented as an intangible substance existing apart from other substances. A person is always linked to the rest of reality. By irreducibility we do not mean independence of relationships. We mean a capacity for communion so inexhaustible that no person will ever be reducible to this or that *particular* kind of interconnection. Every person will always be able to transcend all of his or her actual links with the rest of reality. After all, each person is open to the creation of new and different bonds. The person is not bound by these or those particular situations and structures, then. But the person is not free to do without any relation whatsoever. Inherent in the human being is the capacity and need for communion.

Thus, the structure of the person explains the profound solidarity obtaining among all human beings. There are no solitary islands. They are all connected by water. In like manner, we all share in the lot of all human beings. Not only do we breathe the same air as they, not only do we live on the same earth and under the same sky; much more basically, we share the same human nature. Of course, human nature must be understood not as an invariable substrate, but as a series of anthropological constants—openness to the world, the capacity to transcend a given situation, to produce symbolic actions, and so on. Now, we are all affected by the cultural expressions of this human nature. At the same time, each of us influences these expressions. The basic solidarity obtaining among human beings is not a matter of choice. It does not come into being because we wish it so. It exists independently of our decisions. It is an anthropological fact. Freedom may determine the type, mode, and quality of our relationships, but not the *fact* of these relationships.

This will be the setting for the reflections that we are about to make on the subject of Mary's universal mediation. By mediation, we mean the links that unite persons, the bonds that bring them together. For human beings, mediation is an absolute and fundamental datum of existence. The relation of mediation is not basically one that needs to be created. It is a given of human reality, something that preexists derivative realities, and it needs only to be acknowledged as such. People live in a network of mediations. Everything one person does, does not do, or intends to do, is realized in communion and solidarity with others. The whole fabric of relations is influenced by each person's every act, and suffers the effect of any trauma that may issue from that act. This is true not only in the realm of culture, history, and our collective lot; it is true on the spiritual level, as well. This is why we say that we have all sinned in Adam and been redeemed in Christ. In the Creed we profess belief in a "communion of saints," thereby acknowledging that all of the good practiced in the world, all of the heights attained by the spirit, all growth toward others and God, however it may begin within the compass of a single individual, thereupon circulates among all, to attain the heavens themselves.

We are responsible for one another, then. All that we are, the institutions we create—even the institution of language, and the codification of our habits and gestures—are mediations by which we present ourselves to one another, communicate blessing or curse, and render life sterile or fertile. As we see, then, we must not understand mediation as something arising among discrete, detached beings that then has the effect of uniting them. These beings have never been separated or detached to begin with. Before we undertake the following reflection, we wish to make clear that persons are always intertwined with one another through a whole network of threads. Indeed, this network is the very essence of the person. Persons, then, on absolutely all levels of existence, from the corporeal to the supernatural, are interlaced by mediations.

A SINGLE CHRISTOLOGICAL AND PNEUMATOLOGICAL MYSTERY AS THE BASIS OF MARY'S MEDIATION

The picture we have just sketched will help us understand the mediation of Jesus and Mary. The deeper one sinks, through love, goodness, and moral rectitude, into the authentic roots of existence, the more fully one enters into communion with others—the more one becomes a mediator of the meaning of things, incuding the meaning of all graces. As one spiritual master has well said, "If you were alone in your room and had a true thought, you would be heard thousands of miles away." There are no barriers to good. There are no walls where truth is concerned. Once true thoughts are born, they run their secret ways to the hearts of all the just. The best way to be in communion with others, the best way to be near them, is to place yourself in a true and correct position, a just position, before life, before others, and before God.

Jesus Christ did only good in this world. There was no halfheartedness or duplicity in any of his affairs. Jesus lived a radical purity of life, the kind of life that had been planned and intended by God from the beginning. And he did so not simply as an expression of his will, but as an expression of the incarnate presence of God in his human nature. As both God and human being at once, Jesus was surely the absolute Mediator (1 Tim. 2:5). Jesus' link with the mystery of creation is such that all things have been actually planned and accomplished in him, through him, with him, and for him (John 1:3, Col. 1:16–17). He inheres in the substrate of every being. By this very fact, all human solidarity and communion must be understood as flowing ontologically from the radical solidarity and communion maintained by Jesus Christ with all beings.

However, this unique mediation on the part of Christ does not dispense with the mediations of his sisters and brothers. Rather it grounds them, penetrates them, confers upon them their raison d'être. We shall have to think of Christ's mediation in two ways, then. First, from the top down: Jesus has been constituted by God the principle and foundation of all mediation, solidarity, and communion. The mystery of Christ penetrates all creation, including humanity, and causes it to be "christified," at least anonymously and in its real and objective, or ontological, order. Everything springing from the world is swept up in that openness and communion that is the mystery of Christ.

Second, considering reality from the bottom up: Christ prolongs, radicalizes, and consummates the network of mediations already existing among persons, elevating these mediations to their perfection in God. In both respects, from above and from below, Christ is the Mediator par excellence, the realization of the ideal prototype, in light of whom we are enabled to comprehend other forms of mediation. All other mediations are participatory expressions of his. They are also all oriented toward his. Christ's mediation, then, is at once the source and the goal of all others.

Now, which other mediation, in immediate light of the mediation of Christ, has provided the mightiest and most intimate link among human beings? That of the Blessed Virgin Mary. No one has ever been more intimately united to all of humanity than Mary, through her righteousness and her exemption from all sin.

Thus, Mary and Jesus must be conceived of as discrete moments in the same mystery of God's salvific self-communication. God has saved us through the Holy Spirit in that Person's mission to Mary and through her to the community of the saints, in whom the Holy Spirit now dwells until the consummation of the world. We have also been saved, of course, through the mediation of the eternal Son, who became incarnate in Mary's womb and through her in the universal masculine (present in both male and female) and in the Church, which is his Body. We need not establish a wall of separation between these two aspects of the one divine mystery. We must see them as two moments of the realization of the mystery engulfing the whole of human reality. Mary is mediator in union with Jesus. The Spirit, in spiritualizing Mary, is mediator together with the Son, who "verbalizes" Jesus of Nazareth in taking flesh in him. The sacred liturgy expresses this in all of its solemn prayers or orations, concluding them with a profession of faith in the united mediation of the eternal Son and the Holy Spirit in their oneness with the Father: "Through Jesus Christ, your Son, our Lord, who lives and reigns with you in the unity of the Holy Spirit forever and ever." In Marian liturgies, the Church applies the Wisdom texts of the Old Testament, in their eternal dimension, to Mary:

> The Lord begot me, the firstborn of his ways,
>   the forerunner of his prodigies of long ago;
> From of old I was poured forth,
>   at the first, before the earth.
> When there were no depths I was brought forth,
>   when there were no fountains or springs of water. . . .
>   (Prov. 8:22–24; see 25–36)

The application of these passages to Mary is meaningless unless we place Mary in the eternal design of God as the planned, beloved receptacle of God's total self-communication in the Person of the Holy Spirit. Thus, all salvation—as we have seen—has a feminine, a virginal, and a maternal dimension. Jesus' mediation includes the feminine with the masculine, just as Mary's includes the masculine with the feminine.

The reduction of the salvific mediation solely and exclusively to Christ's mediation curtails our understanding of the mystery

of God and of the human being. The almost neurotic preoc-
cupation of so many Christian confessions of the Reformation
with the exclusion of Mary is surely to be understood as the
outgrowth of the cultural conditions of the modern world and
its profoundly masculinizing tendency. Modernity has chosen to
define itself as "logocentric"—to assign the primacy of the spirit
to rationality and the power of ideas. In light of this cultural
choice it has marginalized the feminine, and with it all dimensions of human reality having anything to do with tenderness,
the symbolic, or pathos.[2] Our culture is rigid, violent, necrophil-
ic, and desperate. This is the price it has had to pay for tram-
pling the feminine underfoot. It is in the feminine that we find
the humanization of life and the source of morality, which implies a renunciation of the will to power. It is in the feminine
that we find purity, self-sacrifice, and the protection of the weak
and oppressed. The great Christian mystics and sages who have
cultivated a feminine sensitivity and tenderness toward nature
and humanity have found their inspiration in their worship of
the *Theotokos,* the Virgin Mother of God. Best known is surely
Saint Francis of Assisi, dubbed *Stella Matutina,* or "Morning
Star," who addressed all creatures as his brothers and sisters,
regarding them with great tenderness, and expressing the most
touching humanism that had ever been seen in the West. He
even apostrophized his "Sister, Death," and we read that he
"died singing": "*mortem cantando suscepit.*" The inspiration for this
striking feminine dimension of his spirituality came from his
tender devotion to the Blessed Virgin Mary.

The Mother of God, and our Mother, is archetypically represented by the great mother earth, who nourishes us and embraces us as the source of all life. We never feel more whole than
when we feel ourselves reconciled with the earth. Earthly and
heavenly happiness alike, then, are linked to Mary, as so many
liturgical texts proclaim. Through the (divinized) feminine, we
integrate our shadowy, nebulous world, and recover the protection of the all-embracing Mystery.

Mary's yes to God's proposal to become definitively humanized in her, links her to all humanity. Hers is a unique function
in salvation history. Her *fiat* allowed God to touch human nature
ontologically. The flesh of God, by which God became our

Brother, is flesh received from Mary. These facts are not fortuitous. Nor are they a matter of a long-ago past. They are definitive events for the history of humanity and even for the history of God. They have an eternal dimension. Mary's amen resounds down through the ages, and it will ring for eternity. Risen from the dead and assumed into heaven, Mary speaks her response to God still today. Still she wills what God has always willed, and what God has brought to pass in history: the salvation of humankind through the incarnation of a Son born of the Virgin Mary and her spiritualization by the divine Spirit.

Mary represents the whole of humanity because she was one with humanity. Now she reinforces this union. She makes it stronger and deeper than ever. In union with her Son Jesus, Mary plunges deeper into the heart of every human being than does any other creature. Accordingly, she can be invoked as our mediator and advocate. In heaven, she accompanies her brothers and sisters along the pathways of their earthly pilgrimage. No one is regarded as completely happy without knowing his or her brothers and sisters are happy, too. Even in her condition of absolute glorification in God, then, Mary has not yet received all of the glory and happiness promised her, any more than has her Son, Jesus. They will receive the plenitude of the fulfillment of that promise only at the end of time, when all of the just have entered the Reign of God. Then will the circle of solidarity and communion of the redeemed be closed and sealed. Until then, it will remain a promise, and the personal destiny of every woman and man will remain open. Mary intercedes with God, with her Son, and with the Holy Spirit with whom she is united, by virtue of her participation in and solidarity with our lot, which is therefore her lot, the Spirit's, and Christ's, as well. Her glorious destiny is ours, too. Her unique situation of intimacy with the triune God has led human nature into the final phase of its maturation and divinization. This event of grace wins us grace upon grace, until the greatest possible number of us reach the everlasting Reign of God, where Mary has preceded us.

MARY'S LIFE OF SOLIDARITY WITH US

We have considered Mary's solidarity and mediation on an ontological level—on the level of the structure of being and consciousness. Now we must examine how Mary lived this solidarity concretely in her personal life. Facts are hard to come by, but they are sufficient to afford us a glimpse of Mary's service to and solidarity with men and women in a context of altogether concrete situations.

First we have her yes, given to God in all freedom, and rendering her available to become the mother of the Messiah and the temple of the Holy Spirit. Mary stands in solidarity with every human being who ever longed for liberation. She also represents and assumes the openness to the divine that humanity has always had, and still has today. Her *fiat* binds her to the incarnational form in which God assumes the task of a human liberation that, henceforth and forever, will have a feminine, Marian dimension. For in Mary, the feminine is inserted in God.

Mary's visit to her cousin Elizabeth shows the solidarity linking human beings in their everyday affairs through the infrastructure of their basic needs. It also shows how this everyday solidarity can be the vehicle of grace, and a genuine experience of God. Elizabeth's greeting and Mary's hymn of praise celebrate this (Luke 1:39–56). The Magnificat reveals Mary's profound solidarity with the oppressed of the earth. She is the mighty woman of liberation, calling down God's justice on the unjust of this world and begging the divine intervention in favor of the lowly and hungry. She knows whose side God is on. She knows that God is genuinely sensitive to the humiliation of the poor. "For he has looked upon his servant in her lowliness . . . " (Luke 1:48). It is God's liberation of a woman who was poor that Mary is celebrating when she sings, "God who is mighty has done great things for me . . . " (Luke 1:49). The spirit of the Old Testament is in Mary's heart, as its words are on her lips, as she sings of the latest "wonderful work of the Lord" wrought in the liberation of Israel.

Giving birth to Jesus in a stable, surrounded by beasts, and laying him in a manger, Mary is in solidarity with the countless men and women who live and die without a roof over their heads—with all the marginalized for whom "there was no room" (Luke 2:7). Salvation is rarely bestowed through spectacular deeds or accompanied by grand words. Salvation comes through a praxis of solidarity with human beings' lowly, and so often horribly cruel, lot.

We may prescind from the dispute over the historicity of the flight into Egypt, since what is important here is the human solidarity portrayed by the inspired writer. In all flight, fear and uncertainty, insecurity and risk, and every type of privation have the upper hand. Mary shares the lot of every just fugitive, every persecuted victim throughout history. Her faith sustains her, but it does not guarantee specifics. That is why she flees. If she had lived with an alienated faith that claims to exempt men and women from doing everything within their power to right their wronged condition, she would not have fled. She would simply have thought, "God will surely protect his Son. There is no need for me to be concerned. Why not just stay here?" But Mary does not think or act in this way. She is aware of the mortal danger she and her Son are in. She does what anyone else would have done: she flees, and awaits better times. Faith penetrates all things, but it is not a substitute for human effort or intelligence.

Mary expresses her faith through the practices of the popular piety of her time. She goes on a pilgrimage with her husband and Son, her relatives and friends, to the temple in Jerusalem. Her Son wanders off and is nowhere to be found. His parents are terribly frightened. As any mother would, Mary fears the worst. And so when she finds him, she asks, "Son, why have you done this to us? You see that your father and I have been searching for you in sorrow" (Luke 2:48). There is reproach in her words. At last Mary can breathe easily, but she has not forgotten the pain, the pain that plagues the hearts of so many other mothers. She must still grow in an understanding of her Son's mission. Again, at the beginning of Jesus' public life she feels a special anxiety for him, and goes in search of him in the company of her relatives. She simply must speak with him (Mark 3:31). After all, some of the relatives have reported that Jesus has gone mad (Mark 3:21). But by now, Mary has grown in an understanding of his mission, and she becomes his disciple, in faith, not knowledge, following the Savior of the world despite the atmosphere of scandal that accompanies him wherever he goes.

At Cana, Mary shares the joy of a wedding and the hosts'

embarrassment when there is nothing more to drink. She is concerned, and she determines to do whatever she can to help. She feels a solidarity with her hosts. And through her intercession Jesus performs his first miracle (John 2:1–11).

The tradition of the Jerusalem church has preserved for us the story of Mary's meeting with Jesus on the road to Calvary. Everyone else has fled Jesus' debacle. But Mary stays. She walks with her Son, suffers at his side, encourages him—and becomes Co-Redemptrix of the human race. At the foot of the cross, she is powerless to interfere with her Son's execution, and her heart is pierced as if by seven swords. But she offers herself, along with Jesus, and in solidarity with all humankind, to the divine mercy. Here at the foot of the cross, in the moment of our redemption, Mary gives birth to us as her children.

Mary maintains her solidarity with her Son in his resurrection as in his death. She is present at the birth of the apostolic Church on the day of Pentecost. She accompanies the inauguration of the process of faith that will now spread out in all directions, all down through the centuries, as a Church is built that takes up the cause of Jesus until he comes again. The Spirit dwelling in Mary now dwells in the Church of her Son.

Nor has Mary abandoned humanity in her glory. Still she abides in the hearts of God's people, as they maintain a constant veneration of her life, her virtues, her mission, and her mystery. She has become the Mother of all Christians and all human beings. Mary's apparitions down through the ages demonstrate her motherly solicitude for persons and their needs. Assumed into heaven, she intercedes constantly for her children, drawing the feminine in all of us toward its eschatological divinization.

Today, inserted forever in the Source of all life and grace, she touches each one of us, exercising a universal mediation—not from without, but from within the mystery of each and every male and female human existence.

The solidarity Mary lived while she was among us demonstrates her preference for being where human need is most crying—where the drama of suffering threatens to stifle the very meaning of life, or indeed where any decisions are made that will mold the framework of the future. Today, from heaven, she is with us in solidarity in these situations, and more so than she ever was in her life on earth—more intensely still, and we know that this will be the pattern of her mediation until all creation reaches God. *"Et tunc erit finis"* ("Only after that will the end come": Matt. 24:14)!

12. Mary, Prophetic Woman of Liberation

As we saw in Chapter 11, one form of Mary's mediation is of special importance for the context of our faith as that faith must be lived in conditions of oppression, as in Latin America. The fonts reveal Mary as a woman in solidarity with the passion of her brothers and sisters. This dimension is of special interest to Christians committed to the liberation process.

One of the most characteristic and beautiful aspects of Latin American piety is precisely its Marian inspiration. Our people associate Mary with their whole passion and their whole joy. Many of our towns and cities, and countless numbers of our churches, bear her name or that of one of her feasts. Until recently, this devotion was mainly a matter of veneration and worship rather than of following or imitation. More recently, however, and more and more noticeably, another form of Marian piety is developing—one strongly centered on the following of Mary. In the *comunidades de base* (base communities), wherever the political dimension of the faith is discussed, a special appreciation of Mary's role of denunciation and proclamation (*denuncia y anuncio*), of prophecy and liberation, stands out as a key aspect of the people's devotion to her. Mary's hymn of praise, the Magnificat, is regarded as a special illustration of these elements.[1] True, our Marian tradition has paid these elements precious little heed in the past. After all, they are intimately bound up with the feminine, and we live in a radically masculinizing culture. The image of Mary in popular piety has been that of the kind, sweet, pious, humble virgin mother, completely devoted to Jesus and the Holy Family. And as we know, theology has supplied this image with abundant theoretical justification.

In a law-and-order society whose masculinizing powers have received such wholehearted ideological support from Christianity, will it ever be possible for people to assimilate the ethical indignation of a Mary who prays of God to scatter the proud in the conceit of their hearts, to topple the mighty from their thrones, and to send the rich empty away, so as to be able to exalt the lowly and fill the hungry with good things? Christian ideology, always in charge here, has had a difficult time deciding between not ascribing any importance to Mary's prophetic words, superficially so male and so strange-sounding on the lips of a woman, and spiritualizing them—bestowing upon them a meaning calculated to reinforce the privileged position occupied by Christians here, or even simply applying them to "the others" (Jews, pagans, or "forces of evil"). In any event, they have not been applied to the Church or to Christians. As a result, for centuries, Christianity has rendered the critical, liberating content of the Magnificat impotent. It is our task, then, to develop a prophetic image of Mary—an image of Mary as the strong, determined woman, the woman committed to the messianic liberation of the poor from the historical social injustices under which they suffer. And today we see this image taking shape, deep in the heart of an oppressed people, who long for a voice in society and liberation from its evils.

PRESENT OPPRESSION AS THE HERMENEUTIC LOCUS OF LIBERATION

A prophetic, liberating image of Mary is the only legitimate conclusion theology can come to against the backdrop of our situation of captivity and oppression. We in Latin America read a divine revelation written in other times—some two thousand years ago—with today's eyes, eyes full of questions, expectations, and interests springing from our own present reality. This is how we approach the Marian texts of the Christian Scriptures. The sacred texts then send us a message that may be gathered right from the words themselves—but our eyes are looking for a revelation for our own time and place, and so we assign priority, in a whole series of inspired texts, to the particular passages that seem most suggestive for our situation. We underscore those passages in red, and we write in the margin, "Very Important!" We accept all of the texts. They all contain God's message for us, and we make an effort to grasp the totality of that message as contained in these fonts of our faith. But our present situation has its own demands and priorities, and those demands and priorities direct our attention especially to certain texts and contexts. We hear a voice that speaks to our ears of today. The meaning of a time long past acquires relevance for the present. We receive a meaning that derives from the texts, of course, but we create new meaning thanks to the echoes of those texts in the context of our own history.

Biblical meaning, of course, cannot be altogether fixed or frozen in the past. There is a vitality of meaning here, a "meaning potential," that becomes explicit only in contact with new sociohistorical situations. Consequently, we find ourselves caught up in the dynamics of a hermeneutic circle. We read the sacred texts with today's eyes, and so our interpretation of what we read cannot but be a modern one. At the same time, these texts send their own message to our modern ear, and thus the ancient message rides the soundwaves of today—again, to be interpreted on the wavelength of our times. The interpretation of a text is always a two-way street, then. Sacred Scripture is not a cistern of stagnant waters, in which all legitimate meanings lie submerged and "ready to go." Sacred Scripture is a fountain of fresh, living water, from which new meanings emanate in light of the times in which we live, suffer, and seek meaning.

But we are not caught in a vicious circle, one that denatures the original meaning of Scripture, imposing upon it our homemade *answers,* constructing *a priori* meanings sprung wholly from the times in which we live. We should have to call the hermeneutic circle a "virtuous circle," for it reveals the richness of meaning implicitly but really present in the texts and uncovered by the *questions* that arise out of our new sociohistorical situations. Thus, our present situation, once it has been diagnosed as captivity and social and political oppression, becomes a privileged hermeneutical locus for the reading of Mary's Magnificat and for becoming hearers of its message. Actually, of course, the Hymn of the Virgin sprang from a network of relationships very much like those in which we in Latin America live today. That is why it seems so realistic, so easy to interpret. To be sure, the terms of Mary's situation were different. But the type of relationships between the terms, and the spirit in which she acted and reacted in view of these terms, are strikingly analogous. As if by magic, Mary becomes our contemporary.

We in Latin America live a life characterized by injustice and oppression. The vast majority of our sisters and brothers are affected by it. The cries of our poverty-stricken people rise to the heart of our God, pleading for dignity, basic human rights, equal societal relationships, and the means for the most effective possible societal participation on the part of all. A tiny elite, possessed of a monopoly over the power, knowledge, and wealth needed to dictate the universal destiny, are in a position to confiscate the lives of whole peoples and appropriate them for their own sole advantage. They institutionalize Christianity itself, with all its symbols and concepts, and reduce it to the service of their selfish cause. Internal colonialism—the only name for the "progress" under which we suffer—is nothing more than the reproduction in microcosm of the great neocolonialism under which we in the Western world must live. The nations of the Center—the countries of the North Atlantic—maintain a ring of satellite nations, dominating and exploiting them for the maintenance and acceleration of the opulent nations. This is a wicked, iniquitous "progress," built on the blood of millions of brothers and sisters.

Against this backdrop we hear the cry of an oppressed people clamoring for liberation. Today's poor Lazaruses plead with every modern Dives for one thing alone: to be taken for human beings, to be allowed to pass from a condition of nonpersons to a condition of persons. The churches must understand the messianic mission with which they have been charged: to stand in solidarity with, to be the mouthpiece of, those with *nem voz nem vez*—neither voice nor a turn to express themselves when it comes to decisions that will affect their whole lives. The churches are called upon to suffer, in their own flesh, the painful passion of their people.

And so the churches now read this negative social reality with the eyes of faith. No longer do they speak of mere structural injustices. Now they denounce a genuine situation of collective sin. No longer do we say merely that the social diagnosis is a gloomy one. We come right out and denounce this social situation as contrary to God's plan for history. Liberation is not only an all-encompassing social process. It is also a form of making concrete and anticipating the absolute liberation to be accomplished in Jesus Christ.

This is the sound box that amplifies the echoes of Mary's prophetic hymn, with all its challenge, propheticism, subversion, and liberation. Mary does not simply open her ears to the message of the Most High. She has one ear open completely to God, and the other open completely to the cries of the oppressed Jewish people. She is the woman of true fidelity, a fidelity equal to that of all of the great prophets. All prophets, along with their fidelity to God, demonstrate an equal fidelity to an afflicted people. Loyalty to the one is loyalty to the others. Anyone deaf to the cries of the poor is also mute before God. But Mary raises her voice and speaks out. She praises God, and she intercedes for the people. She praises God's mercy, and begs his liberation of the lowly and the starving.

MARY, MODEL OF AN OPPRESSED PEOPLE'S LONGING FOR LIBERATION

The liberating dimension of Mariology was solemnly emphasized by Pope Paul VI in his 1974 encyclical, *Marialis Cultus*. We here take the liberty of transcribing the paragraph that offers us the real key to a hermeneutics, or interpretative method, for translating yesterday's message for our faith today.

A reading of the divine Scriptures, under the influence of the Holy Spirit, and keeping account of the achievements of the human sciences and the various situations of the contemporary world, will lead one to discover that Mary can very well be taken as a *model in something that human beings of our time yearn for*. For example . . . we observe, with agreeable surprise, that Mary of Nazareth, while living in absolute surrender to the will of the Lord, was anything but a passive, submissive woman, pious to the point of being out of contact with reality. No, here was a woman who did not hesitate to assert that God is the avenger of the oppressed, that he topples the mighty of this world from their thrones (see Luke 1:51–53); in Mary we recognize the "first among the Lord's lowly and poor" (*Lumen Gentium*, no. 55), the "valiant woman" who has known poverty and suffering, flight and exile (see Matt. 2:13–

23), situations that can scarcely escape the notice of those who seek to endorse and further, in the spirit of the gospel, the *liberating energies* of human beings and society. . . . In this example we see how inescapably clear it is that the figure of the Virgin Most Holy, far from disappointing certain profound aspirations of men and women of our time, actually furnishes the finished, *perfect model* of a disciple of the Lord: laborer of the earthly and temporal city, and at the same time diligent pilgrim toward the heavenly, eternal city; promotor of the justice that liberates the oppressed and of the charity that succors the needy, but above all active witness of the love that builds Christ in hearts. (*Lumen Gentium*, no. 37) [italics added]

One could scarcely ask for greater lucidity in an official text. Mary is presented as the liberating woman, and as prolonging the lineage of the heroic women of the Old Testament who committed themselves to the justice of God and humanity, as Deborah (Josh. 4–5) or Judith (Jth. 13:20, 15:9).

Spiritual Context of the Magnificat

For a better understanding of the liberating content of the Magnificat, we must place it in its context in the history of spirituality.[2] The context of the Hymn of the Virgin is the same as that of the liberating message of the Messiah, and Mary sings her song in the same spirit as Jesus proclaims his message of liberation. The Magnificat is a prelude to the proclamation of the Reign of God, which, of course, is the core and center of the glad tidings of Mary's Son, Jesus, the crowning of the longings of the whole Old Testament,[3] message first to the poor, the unjustly treated, the downtrodden. Their situation is a challenge, and his messianic might rises to the occasion. Blest are these poor, therefore, for theirs is the inauguration of the Reign of God (see Luke 4:18–21, 6:20).

The God of this Reign is absolutely *holy*. "Holy" denotes the one who surpasses everything we can think or imagine, the Utterly Other, before whom, like Moses at the burning bush (Exod. 3:5), we can only fall to our knees and remove our sandals, thereupon to approach with trust and reverential fear. One does not toy with the holy God. Before us we see the *Tremendum*, the one, single Something in our whole life that is absolutely serious. Were God not to prevent it, we should die of the contemplation of this divine glory.

But this God, so holy, is also *merciful*. We have the word *mercy* from the Latin *misericordia,* which contains the root *cord-,* or "heart." God is not unaffected by the human drama. God hears the cry of the marginalized, and takes it to heart. God is sensitive to all misery. God takes the side of the poor, owns their cause. God loves the world because it has issued forth from God's almighty word. Yet God protests this world, too, because the injustices and oppressions that his creatures have manufactured displease God. God's Reign will make an end of all of this. God is the *Fascinosum,* as well, the fascinating, the hypnotizing, the riveting, and we feel God's liberating nearness like electricity in the air.

We have a beautiful example of God's merciful heart in the story of Hannah, mother of the prophet Samuel. Her sterility is a humiliation, and she becomes the object of the sneers of her rival, Peninnah, who has given birth. Bitterly she weeps, and in her sorrow she fasts. And amidst her copious tears, she implores: "O Lord of hosts, if you look with pity on the misery of your handmaid, if you remember me and do not forget me, if you give your handmaid a male child, I will give him to the Lord for as long as he lives ... " (1 Sam. 1:11). And God hears the woman's helpless cry. She gives birth to Samuel, and after him to three other sons and two daughters (1 Sam. 2:21). Then, as she presents her firstborn in the temple, Hannah bursts forth in the canticle that will one day become the basis of Mary's Magnificat. The parallelism is so striking that we cannot resist calling the reader's attention to it.[4]

MARY'S MAGNIFICAT

My being proclaims the greatness of the Lord,
    my spirit finds joy in God my savior,
For he has looked upon his servant in her lowliness;
    all ages to come shall call me blessed.
God who is mighty has done great things for me,
    holy is his name;
His mercy is from age to age
    on those who fear him.

He has shown might with his arm;
    he has confused the proud in their inmost thoughts.
He has deposed the mighty from their thrones

and raised the lowly to high places.
The hungry he has given every good thing,
    while the rich he has sent empty away.
He has upheld Israel his servant,
    ever mindful of his mercy;
Even as he promised our fathers,
    promised Abraham and his descendants forever.

(Luke 1:46–55)

HANNAH'S MAGNIFICAT

My heart exults in the Lord,
    my horn is exalted in my God.
I have swallowed up my enemies;
    I rejoice in my victory.
There is no Holy One like the Lord;
    there is no Rock like our God.

Speak boastfully no longer,
    nor let arrogance issue from your mouths.
For an all-knowing God is the Lord,
    a God who judges deeds.
The bows of the mighty are broken,
    while the tottering gird on strength.
The well-fed hire themselves out for bread,
    while the hungry batten on spoil.
The barren wife bears seven sons.
    while the mother of many languishes.

The Lord puts to death and gives life;
    he casts down to the nether world;
    he raises up again.
The Lord makes poor and makes rich,
    he humbles, he also exalts.
He raises the needy from the dust;
    from the ash heap he lifts up the poor,
To seat them with nobles
    and make a glorious throne their heritage.
He gives to the vower his vow,
    and blesses the sleep of the just.

For the pillars of the earth are the Lord's,
    and he has set the world upon them.
He will guard the footsteps of his faithful ones,
    but the wicked shall perish in the darkness.
For not by strength does man prevail;

the Lord's foes shall be shattered.
The Most High in heaven thunders;
  the Lord judges the ends of the earth,
Now may he give strength to his king,
  and exalt the horn of his anointed!

(1 Sam. 2:1–10)

As we see, Mary is a woman of the mold of Hannah. And her reaction is the same. After all, she is in the same situation of oppression. Hannah is the sterile servant girl, while Mary might just as well have been sterile for all the surrounding culture cared for virginity. Mary is the victim of the same overweening domination as Hannah—the despotism of the proud, the powerful, the wealthy. On the other hand, Mary trusts in the same mercy of God, who will surely intervene to reverse these unjust, iniquitous relationships, to exalt the downtrodden and feed the starving to satiety. The spiritual ambiance in which both women cry to God is the expected coming of the Messiah—long to be awaited in Hannah's day, already at hand in Mary's and the very fruit of her womb. Let us remember: the basis messianic expectation of the Old Testament culture, shared by Hannah and Mary, is that of a transformation of the old order, in which the arrogance of might and self-assertion have the upper hand, into a new order of discernment of attitudes and the triumph of justice for the oppressed.

THE DIMENSION OF LIBERATION IN MARY'S MAGNIFICAT

The backdrop of the Magnificat is the tragic character of a world that is unjustly ordered and therefore an obstacle to God's plan for society and human beings. However, God has resolved to intervene through the Messiah and to inaugurate new relationships with all things. All Israel, and all humanity, yearn for this saving moment. Mary has understood: now, in her womb, suddenly the principle and agent of all salvation and liberation has sprung to human life. It is as if Jesus were already exclaiming, "This is the time of fulfillment. The Reign of God is at hand! Reform your lives and believe in the gospel!" (Mark 1:15)—the cry he will one day utter as he starts enthusiastically down the highways and byways of Galilee.

Mary, too, is filled with jubilation, and intones her hymn of laud and joy. Nor is her joy a kind of "whistling in the dark," fingers crossed, hoping but without a real basis for hope. No, Mary is filled with messianic exaltation.[5] God has become the Savior (Luke 1:47), and has looked kindly upon the lowly servant woman (Luke 1:48).[6] And behold, Mary becomes the prototype of what God intends to do for all humanity. Just as Hannah represented all Israel, so Mary represents not only the Church, but the whole of humanity. This is why she can sing that every generation will call her blessed (Luke 1:48).

God is the Holy, and the Utterly Other, who dwells in inaccessible light (see Luke 1:49). But God does not live at a sovereign distance, far from the excruciating cries of the children of God. The Blessed Virgin can proclaim that God's mercy extends from age to age (Luke 1:50). God has left the resplendent shadows of an inaccessible abode, and now draws near the murky light of the human race. God enters the conflict, takes up the cause of the conquered and the marginalized against the mighty. God strikes down those who "make history," a history that they themselves intend to write in books filled with their self-magnification.

The mercy of God is not reserved for the end time alone. The mercy of God will not allow the wound to fester. The mercy of God takes historical forms, is made concrete in deeds that transform the interplay of forces. The proud, with the power in their hands, the wealthy, do not have the last word. They think they have, but the divine justice is already upon them, in history itself. They will be stripped of their power, the mask will be torn from their proud faces, and they will be sent away empty-handed (Luke 1:51–53). The Reign of God is anything but the consecration of this world's "law and order"—the decree of the overambitious. The Reign of God is precisely a protest against the "order" of *this* world. The Reign of Justice is the reign of a different justice. God promised this new world to our ancestors, and this promise is our certitude. And now God begins to bring all to accomplishment (Luke 1:55).

There can be no doubt that this accomplishment, this fulfillment, has a revolutionary ring. Much as it may shock the ears of a Church priding itself on its caution and balance, its political prudence, we must accept this truth, for it is a truth told by the Blessed Virgin Mary.

> He has deposed the mighty from their thrones
>   and raised the lowly to high places.
> The hungry he has given every good thing,
>   while the rich he has sent empty away.
>   (Luke 1:52–53)

The prayers of the valiant women of the Old Testament were no different. As the Israelites made their escape from Egypt, Miriam, Moses' sister, danced to her own song: "Sing to the Lord, for he is gloriously triumphant; horse and chariot he has cast into the sea" (Exod. 15:21). Hannah, feeling in her flesh that God had heard her plea, cried out, "The bows of the mighty are broken, while the tottering gird on strength" (1 Sam. 2:4). Judith, after she had beheaded Holofernes, proclaimed to her people: "Praise God, praise him! Praise God, who has not withdrawn his mercy from the house of Israel, but has shattered our enemies by my hand this very night" (Jth. 13:14).

The God of the Bible is not an idol with which to adorn a temple or the nooks and crannies of our homes. This God is a living God, whose real name is justice, holiness, and compassion for the oppressed. God sides with Lazarus in the parable, placing him in the bosom of Abraham while the gluttonous Dives, the Rich One, writhes in the flames of hell (Luke 16:19–31). God calls the poor—those who hunger and thirst for justice, the persecuted, the calumniated, the murdered for justice's sake— blessed. And God hurls a cry of woe against the rich, the filled, the exploiters, and the sycophants (Luke 6:20–26).

What sort of God is this? What is this sudden partiality? Did not Jesus tell us that God makes the sun to rise on the good and the bad alike, and the rain to fall equally on the just and the unjust (Matt. 5:45)? Did Jesus not tell us that God is "good to the ungrateful and the wicked" (Luke 6:35)? Is this not an undiscriminating, evenhanded God, then? Our answer to this is that, yes, God loves everyone, and wraps everyone in compassionate embrace. Everyone in the world is God's daughter or son.

But there are good and obedient daughters and sons, and there are evil and rebellious ones. In a dehumanized, twisted world of oppressors and oppressed, the *form* God's love takes is different toward different persons. Jesus did not treat the poor, the sick, the Pharisees, the tax collectors, and Herod all alike. He called the poor blessed. He called the Pharisees whitewashed mausoleums, and Herod a fox. He showed tax collectors like Zacchaeus the wickedness and injustice of their fraudulently acquired wealth.

The liberation willed by God for all finds different paths to all, then, in view of the variety of forms of oppression that plague our world. This is why God exalts the humble and works deeds of justice for the poor. God is indignant with selfish, greedy oppressors who engender the impoverishment and humiliation of others. God flings the proud of heart to the earth, in the hope that they will be converted, delivered from their ridiculous vaunting and flaunting, to become free and obedient children of God and brothers and sisters to others. Only thus can the Reign of God come. God casts the mighty from their thrones only in an effort to persuade them to cease using their power for their own ends and place it at the service of the common good, thereby opening themselves to salvation. God's method of offering them salvation is to topple them from their positions of power. The rich are sent empty away in order that, delivered from the mechanisms of accumulation that render them so heartless and cruel, they may recover their humanity and embark on the path of God's Reign.

God's liberation takes the path of conversion. Without conversion, the world continues in its wickedness, its injustice, and its divisions. God's liberation is realized in different ways according to circumstances. Yet, it always points toward the same end. It makes all persons sons and daughters of God, brothers and sisters of one another, free sovereigns of the goods of the earth, and full members of the Reign of God. God does not invert social relationships out of an anthropomorphic spirit of revenge, so that the dominated may now be dominators, and the poor now become wealthy oppressors. No, God turns social relationships topsy-turvy simply to effect the conversion whereby there will be no more rich and poor as antagonistic classes, no more oppressor and oppressed, but brothers and sisters all, dwelling together in the one house of God.

The Reign of God in history, then, is built in confrontation with the evil empire of this world, which is built on the accumulation of wealth, social relationships of domination, and the privileges of the powerful. There is no compromise between God's plan and the designs of the sinner. Only the conversion of sinners, with its concomitant transformation in our manner of thinking, working, and organizing our relationships with one another and with the goods of the earth, opens the path to reconciliation and peace.

It is through Mary, then, that the Reign of God is inaugurated. With what joy she is filled as she celebrates its arrival! God's mercy is now manifest. God has resolved to intervene on behalf of those who most need the Reign of God as a reality.

Let us note well the content of God's mercy. It is concrete and historical. It is not spiritualizing. The powerful are the powerful plain and simple, the hungry are the literally hungry, and the lowly are those who suffer life's humiliations. The Greek *tapeinos* (Luke 1:52), "poor," and *tapeinōsis* (Luke 1:48), "poverty," in Mary's Magnificat denote the situation of someone who is literally needy (see Lev. 19:10, 23:32; Deut. 15:11, 24:12; Isa. 10:2; Jer. 22:16). This situation is the fruit of exploitation at the hands of the rich, and it is condemned by God and the law (Exod. 22:20–24; Deut. 24:12–17; Lev. 19:20, 23:22). This is the class of people—the lowly, the despised, the outcast—who will be the first to enjoy the coming of the Reign. That is why their prayers, their expectations, and their tears are noticed by God, as the Psalms so frequently show us.

Mary is the recapitulation of all of the poor for us, just as Hannah was in the Old Testament. Mary sees that in her life, through the wondrous things the Almighty has wrought in her (Luke 1:48–49), God has heard the cry of the poor (1:48) and of all Israel (1:54). At last God has looked upon the poverty of the servant woman and embraced the servant Israel (1:54). Behold the firstfruits of the eschatological Reign of God. No wonder Mary's heart leaps in a hymn of exultation and thanksgiving.

To spiritualize the Magnificat—reduce it to a private, interior spirituality emptied of all its liberating and revolutionary content—is to let the order of this decadent world stand, which is directly contrary to the unequivocal demand enunciated in Mary's hymn. The dichotomy between matter and spirit—that root of so many evils in Christianity—is very far from the spirit of the Bible. The Bible presents salvation as *human* salvation, as the integral, complete salvation of the whole human being, matter and spirit interpenetrating, and of all interrelationships with other persons and with things. God's activity affects not only select portions of reality—what we like to call our souls, for instance—but all reality, because all reality is in sore need of liberation.

The Protestant monk of Taizé, Max Thurian, one of the great spiritual teachers of our day, wrote in a commentary on the Magnificat, in 1963, when the liberating content of the Christian message, so highlighted by the Latin American theology of liberation, was first being noticed: "Political and social justice, equal rights, and the common good are the signs of mercy of the Messiah King, which his mother and handmaiden sings. Thus the gospel of eternal salvation is also the gospel of human liberation. Mary the first Christian is also the first revolutionary, the first citizen of the new order."[7]

SHOW THYSELF A LIBERATING MOTHER!

The image of Mary conveyed in the Magnificat fully justifies Pope Paul VI's statement that Mary is not a passive, submissive woman. Her religiousness is anything but alienating. Who but a strong, decisive woman will call down God's justice on the heads of the oppressors of the poor? Who but a committed woman will take sides with those who seem destined to lose the battle? God does not fight on both sides, nor is everything in this world of equal value. God and Mary are on the side of those whose dignity must be recovered, and whose justice must be acknowledged and accomplished. Only thus is the Reign of God in this world anticipated and rendered genuinely historical.

And so Mary accepts the inevitable historical conflict. Reconciliation, in order to be genuine, must be preceded by the process of conversion that inevitably gives rise to conflict. But historical conflict does not conjure away horizons of hope, or obscure the presence of joy. It is most interesting that we hear a joyful, exultant Mary in spite of the social contradictions that her hymn itself manifests and denounces. How is this? It is simply that Mary refuses to hypostatize or ontologize conflict. She accepts it in its historical expression as the inevitable concretion of divergent human interests, in which some persons oppose God's plan while others enlist in its service. Some actualize sin, while others actualize grace.

Christians, following in the footsteps of Jesus and Mary, cannot avoid the obstacles present in the society in which they live. Their position cannot be neutral. First of all, there is no such position. And second, even if there were, it would be nothing more than a mask over the option of the powerful of this world, upon whom the Virgin invokes the mighty manifestation of the divine arm (Luke 1:51). There is no room in real life for a platonic, ethereal "love." A love like this is inoperative. What we need is a love in solidarity with the suffering and with those who suffer with them—an intelligent love that looks for concrete, liberating steps to take in developing relationships of justice among human beings.

We Christians, in this task of liberation, have the bitter experience of slow, tedious processes, the experience of the dogged persistence of oppression. Instead of becoming discouraged, let us make Mary's pleas our own, and ask God to manifest, to realize justice by means of mediations beyond our power. Should not the community of the faithful cry out, amidst the oppression of our people, the very petition of the Blessed Virgin Mary when she prayed, "Lord, show us the power of your arm, scatter the proud in the conceit of their hearts, cast down the mighty from their thrones, lift up the lowly, fill the hungry with good things, and send the rich empty away"?

Let us, then, make our own the prayer of Dom Hélder Câmara to Our Lady of the Liberation:

> O Mary, Mother of Christ and of the Church,
> we prepare for our evangelizing mission.
> We must continue it, enlarge it, and perfect it.
> And so our thoughts are on you.
> We think of you in a special way
> because of that perfect model of thanksgiving,

the hymn you sang when your cousin, Saint Elizabeth,
mother of Saint John the Baptist,
called you blessed among women.
You took no complacency in your blessedness,
but concentrated your thoughts on the whole human race.
Yes, you thought of everyone,
but you made your forthright option for the poor,
the same option as your Son would make one day.
What is it in you—in your words, in your voice,
when you announce in your Magnificat
the humiliation of the mighty
and the exaltation of the humble,
the satisfaction of the starving
and the dismay of the rich—
what is it in you that no one dares to call *you* a revolutionary,
or regard *you* with suspicion?
Lend us your voice!
Sing with us!
Beg your Son to accomplish in us, in all their fullness,
his Father's plans![8]

V. MYTHOLOGY: MARY, TEMPLE OF THE SPIRIT: THE NEW AGE

13. Myth and Its Conflicting Interpretations

We have considered the *history* of Mary of Nazareth, where details are so exceedingly scarce. We have also contemplated the *theological* elements that transcend the raw historiographical facts, understanding Mary, our Lady, in her relationship with the great mysteries of God, the perennial questions of human beings, and the designs of Mystery, and on this level we have encountered the grandeur that lies concealed beneath the fragile veils of historicity. Not that we are speaking of two different realities. Theology is only the explication of history. The *theological* image of Mary, our Lady, is built precisely on the image of Mary the woman of *history*, with the aim of shedding light on that history. The purpose of theology is not to mystify her humble, not very messianic, origins, but to underscore the greatness of her lowliness precisely as lowliness, the profundity of a humility that continues to be humility.

History simply recounts. It really tells us almost nothing. Theology understands. It is conceptual, and this is better. But we want more. Life calls for realization, life postulates depth. Life will have celebration and exaltation. But in order to celebrate, it is not enough just to hear a formula. It is not enough even to know and reflect. We must open our heart, we must project our enthusiasm outward. We must magnify what we wish to celebrate. Praise and enthusiasm thrive in grandiloquence, exaltation, excess. Generosity and exuberance are of the essence of festival. Here is where image, symbol, myth, and archetype appear. None of this, however, is invention of reality, but only its exaltation and sublimation. In history and theology, reason speaks: *logos*. Symbol expresses the heart: *pathos*. It is merely a matter of two different approaches to the same reality. History tells; reason seeks explanations; and symbol uncovers meaning.

Each approach has its own logic and grammar and its appropriate syntax. One must not mix the idioms. Each had its specific rules. Each tells and sings—in its own way, and within the limits of its own potential—of the same person, Mary. One must listen to the music of all of these languages together if one would capture all of the richness of this most singular of women.

SYMBOL REMAKES AND RETELLS REALITY

So let us now enter into the realm of symbolic Mariology, the most fertile part of all Mariology. Symbol—or myth or image—remakes and retells reality on the level of the imaginary. The entire archetypal weight of the realities of our personal and collective unconscious that people the human mind, both sleeping and waking, plays a role in this process. What these realities do for us is to express the experience of the value, the meaning for human life, with all enthusiasm, of the figure of Mary. Their language is one of idealization and eschatology. A person in love exalts the qualities of the beloved. A mother sings the excellence of her child. The emigrant sublimates the beauties of the old country. We think of Don Quixote and his Dulcinea, Petrarch and his Laura, impossible loves and bittersweet exiles. Images arise that represent a most intense call to the unconscious, a call laden with existential meaning. These images do not falsify reality. They translate the reality of feeling. They bear the experience of the heart. One must embrace and understand their formulations in the context of this symbolic realm, where historical reality is remade and retold on another level. Otherwise, reason will only be scandalized, and theology (whose operation is one of analytical reason) will begin to denouce "improper expressions" and "heresies," and assume a repressive role.

Symbol and myth, as such, constitute a legitimate way of expressing Mary's transcendent meaning. It is not a matter of an archaic primitivism valid only for unintelligent people who can be convinced in no other way. Nor is it a matter of reason's decay, a capitulation to the intimidations of fantasy. Nor is it a matter of a disordered rationality of the unconscious. No, it is merely another approach to the reality and the mystery of Mary. The symbolic approach has its own logic—not an irrational one, but a logic that is rational in a different way. It has its own objectives and its own messages, which it seeks to convey in its own way, perhaps a more concrete and comprehensive way. Anyone willing to take the plunge, to dive headlong into these realities that can scarcely leave one indifferent—love, the self-revelation of one life to another, a crucial decision, an illness, the death of a loved one, and so on—will immediately agree that concept is inadequate, cerebral recital cold. Color, image, symbol are the only beds that can hold this wide a load: they alone can adequately, definitively express what holds human beings in this tight a grip. Symbolic Mariology is no exception: it is the heart of Marian theology because it is the *theo*logical part of that theology.

Symbolic Mariology abounds in analogies, types and antitypes, evocations of and allusions to future realities. This is how symbolic, mythic discourse is structured. Seeing one reality, one thinks of another. Thus, for example, in speaking of Eve, the mother of all the living, one thinks at once of Mary, the Mother of all those living the inauguration of the divine re-creation. One hears of the rainbow, the burning bush, Yahweh's tent in the desert, the Ark of the Covenant, the temple of God, Elijah's cloud, Deborah, or Judith—and one is immediately transported to Mary, who fulfilled these type-realities to a supereminent degree.

This is the context, then, these the archaeological depths of the unconscious mind that constitute the matrix of all the archetypes, and first and foremost those that are linked to the mother and the fertile earth. The Advent liturgy sings, "May the earth blossom, and the heavens open to shower the dew of our salvation!" An ancient hymn prayed: "Mary, Thou blessed Earth, Thou pure, Thou beautiful, Thou beloved! Chosen wert Thou by the Eternal to bear the divine Seed in Thy womb!" So many representations place Mary in a garden of blossoms and roses. A garden is an archetypal symbol of a woman's body, and so it becomes the symbol of Mary, who engenders new life in a paradise (literally, garden) from which no one will be expelled because all that it contains will ever maintain its purity and innocence.

Countless titles proclaim the glory of Mary. All that is great, beautiful, gentle, good, and sublime, all of the marvels the mind can imagine, has all been attributed to Mary. This process took a particularly free and spontaneous quantum leap in the fourth century with the great Syrian poet Saint Ephrem (d. 373). But even earlier, in the celebrated Anaphora of Saint Hippolytus (ca. 218), Mary was venerated as Mother and Virgin, and the familiar antiphon "*Sub Tuum Praesidium*" ("To Thy Protection"), the oldest extant prayer to the Virgin Mary, appeared in a third-century Coptic papyrus, passing later into the Roman and Ambrosian liturgies. Finally, the Council of Ephesus (A.D. 431), where Mary's divine motherhood was defined as of faith, developed a whole Marian symbology, and later centuries had only to follow the same path. A now-forgotten theologian, in a sermon preached at the solemn closing of the Council of Ephesus, declaimed a prayer:

> We greet Thee, Mary, Mother of God,
> venerable Treasure of all the world,
> Light unquenchable . . .
> indestructible Temple who hold the Uncontainable,
> Mother and Virgin!
> Through Thee the Holy Trinity is glorified,
> through Thee the Holy Cross is venerated in all the world,
> through Thee holy Baptism reaches all believers,
> through Thee oil gives joy,
> through Thee churches are founded in every place,
> through Thee peoples are led to conversion![1]

Just as we have had to construct a more adequate category of the feminine, through recourse to the analyses of psychology and the reflection of philosophy, before we could employ it in our theological meditation on the Marian truths, so now we must construct a more scientific category of myth. Here too, then, we must take certain analytical and philosophical steps before applying this category to Marian theology.

MYTH IS TIMELESS

In the years following the Second World War, myth came in for a great deal of discussion, especially in biblical exegesis, theology, and the social sciences.[2] The discussion has scarcely lost its timeliness. It never will, for myth is not something from the past to be demythologized. Myth is an ever-present reality. Our mythologizing faculty, our ability to produce new myths—advertising myths, science fiction novels and films (Bionic Man, Bionic Woman), a good deal of our literature, the comics (Superman, Wonder Woman), animated cartoons, even the scientific myths of theoretical physics and sociology—is inexhaustible.

Mircea Eliade, the great scholar of myth, wrote, in 1952:

Today we are prepared to understand something the nineteenth century would never even have suspected: that symbol, myth, and image belong to the very substance of the spiritual life—that they can be camouflaged, mutilated, and degraded, but never destroyed. . . . Myths can be degraded and symbols secularized, but they never disappear, not even in that most positive of civilizations, the nineteenth century in the West. Symbol and myth come from too far away. They are part and parcel of human existence, and it is impossible for them to be absent from any existential situation of man in the cosmos.[3]

Our age, then, has done nothing more than switch myths, and thus continues to do justice to a dimension of knowing without which we should be incapable of arriving at any human or transcendent meaning.

Theological tradition, from biblical times, has maintained a twofold tendency. On the one hand, there is the demythologizing force, manifested in the Yahwist, the prophets, a Duns Scotus, an Ockham, and modern theologians. On the other hand, there is a creative tendency, which coins new symbols and myths calculated to translate the meaning of faith for a new cultural context. Even in our day, so radical in its critique of the spatial myth of theology—the transcendent versus the immanent, heaven versus earth, above and below, ascension and assumption, descent and incarnation, and so on—we accept other, no less mythological, categories, like depth, interiority, and presence (*Tiefe und Grund*).

THE RECOVERY OF MYTH

Myth, which the last century with its naive rationalism sought to eliminate, is gaining more respect by the day, as its value and inner meaning gradually come to light. Myth, we are beginning to see, is primitive not merely in some chronological sense, but in the sense that it plunges into the deepest layers of human cognition, whether in language, in society, or in the psyche. René Laurentin's analysis concludes that there is a confrontation today of two tendencies, the one "restorative," the other "reductive."[4]

The *restorative hermeneutic* of myth, explains Laurentin, states that, delivered from its etiological function (its function as an explanation of the origin of the world and humanity), myth evokes something more than itself. It roots the meaning of existence in a transcendent meaning—life and death, God, and so on. Myth is the testimonial language of transcendence, and as such it is irreplaceable. Levis-Brühl, Mircea Eliade, Carl Jung, and Paul Ricoeur are the best-known representatives of this hermeneutic.

The correlative tendency is the *reductive hermeneutic* of myth, as represented by the nineteenth-century positivists, as well as by the positivism of our own day, especially in linguistics. For these writers, myth is irretrievable, and an indication of a primitive mentality from whose deceit and illusions we must free ourselves. Twentieth-century structuralism, for all the enormous value it has placed on myth and primitive thought, has understood them reductively. The structuralist ideal is to extend the challenges of nineteenth-century scientism and develop the most objective science of person and society that it can, a science delivered from all subjectivity. Structuralism seeks to reduce all reality to basic, structural elements that give rise to its visible structures. Jacobsen applies these ideas to language, Lévi-Strauss to ethnology, Lacan to psychology, Althusser to Marxist sociology, and Michel Foucault to philosophy.

According to this line of thinking, merely because something occurs on a visible, conscious level, it does not thereby cease to be the extrojection of underlying, invisible structures that explain, interconnect, and organize the real. There is actually no such thing as freedom, and it is utterly illusory to regard the individual as self-made. The individual is only the product of latent structures. The same is true of God, the soul, eternal life, and so on. "Man," says Foucault, "is an invention, whose archaeology happily proves our thinking."[5]

Following its proclamation of the death of God, structuralism announced the approaching demise of the human being. On the last page of his *Tristes tropiques,* Claude Lévi-Strauss states that, as the world preexisted and witnessed humanity's birth, though that humanity should rise up to destroy the world's structures, the world will still be here to witness humanity's death.[6] This reductionist understanding of myth has had a profound effect on theology. Theology, contrary to Bultmann's intent, no longer deals with restoring the hidden meaning of myth. It is completely absorbed with salvaging the very possibility of faith, rescuing some meaning for human freedom and the existence of God. Theology is far too busy fighting for its life to have time for much besides. Theology has accepted the restorative hermeneutic of myth, but it has never been able to accept the reductionist, as formulated by structuralism. Structuralism can be useful as a valid method of exegesis and theological discourse, but never as a comprehensive philosophy defining the ultimate realities of the world, the human being, and God.

Myth as an Approach to Reality

Underlying both of these tendencies is a particular acceptation of myth. What is myth? For Bultmann, myth is "a manner of representation under which what is not of this world appears as if it were. For example, the transcendence of God is represented as spatial distance."[7] For Lévi-Strauss, myth is a "matrix of meaning."[8] Myth can be understood positively and negatively. Laurentin renounces the possibility of its definition and contents himself with description: "Mythic thought, as opposed to rational thought, is characterized by vital, dynamic representations, charged with images, actions, and thoughts by which man becomes conscious of his relationship with the world and his destiny."[9]

Myth is neither *a priori* nor *a posteriori.* According to the great French anthropologist Gilbert Durand, myth is the fruit of

the incessant change that exists on the level of the imaginary between subjective and assimilative impulses and the objective intimidations of the worlds of the cosmic and the social. Myth has two sources, then: one internal, and the other external. In other words, man is endowed with certain matrices, archetypes, or symbolic representations, which assimilate meanings stemming from external reality and thereupon generate historical and concrete myths and symbols.[10]

For our part, we doubt that the question of myth can be posited in terms of the *logos,* or rationality. Here myth will always appear as a deficient, primitive form of cognition. But the basis of myth is a good deal broader than this. Myth constitutes a different, nonrational way of thinking. It is another approach to reality, a specifically different way of totalizing human experiences. There is an approach to reality by way of *logos,* and the tool of this approach is the concept, which attempts to capture the essence of objects by means of a process of abstraction from the concrete. Then there is another approach to reality, by way of *pathos,* whose tool is image and symbol. In the latter modality, the human being approaches reality with the feeling of a vital insertion into that reality. He or she understands in an interior, visceral way, through an emotional sympathy. The operation of *pathos* places the operating subject entirely in the presence of living reality. Here the knower is not distant, performs no abstraction, defines nothing, but is in-serted into ("sown within"), is con-scious of, "co-lives" the reality investigated. This cognition is the "loving knowledge" of which the mystics, like Saint John of the Cross, speak. This knowledge is love in the meaning the word has in John's Gospel. After all, love implies an approach that takes a headlong plunge into the very reality before it, and dives deep enough to *know* that reality.

For our ancestors, who had a better experience of this way of being and understanding than have we, this meant an interpersonal act, grounded in a loving surrender to realities hitherto unknown, realities distant and beyond their reach. And this was valid not only for the interpersonal sphere in the strict sense, but for the realm of the things of nature as well. Myth, then, emerges from an atmosphere of loving symbiosis, where breach and division are absent, an atmosphere of what *logos* will call that of opposites, of subject-and-object. In this modality, cognition is not domination of the world, a way of being "on top of" the world, but rather a form of being more profoundly "with" the world, a way of living an open, accepting communion with the whole of reality. The vehicles of this cognition are images and symbols, which, in order to perform their vehicular function, must be open to a polysemy—a potential multiplicity of meaning, including the rationally contradictory. Myth is precisely an organization and network of a variety of images and symbols that weave a fabric of meaning.

At the root of myth is a praxis, a way of being within the world that expresses itself in a corresponding way of feeling and approaching reality, including the Supreme Reality that wraps all things around, God.

This way of being is still very much a part of human life. Generally speaking, it is the realm of the lived, in French the *vecu*, life within daily reality and primary relationships among persons.

The realm of myth and the *vecu* is especially evident in children. Children live altogether within a mythical universe. A child will leap to her feet, strike her head on a corner of the table, and begin to weep. She feels wounded, attacked by the table, and now will angrily strike the table in her own turn and call it, "Bad table!" The tears will flow until the child finds her mother, who will grasp the situation at once, strike the table herself, call it "bad" and "stupid" for injuring her child—and at last the child will grow calm, for now the mother, too, has awarded the table its just deserts.

We are dealing with the mythical process. Things are animated, alive. They live in human space. Speech itself is peopled with living beings rather than with concepts, for it is controlled by *pathos* rather than by *logos*. Nor is it only children who create myths because they have not yet tamed the conceptual, logical tools with which human nature is endowed. Adults, too, create myths, in their way of living reality, in their emotions, their feelings, their judgments. Poetry, art, all creativity is but a systematic articulation of the mythic mentality. The poet, the singer, the artist speak with the sea, exhort it, berate it, altogether as earnestly and realistically as a mother negotiating with the wolf who has made off with her children and pleading with him to return their bodies. The sea becomes a living being, and a dweller of the rain forest, on beholding the sea for the first time, will approach it only with the greatest reverence, a kind of curiosity mingled with respect, touch it, and exclaim, "It is like a great beast!" And, of course, we have the anecdote of the man from

Aragon who, upon seeing the ocean for the first time in his life on a wild, stormy day, solemnly cautioned it, "Just wait till you're married—you'll calm down a bit!"

We had rather express the whole, profound universe of human life, the dimension of love, friendship, relationship, the ultimate meaning of life and death—all the dimensions that affect us existentially—in terms of the symbolic and the mythic, than in dry, analytical, rationalistic terms of the concept.

Experiences and concepts bound up in some way with our parents, which constitute primary, structuring realities of human life, are often expressed in symbolic and mythic complexes.

Now we begin to perceive the importance of a consideration of myth and symbol for the subject of this book. Mary can be presented as the living experience of the living faith of believers, in the universe of myth and symbol rather than in that of logic and concept. The notion of Mary the Virgin, the Mother of God, the Bride of the Spirit, and so on, has emerged in a magnificent Marian mythology, and now our Lady lives in the deepest heart of a humanness that finds expression only in the symbol—in the images that surge and tumble in the unconscious, archaeological layers of our psyche.

14. Mary in the Language of Myth

We should surely do very well to begin our reflection on Mary in the language of mythology with an inventory of the catalog of Marian symbols assembled by René Laurentin from Marracci's edition of *Polyanthea Mariana* (1683).[1] Here we have all the titles of the Blessed Virgin that faith has been able to imagine. We may range them in five classifications.

1. The four elements of archetypal importance to the human psyche, as Gaston Bachelard has shown in his various writings (*Psychanalyse du feu, La terre et ses rêveries,* and so on)—earth, air, fire, and water—with the entire gamut of their combined symbols, are the symbols most often applied to Mary.

2. Sacred objects, especially those of our Judeo-Christian tradition: the Tabernacle, or tent, of the Covenant, the Ark of the Covenant, the Temple, and the altar. Mary is regarded as the definitive realization of these types. Symbols of dwelling—temple, tabernacle, ark—predominate, and appear in Luke 1–2 and Revelation 12.

3. Symbols of animals and plants: from dove to elephant! Flowers, however, predominate: lily, rose, night-blooming jasmine, and so on.

4. Feminine and maternal symbols: These two great realizations of woman are regarded as being made concrete in Mary. First, Mary is the intact virgin, sublime, immune to the pitfalls of human weakness, and free from all of the sin and other defects of the world. The motherhood theme, however, is the one most exploited in Marian poetry: *mulier, femina, mater, genitrix.* The underlying archetype is that of woman charged with vitality and life, connatural with all that is life, echo of the cosmos, whose calling it is to en-

gender, protect, nourish, and prefer. The theme of the Virgin Mother spreading her protective mantle over her children has pierced the human psyche, to emerge in the encounter with the experience of helplessness and the search for refuge, so absent from human life.

The motherhood symbols are closely tied to those of the earth (*Magna Mater*) and water, the life principle par excellence.[2]

5. The biblical woman, seen as types of Mary: Frequently cited are the Sulamite woman, Judith, Rebecca, and Eve, among others.

PAGAN MYTHOLOGY AND MARY: COMPARATIVE HISTORY OF RELIGIONS

These magnificent titles, applying all of the numinous attributes of the feminine to Mary, all come very near those of pagan, especially Greek, mythology. There we find a whole colorful gallery of goddesses, under countless titles. Christianity, which took root in a Hellenic culture, was naturally influenced by the mythology of that culture. When the pagan devotees of the goddesses and virgins were converted, they simply substituted Mary for the goddess known by such and such a title, often retaining the corresponding ritual forms and even the statue of the goddess or virgin in question, with just a change of name. Thus, for example, we know that in the fifth century a sanctuary dedicated to Artemis (Diana) in Ephesus (known to Paul—Acts 19:23–40) was simply rededicated to Mary. The famous cathedral at Chartres, dedicated to the Virgin Mother and a favorite place of pilgrimage to this day, was constructed on the site of the Celtic temple of the *Virgo Paritura,* the Pregnant Virgin who had been honored by so many pilgrimages in bygone, pagan times. In Rome, the church of Santa Maria Antiqua was erected on the site of the temple of *Vesta Mater,* while that of Santa Maria del Capitolio stands on a site that once was Juno's. On the Athenian acropolis, the church of the *Theotokos* has replaced the ancient temple of Pallas Athena.

The devotion to the Madonna of the Pomegranate, in Paestum

in the Italian province of Campagna, totally absorbed the ancient veneration of the goddess Hera Argiva, who was probably transported to Paestum by the argonauts (hence the surname Argiva) and was represented as seated on a throne, holding a child on her left arm and the fertility symbol in her right. Hera was always represented with the sweet face of a generous, fertile mother, without any sign of sexual exuberance, earthly love, or lust. She was the symbol of the *hieros gamos,* the "sacred nuptials" of a supraterrestrial love and fertility. At Samos, where Hera was particularly revered, a rite was celebrated in which a liturgy of her mythical wedding with the god of the sky was followed by the immersion of her statue in a sacred pool. This immersion was regarded as effectuating the restoration of Hera's virginity, so that the goddess was virgin, bride, mother, and virgin all over again, all in the course of the same sacred year.[3]

The statue we see today of Our Lady of the Pomegranate reflects her total identification with the ancient Hera Argiva, down to the least details, including the symbols of the mysterious melodrama of virginity and fertility. Here, then, is substitution pure and simple. Nor is it difficult to understand why this should be. Pagan converts, who had been accustomed to worshiping Hera so purely, and only in her positive attributes, came to see her, along with all of the other true and holy things in their past, as a preparation, prophecy, and anticipation of the truth now communicated to them in Christianity. In Hera, then, they saw the prefiguration of a Virgin and Mother they had not known, one who had actually given them their Savior. The pagan goddess had been the mythical symbol of the true reality of Mary. We must not forget, it was not Christians who became Romans, but Romans with their Roman culture who became Christians, and brought to their new faith all of the richness of their old devotion.

On the other hand, we have to admit the validity of the scholarly conclusions of K. Prümm and Jean Daniélou regarding the encounter between Greek mythology and the Christian faith:

1. The fathers of the Church were extremely mistrustful of the cult of the mother goddesses. Their hostility is one of

the reasons why devotion to Mary was so long in developing, longer than the cult of the martyrs and even the confessors.

2. Many of the church fathers denounced the contamination of Mary's cult with that of the actual worship of pagan goddesses, especially among Montanists and "Coliridians," Phrygians known as worshipers of Cybele. "Others," wrote Epiphanius, "in their madness, wishing to exalt the Virgin, have set her in the place of God!"[4]

3. There is a remarkable difference between mythology and what we say about our Lady. Mythology exalts the symbolic, the fascinating, and the archetype. It organizes the dimension of the oneiric, the spontaneous-imaginary. Cybele never existed. Hera was not a poor woman of the people, anonymous and simple, invited by God to share in the work of redemption. Pagan cults celebrated virgins who became mothers through sexual relations with a god, so that a true physical insemination was involved. With Mary, faith professes the complete absence of the male element: instead, a divine "virtue," or *dynamis,* the Holy Spirit, acted within her, assuming her and making her the living, substantial temple of God, and she discovered that she was with child. The content of the gospel accounts is inescapably historical.

At the same time, while it is surely important to keep in mind all of these differences between Mary and the myths, we can scarcely miss the equally striking fact that Mary, with the wonders wrought in her by God, has meant a great and mighty call to the forces of the collective unconscious. The unconscious is not empty. It is charged with archetypes, reactions, preserved in the depths of the psyche, to the positive or negative experiences that humanity has had with a father, a mother, authority, the sun, the moon, and so on—that is, to the fundamental and central realities of existence. These archetypes are stirred to conscious expression by any encounter with historical realities that correspond to their meaning. Mary, because of her historical content, awakens nearly all of the luminous archetypes of the feminine that lie hidden within our interior archaeology.

MARY AND THE RESTORATIVE FORCE OF MYTH: EXEGESIS

Certain studies in the comparative history of religions attempt to see Mariology as the reproduction of a distinct, yet homologous, version of the myths we know from paganism. According to this school, since myth is simply a primitive fable, Mariology has no real salvific meaning. This is far from the thought of a Rudolf Bultmann, who assigned a positive value to myths, regarding them as vehicles of a transcendent meaning and instruments of God's word.[5] Bultmann introduced demythologization not to eliminate myth, but to capture the *logos* present in myth. In other words, he sought to extract the transcendent meaning embedded in mythic discourse. The content is not mythical. The mythical element is only the means by which the transcendent content is communicated. Bultmann intended only to substitute a rational, critical discourse for the mythical, primitive discourse, with all due respect for content.

Important as this question may be in general terms, we must recognize its scope and its limitations. Surely we cannot erect myth into reality. But neither can we reduce reality to myth. In the case before us, Bultmann's judgment is that the myth of Mary's virginal conception has no historical basis as such. It is mythic discourse pure and simple, calculated to transmit the following content: Jesus of Nazareth's transcendence of history and nature is such that he cannot be understood in human terms alone; he has a divine dimension as well.

According to Bultmann, this myth is no older than Hellenism.[6] The earliest Christian theology did not yet know Jesus as God, and so would have seen no point in highlighting his transcendence by proclaiming his divine birth. The myth of Jesus' birth is the product of a Greek mind, filled with a mythology of virgin-mother goddesses.

Indeed, what we have here is a unique mixture of history and myth. The New Testament proclaims the Jesus of history ("Do we not know his father and mother?"—John 6:42) to be at the same time the preexistent Son of God. History and myth are interwoven here. This creates a series of difficulties, and certain inconsistencies in the New Testament material. It is not easy to reconcile the doctrine of Christ's preexistence as handed down by Paul and John with the legend of the virgin birth as narrated in Matthew and Luke.[7]

This is why the statements of the *protoevangelium* find no echo in the rest of the New Testament, Bultmann explains. They are simply forgotten, and the reason is that we are dealing with a language intended to explain what faith held concerning Jesus as a being who came from God to be the Savior. But today a concept of Jesus' virgin birth is no longer of any help for our understanding of the basis of our faith or for our own faith decisions.[8] This is a language difficult for our contemporaries to comprehend, says Bultmann, and yet our contemporaries need to be led to faith in Jesus as their Savior. Therefore we need another language, one more adapted to our ways of understanding.

Bultmann's interest is pastoral. It is the content of the myth that we must proclaim, he insists, and the content is not mythological. Jesus is God-with-us, God who visits humanity in a salvific manner.

It seems to us, however, that Bultmann presents as myth something that the communities of Luke and Matthew, as well as the uninterrupted tradition of faith, have regarded as *magnalia Dei*—events *to be* explained, as the *explicandum*, rather than precisely an *explicatum*, something already explained in the mythology of the age.

MARY AND THE ARCHETYPES: DEPTH PSYCHOLOGY

More than the history of religions, more than the exegesis of demythologization, it is depth psychology or psychoanalytic theory that has taken the most interest in Mariology. In Mary these schools have seen a figure articulating the mighty motifs of humanity's psychic archaeology. Before embarking on our investigation of the mythological and historical representations of the feminine, with their potential reference to Mary, we should surely do well to look into the question of the *matriarchy*.[9] After all, this is the principal source of analytical material for a psychology of the feminine.

The Matriarchy: Primacy of Woman

By *matriarchy*, we mean that social institution in which the identity, name, and properties of a group are handed down via the maternal line, and in which women occupy the positions of authority in society, family, and religion. We are referring to a genuine gynocracy—the term coined by J. J. Bachofen (1861–1948), systematizer of the question and creator of the still hotly debated theory of the matriarchy. Some scholars regard Bachofen's theory as demonstrably without foundation, and refuse to consider the existence of a "matriarchal age."[10] Others consider the same theory irrefutable—not so much on the basis of any archaeological or iconographical evidence, but because of the evident symbolic existence of the matriarchal in the unconscious, as revealed in dreams, myths, and ancient representations.

Living peoples with matriarchal characteristics include the Iroquois and Huron Indians of the eastern United States, the Hopi and Zuni in the Southwest of the same country, the Nayar and Khasi of India, the Micronesians on the island of Palau, the Miang-Kabau of Sumatra, the Tuareg people of the Sahara, the Brazilian Bororos, the Chibcha of Colombia, and the Txhambuli of New Guinea. There are peoples today, then, who bear witness to the persistence of the matriarchal era that very likely preceded the patriarchal age of Mediterranean culture.

Following are the characteristics of a matriarchal regime. The wife is head of the family. Marriage is uxorilocal (the groom moves in with the bride). Bloodlines are traced through the mother and her female ancestors. Inheritance, along with any title, precedence, privilege, or social role, likewise follows the matriarchal line. The husband is all but a stranger to his children, a maternal uncle having more authority over them than does their father, although he is regarded with respect precisely as father. The wife's word is law in economic, political, and juridical matters, as well as those of war and peace. Polyandry prevails (the wife may have more than one husband at a time). Religious life, characterized by the worship of female divinities, is in the hands of priestesses. Mathilde and Matthias Vaerting, who studied the matriarchal elements in the culture of the Cantabrians, Iroquois, Lycians, and Kamchadales, as well as in those phases of the Egyptian, Spartan, and Libyan civilizations that are marked by matriarchal characteristics, have concluded that many of the psychosexual traits today regarded as feminine—a passive role in courtship, obedience, submissiveness, timidity, sexual modesty and reserve, a special attachment to the home, tenderness with children, and a fondness for jewelry, for example— were characteristic of the males in a matriarchal society; and, indeed, these features have been verified, according to studies by Margaret Mead, in the males of certain New Guinean cultures.[11]

The matriarchal era must have arisen toward the beginning of the Neolithic age (8000 B.C.), when human beings ceased to be hunters and nomads, became sedentary, and began to cultivate the earth. Women, gathering the fruits of the earth while their males did the hunting, began to observe nature and its cycles. They learned to raise fruits and vegetables, and gradually brought the arable land under their control. But agriculture means stability, and so economic, juridical, and psychological relationships were altered. In the process, women assumed the leadership of the tribe.[12] Lafitau writes of the Hurons:

Nothing is more evident than the primacy of woman. The entire nation is actually founded on woman. Nobility of blood, genealogical succession, the preservation of the family, and so on, all depend on woman. All true authority is vested in her. Hers are the city, the fields, and all the farms. Woman is the soul of the council meetings, she is arbiter in matters of war and peace. Hers is the key to the public treasury. Women arrange the marriages, rule the children, and bequeath the scepter of authority to their female descendants. Men, by contrast, are simply isolated and ignored. They are strangers to their own children.[13]

It is scarcely surprising, in these circumstances, that men would organize secret societies (brotherhoods) to try to salvage some minimal identity, and this, Lafitau explains, they did.

As a result of the predominance of woman, matriarchal society generated an ideology according to which the ultimate goal of every human being was to become a woman. This is particularly clear in the East Indian belief of the Shiva-Shatchi, who honored the goddess Tripurasundari. The evidence, again, tends to confirm that men were completely under women's domination.

The most characteristic symbol of the matriarchal era is the moon, Selene. She was regarded as the mother of all living things, and presented herself under all the manifold forms of femininity, such as virgin, mother, wife, companion, protector—or, in her more sinister conception, as witch, sorceress, seductress, devourer, enchantress, and so on. Earth is the source of life, and so the cultivation of the soil—along with water, generation, birth, and so on, with their unmistakable ties to the mysteries of the life of woman—was the last great world revolution, reaching all the corners of the earth and enduring almost unchanged until the appearance of rudimentary technology in the fifteenth century B.C. If agriculture is associated with woman, then it would be self-evident that her influence on humanity—together with her own internal and external history—would have been determining factors in humanity's self-understanding.

The sociological debate rages on as to whether a matriarchal age preceded the patriarchy historically. In the realm of psychology, however, its reality is beyond question, as the entire Jungian school testifies. Erich Fromm has written:

> It may be that Bachofen's theories on the matriarchy will not hold up. But he has certainly discovered a form of social organization, and a psychological structure, that have not received the attention they deserve at the hands of psychologists and anthropologists. The reason, of course, is that for people with a patriarchal mentality the notion of a society managed by women instead of men is simply ridiculous.... Thus for example Freud reduced the mother to a mere object of sexual pleasure. Her divine figure was transformed into a harlot, while the father was elevated to the position of central figure in the universe.[14]

The Feminine Archetype in History

The importance of the feminine is best documented by the research done in the psychology of the complexes—analytical psychology, inaugurated by Carl Jung and continued by his followers, especially Erich Neumann. Psychology attempts to arrive at human origins not just through a study of the historical remnants left to us by culture, but also, and principally, through a study of the remnants deposited in the human psyche by humanity's collective unconscious, and coming down to us in the unconscious psychic component of every individual. In the next paragraphs we shall follow Neumann's classic *Die grosse Mutter: Der Archetyp des grossen Weibliche.*[15]

The Feminine in the Psychology of Freud

We know that the sexual psychology of Sigmund Freud fails to go beyond a *phallocentrism* in which a phallic sexual monism is believed to dominate in both sexes. Before the age of two, Freud states, the only sexual organ children recognize in either sex is the phallus—the penis or the clitoris. Very young children, both male and female, know nothing of the vagina. But neither do they differentiate the penis and the clitoris, thus altogether failing to distinguish the sexes on the basis of genitalia. Only by the age of four have boys and girls finally discovered that they are different with respect to genitalia. The girl, seeing that she seems to be missing something, concludes that she has been castrated. The boy, seeing the same thing, fears castration. This continues until puberty, when both sexes finally become aware of the proper functions of the penis and vagina. Thus, Freud reduces sexuality to male sexuality. Other schools represented by Josine Müller, Karen Horney, Melanie Klein, and E. Jones, recognize two distinct sexualities, a male and a female, each with its own process of experiencing and integrating reality.[16]

At the same time, one of the cornerstones of Freudian psychology is the father figure and the Oedipus complex. Orthodox psychoanalysis is a father-centered psychology. By the Oedipus complex we mean the "group of largely unconscious ideas and feelings centring round the wish to possess the parent of the opposite sex"—the boy wishing to possess his mother, the girl her father—"and eliminate that of the same sex."[17] The Oedipus complex is formed between the ages of three and five, with the development of the libido and the ego. For Freud, this complex must be phylogenetic—genetically determined and universally human—as it is not merely a phenomenon occurring in certain individuals, but is the common property of all humanity. When the primitive horde wished to eliminate their fathers, they did just that, and of course this delivered them from their material superego, but a guilt feeling now entered the picture. In order to exorcise this guilt feeling, held Freud, the clan restored the father to life symbolically by erecting a totem, the particular animal symbol of the clan. Now guilt feelings were repressed and the superego perpetuated. For Freud, the juridical order, the power of the group, the state, even religion, have arisen in reaction to the Oedipus complex.

The Oedipus complex is transcended in both sexes through an identification with the parent of the opposite sex, who is rediscovered in the adult sexual object. Freud sensed the problem here and confronted it honestly. He stated, "What we cannot show is the place in this evolution belonging to the great maternal deities that have perhaps everywhere preceded the father-gods."[18]

The importance of the father for the development of the ego cannot be denied. What is questionable is whether the father holds as radical and structuring an importance as Freud believed he did. Today almost all analytical literature inclines toward a more primordial datum, in the form of a pre-oedipal stage centering on the child's relationship with his or her mother. This stage is all the more basic if it is actually initiated during gestation. Bonds with the father arise only after birth. Every human being has two parents, and confronts them both, in successive, dialectical phases, with the success or failure of the confrontations determining whether the development of the ego proceeds or is frustrated.

The Feminine in Jungian Psychology

We believe that Jung's approach to the fundamental problem of the maternal complex is much more adequate than Freud's. Jung's understanding of the structure of the human psyche is profoundly nuanced. For Jung, the basic question is neither that of the integration of sexuality nor that of the libido and the Oedipus complex. These problems surely exist, but only within a broader and more comprehensive framework.

The major problem—the foundation and axis of the Jungian understanding of the psychic structure—is that of the development of consciousness or self-awareness (*Bewusstwerdung*)—the relation maintained by the ego with conscious and unconscious life. The *Bewusstwerdung* is not a process of developing awareness on the level of the conscious—a development of the light of reason and its establishment as the controlling, dominating psychic force. The *Bewusstwerdung*, or development of consciousness, rather is a process of the reinforcement of the ego as it relates to both the conscious and unconscious dimensions of human life—an assimilation of the energies of both the exterior and the interior in the construction of a gradually fuller, denser, and richer process of individuation. Complexes arise in the course of this difficult process of construction and reinforcement—and centering on the father or on the mother, to be sure, but centering on them not only as physical figures, but as functions and archetypes as well. The ego emerges to freedom from the dark, mysterious world of the unconscious, where it has lived in recollection and latency, in a duality analogous to that of child and mother in the maternal womb. The unconscious is like the mother, whose womb wraps the ego all around. The whole womb tends to give birth to, bring to light, an element that has hitherto lain concealed. Consciousness, then, arises through differentiation, distinction, and breach with the unconscious. The maternal principle is the hotbed of the process of *Bewusstwerdung*. To disengage oneself, to be freed, to be born, to be differentiated, to become aware, to formulate ideals, to emerge toward *logos*—all of this constitutes the paternal principle.

There is a kind of struggle, and a desperate one, between the unconscious (the maternal principle) to retain the ego, and the conscious (the paternal principle) to liberate it. Or viewed from the other side: faced with the difficulties of the outside world (the "father" principle), fragile consciousness tries to escape, to poke its head under the covers, to hide, to submerge toward the matrix of the unconscious (the "mother" principle). Whereupon the unconscious itself, driven by a spontaneous conpensatory impulse, thrusts fragile, teetering consciousness up and away toward liberation.

The myths represent this desperate drama of the psyche or ego in light of a zeal on the part of the myths precisely for the difficult integration of the conscious world with their own respective meanings. It is a matter mainly of the battle between the mythological figures of the hero (consciousness, the "father") and the dragon or monster (the unconscious, the "mother"). The hero strives manfully, is devoured by the dragon or the whale, and then is reborn. Each and every human life repeats the same agonizing cycle. The ego, submerged in its unconscious origins in its "mother," rises to new life and light in the "father," in a process of life and death. But "the fascination of the unconscious is too great for the heroic actions to endure for long. Thus the hero's struggle must be continually renewed, in the form of a symbolic liberation from the mother."[19]

In this wise, through perilous immersions in the belly of the monster (the unconscious, the "mother") and emergence each time into the broad daylight of consciousness (the "father"), the human psyche is developed. And so, in this representation of the psychic forces, the depths of the unconscious are peopled by feminine archetypes and figures, in all of their positive and negative variations, as mother, bride, virgin, companion, lover, and so on. This is what Jung designated by the name of anima in all human beings, male and female alike. There is no one who need not confront the feminine within, accept it, and integrate it. This is part and parcel of the process of building one's personality.[20]

Our brief consideration of some of the main building blocks of Jungian psychology will afford us an understanding and appreciation of the various manifestations of the feminine in history, which in Christian space have been transferred to Mary and used as a tool in the deciphering and communication of the *magnalia Dei* historically wrought by God in Mary. Our grasp of Jung's schema will be improved if we keep in mind an element that facilitates an understanding of the variations of the feminine figure throughout conscious and unconscious history: namely, the fact that the unconscious is always experienced in two distinct ways. However consistently that experience may be represented through the symbol of the maternal womb from which the ego is born, the unconscious presents itself differently in males and females. Man projects the experience of his unconscious upon woman. Woman projects her unconscious upon man. In Jung's terminology, woman experiences the animus that she carries within her—the image of the male—as concretized in man. Man for his part experiences the anima—the image of woman that he bears within his unconscious—as concretized in woman. The unconscious is always experienced as threatening, as it can swallow up the fragile "I" that has freed itself from this same unconscious. It is understandable, then, that the "I" would feel led to suppress the unconscious, and to reassert reason and *logos*. In a society like ours, then—patriarchal, male chauvinist, conducted by males—woman will be trampled underfoot and exorcised, because to the male she represents, she incarnates, his unconscious. In suppressing the unconscious, men repress women. Men are afraid of their own unconscious.

Interestingly enough, the times of the great witch-hunts—times of especial repression of the unconscious—were also the moments of a special flowering of devotion to Mary. The unconscious has a compensatory mechanism. When it represses, it also sublimates. The history of our psychic archaeology demonstrates, as Jung so convincingly argued in his *Psychologie und Alchemie,* the age-old association of woman with the devil, sin, and earth. In other words, the threatening unconscious—the sinner, the devil—is linked to woman or the earth, which for man represents the unconscious.

In the process of humanity's *Bewusstwerdung,* or emergence of consciousness, a matriarchal phase is necessary, then, in which the unconscious predominates, maintaining the conscious, the ego, well protected in the womb. This is the phase represented by the *uroboros,* the serpent of the primitive myths who devours its young. The *uroboros* is the symbol of the symbiosis and primitive unity of the conscious and unconscious parts of the psyche. The matriarchal phase, in which the offspring is still in the womb as part of the "mother's" own reality, makes historical this mythic reality. In a second phase, the *uroboros* no longer eats away at its young. Now it lifts its head from the earth. This is the patriarchal phase, characterized by consciousness, the ego, ideas, and autonomy. This phase, as well, is necessary for the development of the human psyche, on a phylogenetic level as on an ontogenic one (that of the development of each individual). In order for the conscious to assert itself in this phase, it must trample the unconscious to earth. Later this repression will have to be overcome. The obscure, mysterious past will have to be integrated. Patriarchy will have to assimilate matriarchy. Men will have to integrate the feminine they bear within themselves. In today's culture, we are assisting at the shaping of a new constellation of the human psyche, one taking place through the establishment of a new type of male-female relationship that transcends the matriarchal-patriarchal framework.[21]

With these points clarified, we may present some of the basic characteristics of the feminine as it presents itself in dreams, in people afflicted with mental illness, in ancient and modern art—in all of the symbolism of the feminine, wherever we may find it. This area has been researched in great detail by Erich Neumann in the work mentioned earlier (*Die grosse Mutter,* The Great Mother), and we shall follow his lead in our considerations.

Feminine archetypes, like all others, are ambivalent. They preserve both the positive and the negative experiences that people have had throughout their psychic history. We must remember that, for Jung, an archetype is a potentiality, a predisposition, a psychic category established throughout the long process of the human *Bewusstwerdung.* It has no content of its own, no meaning. It is the mold, the condition for the materialization of meanings, which are historical and linked to culture (but which always take shape in the mold of the archetypes).

The basic feminine archetype, then, is experienced as material protection and as strangulation, as mortal aggression and as strength and support. The first pair is eminently feminine. The second is composed of masculine elements within the feminine. The feminine can be the mother who embraces and protects, or the mother or woman who strangles. The feminine can be aggressive and attacking, or inspiring, sustaining, and so on. For example, in the mythologies, the bountiful mother is Sophia, Wisdom, while the terrible, fearsome mother is the Gorgon who throttles her own children. The great, all-engendering mother is Isis—the androgynous goddess who procreates the whole universe alone, representing as she does, in her sole person, both the masculine and the feminine originating principles.[22]

The "I" experiences two further traits in the feminine. The first of these is elementary, the other mutational. The *elementary character* is the basic trait of the feminine: the need to preserve, to protect. Everything emerging from the feminine belongs to her, depends on her, all preserved under the tutelage of the mother. Thus all autonomy is relativized. This is the typical trait of the mother: to preserve, to nourish, to protect, to cherish, to warm, to caress—or just the contrary: to reject, to choke, to stifle.

The *mutational character* (*Wandlungscharakter*) of the feminine is its drive to alter and to be altered, to change and to be changed. It arises when the feminine encounters a Thou. Then the feminine bewitches, charms, and attracts. Woman is modified, and she modifies. Positively, the feminine is experienced as the inspirer. She is Dante's Beatrice, she is any of so many beloved, inspiring women who crowd the fantasy world of the artist. First and foremost the artist projects his own soul, incarnating it in a particular, concrete woman.

The elementary character of the feminine is experienced in institutions, traditions, in the Church, in anything that bestows security. The mutational character is experienced on the personal level, in relationships that produce change, in a loving history, in friendship and creativity, where there is risk, challenge, fear, and so on.

As we have had occasion to observe, the elementary and the mutational character of the feminine each has its positive and its negative side. The feminine can be the mother who engenders, who liberates, who protects and defends. Here she is the good mother: Isis, Demeter, the Madonna with the Child. Or she can be the mother who strikes, who strangles, who destroys and castrates freedom. Then she is the terrible mother: the Gorgon, Hecate, Kali. The feminine can present itself as virgin, spouse, and consort—fascinating, enchanting, inspiring, and supporting (the figures of Mary, or Wisdom); or instead as the virgin-spouse-companion who grasps, who absorbs and devours, who drives one mad: Circe, Astarte, Lilith, chthonic Venus.

To be sure, these characteristics of the feminine, both of which are to be found in men and women alike, never occur pure and unadulterated. In the concrete person, each always suffers the admixture of the other, in a lighter or darker shade of gray. Human reality is never either all bright or all somber.

It will be easier to grasp the import of these two facets of the feminine if we understand them as phases in the process of the individuation and *Bewusstwerdung*, or coming to consciousness, of the individual human being.

1. In the first dim light of self-awareness, early in gestation, a primitive unity prevails. This unity is represented by the

archetype of the *uroboros*. Here all is one, in a great *union mystique:* human being and world, I and nature, God and humanity, mother and child. All of these dualities occupy the same space and live the same life, for the time being. This is the maternal in its character of preserver of the other as her own reality. Acceptance and protection reign unchallenged.

2. Then the child is born. But he or she is still altogether dependent upon the mother—the good, great mother. The child has introduced duality, but dependency still prevails. Without the mother the child will die. Apart from her the child cannot exercise any vital functions.

3. The child grows—the beloved child at the side of the good, great mother. Now the child lives in an "incest" with its mother. She is mother now, but mine only. She belongs to none other. Though mother, still she is virgin. She belongs to no one else—only to me. "Incest" here is not sexual in the genital sense, but symbolically: the child is still so thoroughly under the mother's influence that she or he wants to return to the primitive *union mystique* the child enjoyed with the mother while still in the womb. The mother, for her part, still protects and preserves the child, but now she loves and guards the child as distinct from herself: as the genuine object of her love.

4. Last, the mythical, archetypal struggle of the hero with the great mother becomes reality. The child becomes independent. The "I" is at last strong enough to assert itself. But the price to be paid is the severing of the child's bonds with the maternal home. Only thus can the child be a self. Here we have the "I," the spirit, the masculine in its self-assertion vis-à-vis the feminine.[23]

This liberation of the conscious, the "I," the spirit, vis-à-vis the depths of the feminine and the unconscious, is a path of struggle. Grave obstacles must be overcome, for all humanity, both men and women. A battle rages between the unconscious and the conscious, with the former giving birth to the latter, yet keeping it under its influence until the moment when its protégé can assert itself in victory, stand on its own, and actualize its own historical reality. The struggle is an age-old one, and humanity bears its scars. Nor has it abated in our own day. It is understandable, then, that this experience of birth, growth, and self-affirmation should leave a negative admixture in its positive features. Shadows still loom—old war wounds, still a molestation, still trouble for men and women alike in their respective syntheses of the positive and the negative. The conscious, in both women and men, has a masculine character: it is the principle of order, self-affirmation, and self-regulation in both sexes.[24]

The key symbol of the feminine is the container, the receptacle (*Gefäss*). Here, throughout all stages of development, from the most primitive to the most advanced, is the symbol that proclaims the feminine. "The symbolic equation, feminine = body = receptable corresponds to what may well be humanity's most basic experience of the feminine. Here the feminine is experienced both in itself and by the masculine."[25] Any container or receptacle has an inside and an outside. The body with its five senses is an excellent example. The senses are experienced as numinous. They are adorned, cared for, and converted into taboos. After all, in and through them something marvelous happens: the very mystery of life. Changes are wrought through the senses. The body experiences itself as a receptacle, an interior, containing and developing the whole world of the unconscious. Passions, mood, speech, thought are all born of it. The interior of the body is archetypally assimilated as part of the unconscious—this is why it is understood as a symbol of the feminine. Everything is born of the interior of our body, engendered to the outside. Universal matter itself, the cosmos as a whole, is symbolized by the feminine, the all-producing, all-bestowing element. ("Matter," *materia*, comes originally from *mater*, "mother.") Mind is universally experienced as masculine (*nous*, "mind"), as the principle of order and organization, of separation and distinction.

All that is elemental and elementary, all that evokes nature, germination, and vitality, is experienced as feminine, by both men and women. All that is experienced and expressed as development, ordering, rationalization (in the original sense), and division is identified with the masculine, again by both men and women. The terminus of this development is the emergence of rationality as rationality. Woman in the flesh primarily represents the feminine, and therefore rationality and the masculine constitute her unconscious. Man in the flesh represents a greater concentration of the masculine. Accordingly, his unconscious is feminine. Hence, a profound, active "woman's intuition." A woman may not do her best work on the level of cold, conscious rationality, which is more a "man's way." A woman has her rationality, but it is unconscious. She need not necessarily "know" a given reality or the solution to problems to which it gives rise. She may "see" both the reality and the solution to its problems. Man, by contrast, as he moves within the parameters of rationality, may be agitated by profound, unconscious feminine passions. After all, his unconscious is feminine. The human ideal will be the integration of feminine and masculine, in a proportion proper to the sex, or psychosexual identity, of the individual in question.

The feminine will always be mysterious, deep and dark. Thus, it will always challenge our very reality. The feminine will ever be the "open question"—the Sphinx, the demand for a response. It will always contain an admixture of the luminous, the clear, the rational—something of the masculine. But none of the answers it inspires will ever decipher the unfathomable *matter* of our deepest roots, of our *mater*. The feminine is bottomless mystery, the mysterious abyss of our own reality as women and men.

Every human being is born of woman. The relations we maintain with her, from gestation onward, through all the phases of childhood, adolescence, and adulthood, mark each of us in a profound, definitive way. It is legitimate, and not a mystification of reality, to speak of an "eternal feminine" that accompanies each of us all our life long, in its positivity and negativity. To confront that dimension, to assimilate it and surrender to it, is the attainment of individuation. In the eternal feminine, we are dealing with the primary, most basic relationship of the existence of each of us. No wonder, then, that it was woman who was first linked with the divine. Long before the father gods, mother goddesses peopled the human mind.

From India to the Mediterranean, is practically all cultures, as Neumann has demonstrated in his masterpiece, are statues of the mother goddesses. Their luxuriant wombs proclaim to us that they engender and nourish all the universe, not excluding the gods themselves. In Sumeria, the mother goddess was called Inana or Ishtar. She ruled earth and sky. She was the Most High, the Glorious One, the all-engendering, and the zodiac was her girdle.

In Egypt, the great goddess was called Isis. Creator of heaven and earth, of gods and human beings, Isis may have been the most worshiped goddess in the world. Her reign outlasted the Greek and Roman civilizations and even penetrated Christianity. We know that early Christians often venerated statues of a black Isis with her son Horus in her arms as the Madonna and Child. Many a Catholic sanctuary of our own day is dedicated to a black Madonna who seems to have her roots in Isis. The black Madonnas of Einsiedeln in Switzerland, Montserrat near Barcelona, Orleans, Marseilles, the black Madonna of the rose window in the north transept of the Cathedral of Chartres, or in the crypt of the same cathedral where she stands beside a deep well, the black Madonna of Rocamadour in France, Our Lady of Czestochowa in Poland, our own Lady of Aparecida, all seem to have originated as a transposed cult of Isis. Isis was the Goddess of the Ten Thousand Names. Everything positive that could be said of the feminine was attributed poetically to Isis.[26]

Again, we know that the whole Minoan culture of Crete worshiped the great goddess Dictyna, or Britomartis, represented in a tunic, her breasts bare, a tiara on her head, her hair falling free, and her arms entwined by serpents. Her special symbols were the sacred tree and column, standing for the union of heaven with earth and the underworld, her three kingdoms.

The Canaanite culture, too, worshiped the mother goddess. The Book of Kings tells of the battles it cost the Jews to vanquish this cult, especially the worship of Ashtarte and her son Baal.

All of the mother or virgin goddesses were represented as mistresses of flora, fauna, and all nature, as they specifically incarnated the principle of life and generation.[27]

It is in this context that the religion of "God my Mother" arose. A like conceptualization is self-evident to a practitioner of the Hindu religion, where Brahman, indeterminate in every way and therefore beyond any differentiation of gender, is the original source of all. The first determination or differentiation appears with the great cosmic mother, Khakti, who constructs and orders the universe as she takes her stand opposite her counterpart and contrary, Kali, goddess-principle of division and destruction.

Even Judaism, so masculine, so patriarchal, displays the feminine characteristics of absolute Mystery. The Book of Proverbs (8:22–30) speaks of Wisdom as if she were God in God's tender sympathy and delight in the creation.

And so the feminine appears as the beginning of beginnings, the principle of principles. Humanity represents its origin as a primordial Uterus, the fecund womb from which all things are sprung. But the archetype of origins is the archetype of the end, and humanity, insatiably hungering to live that primordial unity, can conceive of the end only as the recovery and actualization of the initial integration.

Jung's Acknowledgment of the Psychocultural Validity of the Marian Dogmas

A mind as attentive as that of Carl Jung, founder of the psychology of the archetypes, could not fail to register the importance attributed by Christianity (especially in its Catholic version) to the worship of the Virgin Mary, the Mother of God. Jung was, of course, altogether aware of the paternalism, indeed the male-supremacist ideology, inherited by Christianity from its Old Testament and pagan (Greco-Roman and Germanic) cultural sources. Yes, Christianity had largely become a religion of men. Still, the collective unconscious of the community of faith had managed to assimilate the feminine dimension, primarily in terms of Mary and of a Church as virgin, bride, and mother. Christianity had failed to integrate the dark dimension of the anima archetype. It had only articulated its luminous aspect, in a numinous Bountiful Mother and Virgin Most Pure. But Jung did not regard this as a shortcoming. Rather, and we have seen this for ourselves, Jung regarded it as an argument in favor of Christianity's self-concept not only as the convergence of all the dynamisms of the past, but also, and indeed primarily, as the irruption into history of the eschaton—that definitive framework of the human being, including woman, in God. Jung saw that it was only thanks to the eschatological moment that the face of the feminine, reconciled and finally recovered and re-deemed, appears in Christianity.

Jung considered Mary under four aspects: (1) as an image of the anima archetype; (2) as an expression of the mother arche-type; (3) under the aspect of trinity and quaternity; and (4) in terms of the dogma of her bodily assumption into heaven. Let us summarize his fourfold analysis.

1. The anima is one of the most profound, as well as one of the most palpable, archetypes of the human psyche. It is the expression par excellence of femininity—in both the male (where it occurs precisely as anima) and the female (where it occurs as the animus). In its journey through his-tory it has been articulated as human beings have experi-enced it: as Eve, in a transpersonal, collective sense—as the chthonic, engendering mother who is at the origin of all life; as Helen of Troy, in whom sexual eros occurs in es-thetic and romantic sublimation, in the expression of woman in her capacity for relationship and communication, woman capable of fascinating human beings to the point of exalting them above mere genital sexuality; as Mary, a sublimation and spiritualization of eros so exalted that she becomes the object of a religious devotion, in total divorce from any sexual reference, in the form of the Virgin, or the Mother who is Virgin as well, immaculate and inviolate; and finally, as Sophia, Wisdom, the ultimate, inaccessible form of the feminine archetype, integrating within herself not only the various distinct feminine forms, but the mas-culine as well, and even a reference to God. Christian tra-dition has accommodated Mary in the texts of its scriptures that speak of Wisdom (especially Proverbs 8). In this con-ceptualization, Mary of Nazareth represents, in Christian culture as throughout humanity, the most magnificent splendor of the feminine. The feminine will not be content with an occasional collective concretion. It will have its max-imal expression in history, and in a person. Mary embodies this actualization.[28]

2. In his consideration of Wisdom (Sophia) as the expression of a God in sympathy with creation, Jung has the oppor-

tunity to analyze the importance of Mary as mother, and as the incarnation of the mother archetype. God as Wisdom is God yearning to change, God longing to draw near creation. God has an "incarnational intention." There will be a second Adam. Unlike the first, however, who burst into being directly from the hands of his creator, the second Adam will be born of the womb of a virgin mother. Because she is to be the mother of God, Jung explains, she must be purified, posited in a condition prior to the Fall. She will not only be God's daughter, and supereminently so, but his bride and spouse, as well. A sacred, heavenly marriage, a hierogamy, will be consummated, and of this union will come the Son of God. Immaculate, free of the snares of the devil, Mary will live the condition of one who dwells in paradise. For she leads a divine life, a life of pleromatic existence. Jung concludes that Mary's closeness to God is such that she enjoys the *status* of a goddess. As the instrument of the birth of God, Mary and the humanity she represents are swept up in the divine drama. As Mother of God, Mary is able to assume and represent humanity's substantial participation in the Trinity.[29] And here we touch on the third aspect of Mary in Jung's study, that of her relationship with the Trinity.

3. In a celebrated passage, Jung examines the psychological meaning of the Christian dogma of the Holy Trinity. First he calls our attention to the fact that a Trinitarian theme, a oneness in trinity, constitutes a commonplace in the history of religions. Christianity here prolongs a line that goes back to the most ancient mythologies and religions. For Jung, the Holy Trinity has the characteristics of an archetype springing from one precise moment in the process of individuation. It contains the symbol of development, of split, of one that becomes two, engendering division and conflict. At the same time, the Trinity signifies the resolution of that conflict, the integration of the division engendered by the becoming-two. The archetype of trinity, then, of threeness, is an element corresponding to a stage in which humanity makes a qauntum leap in the direction of reflection and consciousness.[30] Were we to wish to locate

this stage in the history of humanity's individuation, we should have to concede that it occurred in the age of patriarchalism. Trinity is a masculine archetype par excellence.[31] It suggests perfection and completion. (We have the three theological virtues, the family trinity of father, mother, and child, and so on.)

However, in Jung's view, the perfection expressed by trinity, by threeness, does not exhaust the process of personal identification. A fourth element is needed. In the Holy Trinity this will be the feminine in God. This is where Mary enters the picture as Mother of God, bride of the Holy Spirit, and the one who, through her bodily assumption into heaven, has penetrated the intimacy of the Trinity. For Jung, quaternity, fourness, represents a greater fullness than does trinity, because quaternity integrates precisely the forgotten feminine. This, explains Jung, is why, in Christian representations, in visions of some of the saints, in dreams, or in the writings of certain emotionally disturbed persons, there almost always appears a fourth element along with trinity, even the Holy Trinity, be it creation, matter, or Mary. The dogma of the Assumption, proclaimed by Pope Pius XII in 1950 (in the encyclical *Munificentissimus Deus*), endorses one of the most basic attitudes of the human psyche in its thirst for total integration. And this brings us to the fourth aspect of Mary in Jung's reflection, the meaning of her assumption into heaven.

4. The proclamation of the Marian dogma of the Assumption occasioned a grave crisis for the ecumenical efforts of so many Christians. Jung, however, does not hesitate to refer to it as the greatest religious event since the Reformation. Our approach to an understanding of this dogma should not be religious, he explains, but symbolical. We should approach it by way not of the conscious, but of the unconscious. On the unconscious level, it is the perfect response to a demand on the part of our integral archaeology. Not only the masculine has been raised to divinity, by means of Christ, but in a certain way the feminine as well, by means of Mary. To be sure, Christian faith has never regarded Mary as divine. Jung concedes this. But it has placed her

in such a state of intimacy with the Holy Trinity that she does accede to a position in the circle of the Trinity as a quaternity—as Mother of God. By this very fact she becomes Queen of the Universe, Universal Mediator (in dependence upon Christ her Son), and Mistress of Heaven and Earth. At last the demands of the psyche are essentially satisfied. Now the feminine has achieved its maximum identity.[32]

At the same time, this new dogma contains the solution to one of the oldest problems ever to plague humanity: the integration of matter and spirit, the wedding, for good and all, of heaven and earth. Now the golden dream of alchemy—the construction of an ultimate oneness and unity in which all contradictions are reconciled—becomes living, breathing reality. Through the assumption of the Blessed Virgin Mary into heaven, her corporality, her material reality, has attained to the highest glory. Despite all, matter—deep, dark, heavy, transitory matter—wins a share in God. The human psyche conceives of matter and earth as feminine realities. Mary assumed into heaven is the exaltation of the *Magna Mater* to a oneness with her divine spouse, heaven. The hierogamy, the sacred wedding, has been accomplished. Mary anticipates the universal process of the radical integration of opposites in an ineffable union of matter and spirit, of the dark of earth with the resplendent light of the sky.

THE FEMININE AS REVELATION OF GOD

The perspectives afforded us in our excursion into feminine mythology have clearly manifested the importance of the feminine for an understanding of human beings and their relation to God. The female deities are no less worthy, powerful, or life-giving than the male ones. We have seen how useful the category of the feminine can be for an articulation of the human experience of contact with absolute Mystery—which does not permit itself to be captured solely in categories of the masculine. This awareness must surely lead us to a certain relativization of our religious horizons, which are, of course, organized primarily

in a masculine framework. God is beyond both sexes, hence beyond the qualifications of masculine and feminine. However,
God is also the foundation of these qualifications, and when God
undertakes self-revelation God uses their categories, thereby
erecting masculine and feminine into sacraments of divine presence and activity. God may be correctly regarded both as Father
and as Mother, even though transcending both categories in the
divine reality, where God dwells in inaccessible light.

These categories, furthermore, have both penetrated the entire area of religion. For Mariology, the feminine becomes the
vehicle for a communication of Mary's transcendent reality. At
the same time, we must distinguish between factual reality and
mythic or archetypal reality. Reduced to its simplest terms, the
question, then, is the following: Is the Virgin Mother of God,
immaculate and assumed into heaven, a variation of the ancient
agrarian myths, or is she the actual historicization of a divine
action in the realm of historical time? Is the principal reality the
myth, so that the Virgin Mary is primarily an elucidation of the
myth? Or is Mary a historical reality injected into the universe
by God, so that the myth is primarily a preparation and elucidation of this mystery? Here we have the decisive question for
Christian Mariology. Now we must draw the line between myth
and history.

Christian faith, and the erudite discourse of that faith called
theology, affirm that Mary and the wondrous deeds wrought in
her by God are duly established historical events. In Mary, the
longings of the most ancient myths, the most radical yearnings
of our interior archaeology, and the dreams of the most primitive archetypes have achieved a historical, personal concretion.
In Mary, the eschaton—definitive reality, reality in its final
phase of absorption in God—has burst upon us for good and
all. The myths only anticipate and point to this event of grace,
then. But then, too, they are laden with meaning and value.
Only now are they seen to be altogether true. Now we know that
they are absolutely authentic. Of course, they must not be portrayed as substantive, terminal realities. Their service is to a reality yet to come. They anticipate a history that one day is concretely actualized. In the Christian interpretation, then, Mary is

the eschatologization of the truth of the feminine myths and archetypes.

Mariology, as a systematic reflection on the mystery of Mary, must employ a twofold expression. First, it must regard that mystery as historical fact and theologize upon it as such. Second, however, it must express Mary in myth and archetype. As theologization upon historical fact, Mariology must insist upon the historicity of its propositions. Mary is *historically* immaculate, she is the Virgin Mother of God *in fact*, she was *really* taken into heaven body and soul. But in terms of a second approach, Mariology will understand that these events of salvation history were anticipated in the human psyche, all through the latter's history, by means of the most varied myths, and under the strangest figures, and that we continue to mythologize Mary today. There is no better language for translating these ineffable historical, factual truths than the language of myth.

15. The Marian Dogmas: Their Existenial and Symbolic Content

Let us conclude our lengthy consideration of the various aspects of the mystery of the Virgin Mother with a brief examination of history's treasury of symbolic statements concerning her.[1] Here Catholic faith has truly surpassed itself in invention and creativity.

THE TRUTH OF SYMBOLS

The Christian songbook of Mary knows no restraint.

> Whiter than the dawn,
> Brighter than the sun,
> My lovely Queen,
> My sweet love!

This is no longer theology, with its systems and refined concepts. This is the exuberance of the heart—*theologia cordis*—in its enthusiasm for the human-and-divine meaning it finds in Mary. This is the universe of symbol and mythology, those vehicles of the meaning and values that confer sense on human life.

THE IMMACULATE CONCEPTION

The great Marian mysteries constitute special points of emergence and intersection for so many of the images of the unconscious. The symbolic experience of Mary's immaculate conception, for instance, contains far more than the bald proposition that she was preserved free of original sin. The Immaculate Conception is precisely the foundation of the whole constellation of Marian symbols. Now the memory recalls the myths of a paradise lost and regained. Now we recognize the flower the serpent did not crush, the paradise made real in historical time, the springtime of fruits and flowers that will never wither or decay. The Litany of Our Lady of Loreto proclaims Mary to be a "Spiritual Vessel, Vessel of Honor, Singular Vessel of Devotion." As we have seen, a vessel, a container or receptacle, is the basic archetype of the feminine. The feminine contains all life. Eternal life, and a new humanity, springs forth in Mary. In her we find all creation in symbolic recapitulation, purified and radiating God. Mary becomes the receptacle, the temple of God. Mary is the antitype of Eve. Eve generated mortal life, Mary immortal life. Mary Immaculate is the symbol of the soul touched by grace and giving birth to the Son of God. She is the image of a Church continually generating new sons and daughters in the Son. As Mary bore the head of the new humanity, Christ, so she continues to bear its body, Christ's new members, all down the centuries.

THE VIRGINITY OF MARY

Mary's virginity, in the world of symbol as in the realm of faith, is a great deal more than a miraculous phenomenon of human biology. In our interior archaeology, the virgin is the archetype of the whole, the complete, the not-yet-touched, the natural, the integral product of the Creator's hands. She symbolizes life in its immortality, life at birth, still uncontaminated, not yet cast to the hazard of the game of possessors and possessed. Mary articulates this recollected fullness, this mysterious, fascinating strength, this secret sheen of the new and untarnished. Mary comes to us as a promise and a possibility—a real possibility, not an unattainable one, not as a coffer all locked up and shut off from others. She is a gift, an offering, like a bud about to bloom, a seed ready to germinate, a hand outstretched to give and receive, an eye opening to the landscape, a voice drawing breath to shout the glad proclamation and the good news, a thought become concept and a concept spelled in words. All this is virginity, fecund virginity. It opens out toward another reality, and behold, the new is born. Virginity is like the concept conceived of the relationship between untried thought and fertile reality. Mary possesses this fertile virginity, this virginal fertility. This is why she is virgin and mother, and not virgin alone. As bride, as wife, she expresses the fecundity of virginity, for the bride is the symbol of patient-and-impatient waiting, of happy, trustful openness.

Is this not the only true, genuine attitude to take in the sight of God? Mary fulfills the archetype of holy creation in the face of absolute Mystery, our future and our meaning.

THE VIRGIN MOTHERHOOD

Mary's virgin motherhood provides the focus for a whole array of symbols, myths, and archetypes. We have already examined the most primitive archetype of harmonious, primeval human life, the *uroboros*, which generally appears in the image of the feminine, the great mother who is also virgin, the woman so perfect and complete that she has no need of male seed. Now, what is true phylogenetically is also true, *mutatis mutandis*, ontogenetically. The individual structurally reproduces the pilgrimage of humanity as a whole. The child develops not only within the mother, but in constant reference to her. The child's behavior molds to that of the mother. The container of the mother is the first "continent" to be discovered by the child. Proximity and estrangement with respect to the mother constitute the child's first contact with reality. The fundamental categories of good and evil, beautiful and unpleasant, great, strange, and so on, are initially maternal qualities, for it is the mother whom the child experiences as good and evil, loving and suffocating, harsh, protecting and threatening, and so on. Mother and child live in a "uroboric" relationship of integration. Whenever anyone or anything comes between them, displeasure sets in, triggering a drive to expel the intruder, even the father. Here, in Freud's theory, the Oedipus complex appears: the unconscious desire to remove the father in order to be alone with the mother, a mother who is entirely for the child and for no one else. Here the image of the virgin mother emerges in the unconscious—the image of a mother who has had nothing to do with that person, the father, a mother who has never had a relationship with anyone but the child. And so the child tries to prolong the cradling, intimate relationship of the primitive, uroboric oneness, for as long a time as can be.

In later normal development, the child will integrate mother and father, feminine and masculine. Still, the initial struggle—to maintain the paradisiacal relationship with the mother while developing and strengthening the ego by separating from her—has left its profound mark. Hence the recollections that well up in the form of archetypes and myths. Thus, for example, the indelible record of a primeval felicity and integration and its subsequent loss becomes the myth of a paradise lost, a golden age of long ago. The intrauterine life is reproduced in the religious myths of mother earth and the *Magna Mater,* earliest of the deities. The mother is experienced as goddess, all holy, all pure, a creature of another, long gone, happy world. This suggests the origin of the incest taboo not in cultural prohibitions calculated to protect the species, but in a celebration and symbolic sublimation of mother love, and a desire to be with Mother once more, as we were during the nine months of our gestation. The incest taboo is the call of paradise, impossible historically, but accessible by desire and expressed in symbol. Indeed, in this schema the whole sexual taboo would have arisen not from the imposition of a cultural censure, but from a sense of sexuality's link with the very mystery of life, a mystery spelled out in the myth of creation. Creation myths see God as masculine and feminine at once, both as father and as mother. It is God who is the ultimate principle of fertility, as it is God who is the ultimate source of perfection and integral unity. Now we grasp the import of the myths of parthenogenesis—of the virginal conception by power from above.

It is this unconscious content that fires the quest of the human conscious for a mother wholly pure, never touched, the perfect woman, and so on. Analytical reason, of course, will be at pains to demonstrate that these virtues have never existed historically. Feeling, however, *pathos,* which lives on an altogether different level, will always feed on such realities. Often enough they are symbolic, to be sure. But even so, these realities are more real than bald, naked facts, for they lie at the foundation of the values and meaning of life itself.

A theological reading of the texts of mythology will reveal God's pedagogy of the human psyche. God has ever guided that psyche toward the historical event realized by the Holy Spirit in the Virgin Mary. Thus, we have Demeter and Artemis of the Greeks, goddesses of fertile mother earth; we have Juno of the Romans, queen and mother; we have Ceres or mother earth, later identified with Demeter; we have the *Mater Idaea;* we have the *Magna Mater,* worshiped under the name of Cybele; and we have Isis of the Egyptians, generatrix of human beings and the gods. Both Cybele and Isis were believed to have given birth by divine power, without male intervention. All of the virgin mother goddesses are reflections of the old dream, and symbolic prefigurations and anticipations of the new reality, the really existing Virgin Mother, Mary of Nazareth, fecundated by the Holy Spirit, inauguration of the utopia of paradise and the Reign of God.

Mythology is part of the divine pedagogy, then. A loving, benevolent God prepared humanity for real divine wonders by bestowing on it an appreciation of anticipatory, symbolic wonders that one day would become reality. Our universal mystification of woman as virgin and mother is God's way of drawing us to Mary, God's Mother and ours, Mary whose reality is no longer merely symbolic, but historical, as well, Mary who is the eschatological event of the Reign and of the new humanity assumed by the Holy Spirit and the eternal Son.

THE ASSUMPTION

Carl Jung has identified the essential archetypal meaning of Mary's bodily assumption into heaven. This event fulfills one of the oldest dreams of humankind: the dream of an earth that reaches up to touch the sky, the dream of the union of the "above" with the "below," of the oneness of matter and spirit, beginning and end, humanity and God. The most frequent symbol of this ultimate unity is in terms of a marriage. No wonder, then, that the texts of the liturgical celebration of marriage recall nuptials celebrated by Son and Mother. Understood symbolically, these texts, which could appear so monstrous on the historical level, articulate one of our most primitive myths—that of the recovery of the pristine unity of mother and son. In and through Mary, all creation is led into the marriage chamber of Trinitarian love. Mary marks the beginning of a new history between Creator and creature, a history without the dark side, without the rebellion that disgraced the first, the old creation.

MARY, SEAT OF WISDOM

Mary's symphony of symbols reaches its climax in her celebration as Wisdom. Here the Old Testament Wisdom theme is applied to Yahweh's loving regard for creation. The New Testament sees Jesus Christ as eternal Wisdom, for it recognizes in him the only-begotten Son of the Father. In many of its Marian feasts, the Christian liturgy attributes the function of Wisdom to the Blessed Virgin. After all, she is the mother of the eternal Son who is the uncreated Wisdom of the Father, and the temple of the Holy Spirit. Now Mary is heard to say:

> The Lord begot me, the firstborn of his ways,
>   the forerunner of his prodigies of long ago;
> From of old I was poured forth,
>   at the first, before the earth.
> When there were no depths I was brought forth,
>   when there were no fountains or springs of water. . . .
>
> When he established the heavens I was there. . . .
> For he who finds me finds life. . . .
>   (Prov. 8:22–24, 27, 35
>   —Mass of the Immaculate Conception)
>
>> Come to me, all you that yearn for me,
>>   and be filled with my fruits;
>>
>> You will remember me as sweeter than honey,
>>   better to have than the honeycomb.
>>   (Sir. 24:18–19)

From the inexhaustible wellspring of the symbolic we draw the most appropriate expressions of the figure of Mary in her glory within the Holy Trinity. The figure of Wisdom is an excellent example. Here, on the eschatological, final, transhistorical level, we have the divinization of a creature in the most excellent form. Mary enters the intimate mystery of the Trinity itself, since she is definitively united to the Spirit and to the eternal Son made flesh. It is through her that God has acquired carnality and visibility. It is through her that God has come into physical contact with human nature. Human language is at a loss, and falls silent.

Only a divine imagery, like that of the Wisdom literature, will ever be able to express the ineffable Marian mystery.

The entire Marian universe is lighted up by the symbolic. All our representations, our paintings, our sculpture, every medium and genre of Marian art articulates the meaning and religious value of Mary through the magnification available through the symbol. We can only comprehend such language by penetrating the world of myth. Here, in the world of myth, historical reality is recreated on the symbolic level. Every generation has its many symbols, pregnant with meaning, and it is in their light that Marian symbology has taken form.

SYMBOL AND HISTORY

In an age when Christianity concentrated so heavily on sin, punishment, forgiveness, Christ's ransom of humanity by blood and crucifixion, heaven and hell—categories that convey an image of God and Christ primarily as judges—the Virgin Mary emerged as providing the balance of mercy. From the fifteenth to the eighteenth centuries, Christian iconography actually portrayed Jesus as a man swept up in a paroxysm of rage and poised to strike sinners with a bolt of lightning—until Mary stepped in to shield them with her mantle. Indeed, the title of the work sometimes ran, "Jesus will condemn, but Mary will save."

In a Christian feudal or slave society, like the one that prevailed for so many centuries in Latin America, Christ was portrayed as the great Lord, the absolute monarch, and Mary the slave freely offering herself in behalf of God and humanity. Thus, Mary was used as an ideological instrument to instill the spirit of submission in women, who were ruled by their feudal lords or slave masters as well as by the male of the species.

In the late nineteenth century, when the old regime was at an end and the social classes acquired greater mobility, a shift occurred from a rigidly ordered society to a conflictive, changing one. Now God began to be portrayed with more human traits, as the father of infinite kindness who loves both the good and the wicked, and Mary's iconography began to show her as a gentle, kind, sweet, loving woman.

Today we are acutely aware of the need for deliverance from

the captivity of a political and economic system that exploits human work. And so now God is represented as the liberator of victims of injustice, and Mary as the woman who

did not hesitate to assert that God is the avenger of the humble and oppressed, and that he pulls down the powerful from their thrones (Luke 1:51–53). Mary is "first among the humble and the poor of the Lord," the strong woman who experienced poverty and suffering, flight and exile, that is, situations which cannot be ignored by those who will toil in the spirit of the Good News for the liberation of the human being and society.[2]

As we see, each new generation finds itself in Mary, projecting its dreams, its sociocultural ideals, upon her. In her, each new generation discovers the revelatory path of the feminine archetypes that crowd our unconscious. With Paul VI we may well say:

When the Church considers the long history of Marian devotion, she rejoices at the continuity of the element of cult it shows, but she does not bind herself to any particular expression of an individual cultural epoch, or to the particular anthropological ideas underlying such expressions. The Church understands that certain outward religious expressions, while perfectly valid in themselves, may be less suitable to men and women of different ages and cultures.[3]

We have said before, and we must say again, that the symbolic must remain within the limits of its specific realm, which is that of the recreation and restatement of historical reality in order to render it explicit and spell out its hidden meaning and secret value. Symbol can neither replace history nor divorce itself from history. And so a symbology of Mary must return again and again to the concrete history of Mary the village woman, the wife of Joseph, and the virgin mother of Jesus the carpenter. She was so like other Galilean women, just as her Son resembled the other men of Nazareth. What distinguished them was only the fact that they knew no sin, for one was God incarnate and the other the Mother of God and the temple of the Holy Spirit.

When we regard Mary from the perspective of the symbolic, her humble condition is difficult indeed to perceive. We hear nothing of hands calloused by hard work, a face creased by a life of suffering, legs thick from long hours of standing. The symbol shows us the lovely maiden crowned with jewels and gold, robed in brocade and silk, with long, delicate hands, translucent flesh, and a face transfigured. What the grandiloquence of symbol must be careful to exalt, however, and not attempt to conceal, is the grandeur of Mary's lowliness. Otherwise Mary will have short shrift indeed, and we shall ourselves become the victims of the confusion of historical and symbolic reality. The faithful who kneel before the statue of the Blessed Virgin Mary must be enabled to see beyond the symbol, to the history of this unique woman of our world, who shared in the life of everywoman. She waited for her husband to finish his work, she prepared his meals, washed and ironed his clothes, supported him during the long days of labor and in times of sickness, she cleaned, swept, sewed, she put the house in order, she sat down with her husband in the evening for long conversations, and then stood to pray with him to ask God, whom they both loved so dearly, the meaning of the mysteries unfolding in their lives and in Mary's womb. She visited neighbors, comforting them in their trials, bearing with the dull and laughing with the merry. The Blessed Virgin Mary experienced the trauma of widowhood, then watched in a paroxysm of anguish, her heart torn asunder and pierced by seven swords, the death by torture of her beloved only son.

If the faithful can discover the daily, quiet heroism of Mary's life, they will begin to understand the grandiose, the sublime, the sacred and holy concealed in the daily routine of home life, in their own lives. Deep in the heart of this simplicity, God concealed the wealth of divine glory and ours. Now the euphemisms, the mystifications, the false interpretations of Mary's glory have no place in our contemplation of the symbols that express her for us. Only in this dialectic between the historical and the theologicosymbolic shall we ever be able to encompass the whole magnitude of Mary's smallness—all of her sovereign humility and humble sovereignty, all of the hidden glory and glorious obscurity of the Virgin Mother of God.

Conclusion: The Radical Feminine

We have come to the end of our study. We trust that the anthropological category of the feminine, in all of its radical, ontological dimensions, has shed some light on the mystery of Mary. At the same time, surely Mary's life and the wonders wrought in her by God will have facilitated an understanding of the feminine, in its historical and eschatological expressions alike.

The reality of the feminine, which we have examined from a number of approaches—analytical, philosophical, and theological—has certainly afforded us a richer perception of the human person as such, and not simply of woman. At the same time, however, the feminine has revealed itself to us in utter mystery. What we might come to know of the feminine is nothing in comparison with what we do not know, with what is hidden from us. The roots of the feminine are lost in God. It is perfectly legitimate to speak of the feminine in God, and of God, our Mother.

The mystery of the feminine is not a fearsome mystery. It is a mystery of intimacy and tenderness. And it is far more of a mystery than a problem. Problems have solutions. Once solved, they are gone for good. But mystery has no solution. The deeper we probe, the more challenging it becomes. Mystery is not dark; it is altogether too light. But light attracts light, and we can understand more and more. Constantly we think and rethink the mystery of the feminine. Each generation makes its contribution to a greater understanding. And so we may speak of a radical feminine. The feminine has its root and source in the ultimate Root and perfect Source. In Mary, the feminine has won historical palpability. It has found its eschatological anticipation, in the concrete, enfleshed symbol of what will transpire when the whole feminine, in every human being in a proportion proper to each, is brought to fulfillment.

The feminine gives us to see another form of being human and civilized. The past several millennia have been lived under the dominance of the masculine, or a very particular way of being human and of relating to reality. This particular way is characterized mainly by *logos*—rationality, concept. *Logos* introduces a division between humanity and nature. It turns human beings into rulers of the earth, who subjugate the forces of nature and alter their balance.[1] This mode of civilized being has produced its positive fruits, as well as the dilemmas that so gravely threaten our life on this planet today.

In this context, the feminine emerges as the possibility of an escape between the horns: neither to continue as we have been, nor to regress to the models of a feminine agrarian civilization, but to make room for the feminine dimension in our own culture. Through the feminine we make ourselves capable of another kind of relationship, more communal, more tender, more in solidarity with our roots in cosmos and earth. All great human beings, all profoundly integrated human personalities, have been gentle spirits who have valued the expressions of the anima.

From this perspective we have tried to recast theological reflection where Mary is concerned. Gertrude von Le Fort called Mary the "Eternal Woman,"[2] and Paul Claudel, "the sacrament of the motherly tenderness of God." We hope we have made it clear that the meaning of Mary extends beyond Mary, beyond woman, to the mystery of the human being, male or female, as such, and to the whole religious mystery of creation. "Mary, representative of the whole of creation, represents at once the human being and woman."[3] Not by chance do the Marian litanies attribute to Mary qualities that our culture usually reserves to one sex alone. Mary is "Mother most pure," "Mother most kind," "Mystical Rose," "Morning Star"—qualities considered eminently (although not exclusively) feminine; but she is also hailed as "Virgin most powerful," "Tower of David," and "Mirror of Justice"—referring to qualities seen as especially (although not exclusively) masculine. Mary is presented as a human ideal, not just as an ideal for women.

The language most adequate for conveying such an all-embracing ideal is not conceptual, but symbolic—not the language of discourse, but the language of myth. Symbolic, mythical language communicates a message inscribed in hieroglyphs, not in an alphabet to which our rationality is attuned. But like any alphabet, the vehicle of this message can be deciphered. We have devoted long pages to a justification of mythical language as the conveyor of the depth of the feminine, especially in its supreme concretion, its insertion into the divine mystery. In the mythical tonality we come to realize that humanity's basic structure is not *sum* (I am), but *sursum* (upward).[4]

Nevertheless, we must clearly distinguish between mystery and myth. Myth is language; mystery is radical reality. Myth is a hermeneutics of this historical reality. This is why we have insisted so strongly that the mysteries of Mary are more adequately expressed through symbol and myth than through theological rationality. The reality of Mary is so fertile and so basic that it attracts almost all of the positive mythological symbols of our interior archaeology. Jean Guitton has said it well:

The Virgin is the prioritarian *locus* of the purest myths. The Virgin is the *bond* of the highest mysteries. We must say this still more profoundly: the Virgin is an original, prioritarian, perhaps unique, focus through which the sublimating *ascension* is realized, by which the lower stages of existence are made to pass to a more perfect state, where they rediscover their essence ennobled, leaving behind only its accidents. Is not this sublimation, this "ascension" the metaphysical mystery of the cosmos, of life, of thought, of spiritual progress, of temporal life elevated to life everlasting? In the idea of the Virgin Mary myths realize their *ascension*—not the annihilation of their body, but its sublimation. As Saint Paul says, we do not wish to see ourselves unclothed, but most elegantly clothed, in order that the mortal in us be absorbed by life. Surely this is the supreme law.[5]

This supreme law must always be kept in mind. And so it must constantly be restated. This is why we must understand the language of symbols and myths in its own grammar. We must be on our guard against an overly geometrical mentality, which is afflicted with a marked, painful absence of finesse and tenderness. In its concern to safeguard mystery, this mentality purifies it of all of its symbolic raiment. The price of this theoretical catharsis is the desiccation of mystery. Mystery dries up and withers away, and all that is left is an abstract idea, which will never fire the spiritual life, never invite a human being to sink to the very roots of reality or soar to the heights of religious experience. We must clearly distinguish between myth and mystery, yes. But if we attempt to put asunder what psyche has joined together, we do so to our detriment.

At the other extreme, we have the tendency to concretize mystery, to bury it in a profusion of symbols and myths to the point where it is no longer recognizable. The result is a dissolution of the Christian and Marian experience. Mystery has its origin not in myth, but in God. It attracts myth, however, and myth is from the human being. The correct standard for the proper use of symbolic language is in historicity. Thus, the symbolic language of faith in Mary, with all of its magnificence, must ever evoke the historical figure of that simple woman of the people who shared in the lowliness of our lives and walked the narrow path of anonymity. No one falls in love with a ghost woman. We fall in love with a real woman, a woman whose actual historical grandeur will underscore the language of symbol and make it more meaningful still. When Don Quixote came to his senses, he forgot his Dulcinea.[6]

We must always keep the spirit and the letter at one. Only then can the historical Miriam of Nazareth be identified with the Mary Most Holy of our faith. Mary's greatness, as we have sought to demonstrate in these pages, proceeds from the twofold relationship that she maintains with the Holy Spirit and the Word. Mary is hypostatically assumed by the Spirit, who eternalizes the feminine in her, conferring an anticipatory eschatological character on human existence in its feminine modality. At the same time, she opens herself to the plenitude of the feminine as Virgin Mother of God when she pronounces her *fiat*, and the incarnation of the eternal Word transpires within her. Through the Incarnation, Mary is enveloped by the eternal Word, as well, and this Word acquires in her historical density. The pneumatic and christological elements, in association with the eschatological, against the background of an anthropology of the feminine, have enabled us to recast systematic reflection on Mary. We trust that we have thus restored her to her authentic position in salvation history, which is the progressive assimilation of the human being to God and God to the human being.

With Pierre Teilhard de Chardin we believe that "the authentic, pure feminine is par excellence an luminous, chaste energy, the vessel of the ideal, and of goodness—the Blessed Virgin Mary."[7]

In her, as in Jesus, God is all in all (see 1 Cor. 15:28).

Notes

Introduction: Theology and the Feminine

1. Augustine of Hippo, *Quaestiones in Heptateucum* 2, 152.
2. Thomas Aquinas, *Summa Theologiae*, I, q. 92, art. 1, ad 1.
3. This exaltation of the feminine in Mary functions as a compensatory mechanism for society's widespread antifeminism. But a polarization of the feminine in Mary alone ultimately redounds to the reaffirmation of precisely what it seeks to rise above: an exaggeration of the importance of gender. See F. A. Hoyer, "Verachtung des Weiblichen," *Erdkreis* 19 (1969):397–416; Yvonne Pellé-Douël, *Etre femme* (Paris: Seuil, 1967), pp. 101–2; France Quéré, *La femme avenir* (Paris: Seuil, 1976), pp. 83–120.
4. For this whole complex question see Clodovis Boff, *Teologia e prática: Teologia do político e sus mediações* (Petrópolis, Brazil: Vozes, 1978), pp. 112–30, 335–53. Translated by Robert R. Barr under the title *Theology and Practice* (Maryknoll, NY: Orbis, forthcoming).
5. See M. Bertola, "Dimensione antropologica del culto mariano," *Marianum* 39 (1977):69–82.

Chapter 1: The Organizational Principle of Mariology

1. For a detailed examination of this question see A. Müller, "¿Un principio mariologico fundamental?" in *Mysterium Salutis*, ed. Johannes Feiner and Magnus Löhrer (Madrid: Cristiandad, 1972), 3/2:419–33, originally published as 4th ed., (Einsiedeln: Benziger, 1978); René Laurentin, *Breve tratado de teología mariana* (Petrópolis, Brazil: Vozes, 1965), pp. 111–17, 173–76, originally published as *Court traité sur la Vierge Marie*, 5th ed. (Paris: Lethielleux, 1968); Edward Schillebeeckx, *Mary, Mother of the Redemption*, trans. N. D. Smith (New York: Sheed and Ward, 1964), pp. 101–28; C. Dillenschneider, *Le principe premier d'une théologie mariale organique* (Paris: Orientations, 1956); Guy de Broglie, "Le 'principe fondamental' de la théologie mariale," in *Maria*, ed. Julien du Manoir (Paris: 1961), vol. 6, pp. 297–365; Cyril O. Vollert, *A Theology of Mary* (New York: Herder & Herder, 1965), pp. 49–112; W. H. Marshner, "Criteria for Doctrinal Development in Marian Dogmas," *Marian Studies* 28 (1977):47–100.
2. The best exponent of this option is certainly René Laurentin, with his classic *Court traité sur la Vierge Marie*, 5th ed. (Paris: Lethielleux, 1968).
3. See *Lumen Gentium*, chap. 8, in *The Documents of Vatican II*, ed. Walter M. Abbott (New York: America Press, 1966).
4. See T. M. Bartolomei, "La maternità divina di Maria in se stessa e come primo e supremo principio della Mariologia," *Divus Thomas* 60 (1957):160–93.
5. See P. Sánchez Cespedes, *El misterio de María (Mariología bíblica: El principio fundamental: Cristo y María un solo principio redentor)* (Santander: Sal Terrae,

1955); Constantine Koser, "A teologia de Imaculada em Duns Scotus," *Revista Eclesiástica Brasileira* 14 (1954):610–76.

6. See Otto Semmelroth, *Mary, Archetype of the Church,* trans. Maria von Eroes and John Devlin (Dublin: Gill & Son, 1964).

7. See René Laurentin, "Maria nel dogma," in *Dizionario teologico interdisciplinare* (Turin: Marietti, 1977), vol. 2, pp. 465–68.

8. See A. Müller, "La mariología y el concilio Vaticano II," in *Mysterium Salutis,* 3/2:416–18; Luigi Sartori, "A posiçao da mariologia na teologia contemporanea," *Nova Aurora* 3 (1977):35–38 (quarterly review of Marian spirituality and pastoral ministry, Belo Horizonte, Brazil); Domenico Maria Bertetto, *Maria Madre universale nella storia della salvezza* (Florence: Libr. Edit. Fiorentina, 1969).

9. See *Lumen Gentium,* nos. 55–60, in *The Documents of Vatican II,* ed. Walter M. Abbott (New York: America Press, 1966).

10. See William of Ware (d. 1298): "Si debeam deficere . . . magis volo deficere per superabundantiam, dando Mariae aliquam praerogativam quam non habuit, quam per defectum, diminuendo vel substrahendo ab ea aliquam praerogativam quam habuit" ("Were I to miss the mark . . . I should prefer to miss it through excess, giving Mary some prerogative she did not have, rather than by falling short—diminishing her, depriving her of some prerogative she actually had"): *In III Sent.,* q. 25. Or again, the celebrated statement of Duns Scotus in regard to Christ, which can be applied to Mary as well: "In commendando enim Christum malo excedere quam deficere a laude sibi debita si propter ignorantiam oporteat in alterutrum incidere" ("For in recommending Christ, I had rather exaggerate the praise due him than fall short of it, if through ignorance I must needs fall into either extreme"): *Ordinatio III,* d. 12, q. 4.

Chapter 2: Basic Epistomological Obstacles in the Area of the Feminine

1. See Gaston Bachelard, *The Philosophy of No: A Philosophy of the New Scientific Mind,* trans. G. C. Waterston (New York: Orion, 1968), p. 6.

2. See Gaston Bachelard, *La formation de l'esprit scientifique: Contribution à une psychanalyse de la connaissance scientifique* (Paris: 1938), p. 16: "It is impossible suddenly to have a *tabula rasa* with respect to usual knowledge. Faced with the real, what we think we know clearly obfuscates what we ought to know. Confronted with scientific culture, the mind is never young. It is already too old, for it has the same age as its prejudices. To have access to science is to be rejuvenated spiritually, to accept a sudden change that will surely contradict a past."

3. For an incisive critique of the logocentrism typifying our culture and especially pernicious where woman is concerned (Freud, Hegel, Plato), see Luce Irigaray, *Speculum of the Other Woman,* trans. Gillian C. Gill (Ithaca, NY: Cornell University Press, 1985). See also Paul Evdokimov, *La mujer y la salvación del mundo* (Barcelona: Ariel, 1970), pp. 148–51, originally published as *La femme et le salut du monde* (Paris: Desclée de Brouwer, 1983), for a denunciation of the male supremacy and antifeminism of the whole of modern atheism, the despair and anguish of our century, and the rigoristic doctrines of Christian tradition (Jansenism, eternal reprobation, and so on).

4. See Janine Chasseguet-Smirgel, C. J. Luquet-Parat, *La sexualidad femenina* (Barcelona: Laia, 1973), pp. 11–24, for Freud on female sexuality, especially

pp. 21–24 (Freud's celebrated address on the feminine, 1932). In English: *Female Sexuality: New Psychoanalytic Views* (Ann Arbor, MI: University of Michigan, 1970; London: Virago, 1981).

5. See F. V. Joannes, ed., *Crisi dell'antifeminismo* (Milan: Mondadori, 1973), especially the article by Moore and Buysseret, "La donna in una Chiesa mascolinizzata," pp. 197–218.

6. See F. J. J. Buytendijk, *La mujer: Naturaleza-apariencia-existencia* (Madrid: Revista de Occidente, 1955), pp. 299–311, on the maternal vocation and calling. Translated by Denis J. Barrett under the title *Woman: A Contemporary View* (Glen Rock, NJ: Newman, 1968).

7. See Heloneida Studart, *Mulher, objeto de cama e mesa* (Woman, object of bed and board) (Petrópolis, Brazil: Vozes, 1974), for a biting critique of male prejudices against women.

8. We do not mean to deny the respective characteristics of the sexes. We only criticize their irreducible polarization to the point of rendering incomprehensible the basic phenomenon of their reciprocity. For example, as Schiller so correctly intuited, woman's form of self-giving is different from man's: "Give what thou wouldst: ever is it thyself thou givest, thy whole self!" Or as Rainer Maria Rilke wrote to a young poet, "In woman, life abides, dwelling in more immediate, fecund, and trustful form."

9. See Jean-Marie Aubert, *La mujer: Antifeminismo y cristianismo,* trans. María Colóm de Llopis (Barcelona: Herder, 1976), pp. 125–28. Originally published as *La femme: Antiféminisme et christianisme* (Paris: Cerf/Desclée, 1975).

10. Paul VI, *Marialis Cultus,* 1974, no. 37.

11. Ibid.

Chapter 3: The Feminine: An Analytical Approach

1. The bibliography is immense. We shall not even attempt to list the principal works on the subject, and note only bibliographical material here: M. T. Bellenzier, "Panorama bibliografico sulla 'questione femminile,' " *Rasegna teologica* 16 (1975):522–65, 17 (1976):81–91; entire issue 106 (1972) of *Lumière et vie: Masculin et féminin;* M. A. O'Neill, "Toward a Renewed Anthropology," *Theological Studies* 36 (1975):725–36; one of the most lucid contributions up to the present is that of Erwin Metzke, "Anthropologie des sexes," *Lumière et vie* 43 (1959):27–52; Evelyne Sullerot, ed., *Le fait féminin* (Paris: Fayard, 1978) is the most complete work at present and will continue to serve as a basic reference work for some time to come.

2. Norbert Bischof, "De la signification biologique du bisexualisme," in *Le fait féminin,* pp. 34–49.

3. Susumu Ohno, "La base biologique des différences sexuelles," in *Le fait féminin,* pp. 57–68.

4. This datum of man's derivation from woman could be adduced in justification of an ideology of male supremacy. Man has all that woman has, and more. However, the tables could be turned: man could be regarded as a "spin-off" of woman, according to the "law of the castrated hen." If the left ovary of a hen is removed—the functional ovary—the right develops into a functional testicle and the hen becomes a rooster. According to this understanding, the rooster is simply a castrated hen. Then why might not maleness as such be regarded as the collective by-product of the feminine? As we see, we are in a hellish maze of ideologies.

5. G. Raisman, "La différence de structure entre les cerveaux mâle et femme

chez le rat," in *Le fait féminin,* pp. 93–96; compare the commentary by Odette Thibault, ibid., pp. 97–98.

6. There is a vast scientific literature on this subject: R. L. Connor, "Hormonal Influences on Aggressive Behavior," in *Aggressive Behavior* (Amsterdam, 1969); Roy G. D'Andrade, "Sex Differences and Cultural Institutions," in *The Development of Sex Differences,* ed. Eleanor E. Maccoby (Stanford: Stanford University Press, 1966); Milton Diamond, "A Critical Evaluation of the Ontogeny of Human Sexual Behavior," *Quarterly Review of Biology* 40 (1965):147–75; A. Erhardt and S. Baker, "Fetal Androgens, Human Central Nervous System Differentiation and Behavior Sex Difference," in *Sex Differences in Behavior: A Conference,* ed. Richard C. Friedman, Ralph M. Richart, and Raymond L. Vande Wiele (New York: Wiley, 1974); Eleanor E. Maccoby, "The Development of Sex Differences," in *Human Behavior* (Stanford: Stanford University Press, 1966); Peggy R. Sanday, "Toward a Theory of the Status of Woman," *American Anthropologist* 75 (1973):1683–1700; R. Larse, "Les fondements évolutionnistes des différences entre les sexes," in *Le fait féminin,* pp. 337–58, with an extensive bibliography.

7. See, for example, F. J. J. Buytendijk's classic, *Woman: A Contemporary View,* trans. Denis J. Barrett (Glen Rock, NJ: Newman, 1968).

8. See, for example, M. Leibl, *Psicología de la mujer* (Buenos Aires, 1955); likewise the familiar work of Helene Deutsch, *The Psychology of Women: A Psychoanalytic Interpretation,* two vols. (New York: Bantam, 1973).

9. Abel Jeannière, *The Anthropology of Sex,* trans. Julie Kernan (New York: Harper & Row, 1967), p. 132.

10. See Metzke, "Anthropologie des sexes," p. 50.

11. See the classic work by Simone de Beauvoir, *The Second Sex,* trans. and ed. H. M. Parshley (New York: Knopf, 1953).

12. Claude Lévi-Strauss, *As estructuras elementares do parentesco* (Petrópolis, Brazil: Vozes, 1976). Translated from the French by Claire Jacobson and Brooke Grundfest Schoepf (vol. 1) and Monique Layton (vol. 2) under the title *Structural Anthropology* (London: Allen Lane, 1968).

13. Ibid. (Portuguese), p. 520.

14. Ibid., p. 537.

15. See the critique of de Beauvoir's position in Abel Jeannière, *Antropologia sexual* (São Paulo, 1965), pp. 94–99. Translated as *The Anthropology of Sex.*

Chapter 4: The Feminine: A Philosophical Reflection

1. See Thomas Aquinas's celebrated proposition: "The philosopher is like the poet in that both are concerned with the marvelous" (the *mirandum*), *In Metaph.,* bk. 1, chap. 3.

2. Paul Evdokimov, *La mujer y la salvación del mundo* (Barcelona: Ariel, 1970), p. 7. Originally published as *La femme et le salut du monde* (Paris: Desclée de Brouwer, 1983).

3. Here, with a few variations, we follow our "Masculino e feminino: O que é? Fragmentos de uma ontologia," *Vozes* 68 (1974):677–90.

4. See, for example, B. del Valle, "Versão masculina e versão feminina do humano," in *Filosofia do homem* (São Paulo, 1975), p. 172: "The human being occurs in a sexed situation. Let us not confuse sexuality with sex. While sexuality is exercised during a period of life, our sex accompanies us from the cradle to the grave. One is born a man, or one is born a woman."

5. See the classic work we have already cited, F. J. J. Buytendijk, *Woman: A*

Contemporary View, trans. Denis J. Barrett (Glen Rock, NJ: Newman, 1968). This writer characterizes man by work (*travail*) and woman by care and concern (*souci*). Work and concern are relationships the human being has with the world, and they bestow perfection on existence.

6. Margaret Mead, *Male and Female: A Study of the Sexes in a Changing World* (New York: Morrow, 1949); idem, *Sex and Temperament in Three Primitive Societies* (New York: Morrow, 1935); compare the classic Johann Jakob Bachofen, *Das Mutterrecht: Eine Untersuchung über die Gynaikokratie der alten Welt nach ihrer religiösen und rechtlichen Natur*, 2nd ed. (1897; reprint, Brussels: Culture et Civilisation, 1969), vol. 3. (selections from Bachofen translated by Ralph Mannheim under the title *Myth, Religion, and Mother Right: Selected Writings of J. J. Bachofen*, Princeton, NJ: Princeton University Press, 1973).

7. Erich Neumann, *The Great Mother: An Analysis of the Archetype*, trans. Ralph Mannheim (New York: Pantheon, 1955); idem, *The Origins and History of Consciousness*, trans. R. F. C. Hull (Princeton, NJ: Princeton University Press, 1970); idem, *Ein Beitrag zur seelischen Entwicklung des Weiblichen: Ein Kommentar zur Apuleius Amor und Psyche* (Zurich, 1952).

8. Paul Ricoeur, "A maravilha, o descaminho e o enigma," *Paz e terra* 5:36; compare Paul Guilluy, "Filosofía de la sexualidad," in *Estudios de sexología*, ed. Jean-Pierre Trempé et al. (Barcelona: Herder, 1968), pp. 107–34, originally published as *Etudes de sexologie* (Montreal: University of Québec, 1976); Philipp Lersch, *Vom Wesen der Geschlechter* (Munich: Reinhardt, 1950).

9. We recall the utopian prophecy of the Saint-Simonians (Claude-Henri Saint-Simon, 1760–1825): "I believe in the imminent regeneration of humankind through equality of male and female. I believe in the coming of a woman who will effectuate this regeneration." Cited by Marguerite Thibert, *Le féminisme dans le socialisme français de 1830–1850* (Paris: Giard, 1926), p. 53; compare A. Lion, "Hommes et femmes en utopie," *Lumière et vie* 106 (1972):33–45.

10. Paul Ricoeur, *Finitud y culpabilidad*, vol. 1, *El hombre lábil* (Madrid: Taurus, 1969), pp. 135–209.

11. The *Tao Te Ching* expresses this mystery thus:

> Chasm, spirit, immortal:
> behold the Mysterious Feminine.
> Lintel of the Mysterious Feminine,
> root of heaven and earth!
> Ceaselessly
> she appears to exist, ever:
> never her force is spent.

Chapter 5: The Feminine: A Theological Meditation

1. See Phyllis Bird, "Images of Women in the Old Testament," in *Religion and Sexism*, ed. Rosemary Radford Ruether (New York: Simon & Schuster, 1974), p. 41.

2. See Phyllis Trible, "Depatriarchalizing in Biblical Interpretation," *Journal of the American Academy of Religion* 41 (1973):31–34.

3. The bibliography is extremely extensive. Let us indicate only selected titles, as: Bird, "Images of Women"; Johannes Leipoldt, *Die Frau in der antiken Welt und in Urchristentum* (Leipzig: Koehler & Amelang, 1954), pp. 49–80; Helga Rusche, *They Lived by Faith: Women in the Bible*, trans. Elizabeth Williams (Bal-

timore: Helicon); Jean-Marie Aubert, *La mujer: Antifeminismo y cristianismo,* trans. Maria Colom de Llopis (Barcelona: Herder, 1976), pp. 15–20, originally published as *La femme: Antiféminisme et christianisme* (Paris: Cerf/Desclée, 1975).

4. See Raphael Patai, *Sex and the Family in the Bible and the Middle East* (Garden City, NJ: Doubleday, 1959).

5. A fragment attributed to Saint Irenaeus (frag. 14) and cited in the *Anagogicarum Contemplationum* of Anastasius Sinaita (*PG* 89:1013–14) asserts that, contrary to tradition, woman, in the account of the Fall, emerged as stronger, more active, more intelligent, and more decisive than man. The serpent attacked the stronger flank. See Irenaeus, *Adversus Haereses* (*PG* 7:1235–38). For an analysis of this fragment, see J. M. Higgins, "Anastasius Sinaita and the Superiority of the Woman," *Journal of Biblical Literature* 97 (1978):253–56.

6. See Albrecht Oepke, "*Gunē,*" in *Theological Dictionary of the New Testament,* ed. Gerhard Kittel, trans. Geoffrey W. Bromiley (Grand Rapids, MI: Eerdmans), vol. 1, p. 777.

7. Evelyn and Frank Stagg, *Woman in the World of Jesus* (Philadelphia: Westminster, 1978); Thierry Maertens, *The Advancing Dignity of Woman in the Bible,* ed. Lisa McGawl, trans. Sandra Dibbs (De Pere, WI: St. Norbert Abbey Press, 1969); Peter Ketter, *Christ and Womankind,* trans. Isabel McHugh (Westminster, MD: Newman, 1952); and an infinitude of studies in dozens of periodicals, such as M. Merode, "Une théologie primitive de la femme," *Revue Théologique de Louvain* 9 (1978):176–89, with its rich bibliography.

8. A reported saying of Jesus cited by Clement of Alexandria (*Stromata* 3, 9) runs: "I have come to destroy the woman's deeds." Its sense is not pejorative of women, however, since the meaning is simply: I have come to destroy sin. "Woman's deed" was a synonym for "sin" in light of Genesis 3.

9. See the fine reflections along these lines by Aubert, *La mujer,* pp. 26–32, 91–94.

10. See Ludwig Hick, *Die Stellung des hl. Paulus zur Frau im Rahmen seiner Zeit* (Cologne: Amerikanisch-Ungarischer Verlag, 1967); Elisabeth Schüssler Fiorenza, "Presencia de la mujer en el primitivo movimiento cristiano," *Concilium* (Spanish language edition) 111 (1976):9–24.

11. Elsie Gibson, *Femmes et ministères dans l'Eglise* (Paris: Casterman, 1971), pp. 40–46, originally published as *When the Minister Is a Woman* (New York: Holt, Rinehart & Winston, 1970); Constance F. Parvey, "The Theology and Leadership of Women in the New Testament," in *Religion and Sexism,* pp. 117–49.

12. See Hick, *Stellung des hl. Paulus;* see also E. Kaeler, *Die Stellung der Frau in der paulinischen und deuteropaulinischen Briefen* (Zurich, 1960).

13. See Leonardo Boff, *Ecclesiogenesis,* trans. Robert R. Barr (Maryknoll, NY: Orbis, 1986), pp. 76–79: "Women's Priesthood in a Perspective of Women's Liberation."

14. Kari Elisabeth Borresen, "Fundamentos antropológicos de la relación entre el hombre y la mujer en la teología clásica," *Concilium* (Spanish language edition) 111 (1976):25–40; idem, *Subordination and Equivalence: The Nature and Role of Woman in Augustine and Thomas Aquinas,* trans. Charles H. Talbot (Washington, DC: University Press of America, 1981). See Aubert, *La mujer,* pp. 99–116, on the conjugal typology or woman as man's body.

15. See Rosemary Radford Ruether, "Misogynism and Virginal Feminism in the Fathers of the Church," in *Religion and Sexism,* pp. 150–84, with abundant

bibliographical material; Borresen, *Subordination and Equivalence;* Georges H. Tavard, *Woman in Christian Tradition* (Notre Dame, IN: Notre Dame Press, 1973).

16. Aubert, *La mujer,* p. 54.

17. Gibson, *Femmes et ministères dans l'Eglise,* p. 54.

18. *Decretum Gratiani,* q. 5, causa 33.

19. Ibid. See Ida Raming, "Inferioridad de la mujer segun el derecho canonico vigente," in *Concilium* (Spanish language edition) 111 (1976):68–77; idem, "From the Freedom of the Gospel to the Petrified 'Men's Church': The Rise and Development of Male Domination in the Church," *Concilium* 134 (*Women in a Men's Church,* ed. Virgil Elizondo and Norbert Greinacher) (1980):3–13.

20. *Pseudo-Augustini Quaestiones Veteris et Novi Testamenti CXXVII,* Corpus Scriptorum Ecclesiasticorum Latinorum (Vindobonae: Temsky, 1908), vol. 50, p. 83.

21. See the periodical *SEDOC* (March 1977):827–84.

22. Thomas Aquinas, *Summa Theologiae,* I. q. 92, art. 1, ad 1.

23. Idem, *Contra Gentiles,* 3, 123.

24. See René Laurentin, "Marie et l'anthropologie chrétienne de la femme," *Nouvelle revue théologique* 89 (1967):486.

25. The bibliography is immense, and we can cite only a few titles: Laurentin, "Marie et l'anthropologie chrétienne," one of the best; Henri Rondet, "Eléments pour une théologie de la femme," *Nouvelle revue théologique* 79 (1957):915–40; Paul Evdokimov, *La mujer y la salvación del mundo* (Barcelona: Ariel, 1970), originally published as *La femme et le salut du monde* (Paris: Desclée de Brouwer, 1983); Yvonne Pellé-Douël, *Etre femme* (Paris: Seuil, 1967); Jean Vinatier, *La femme, parole de Dieu et avenir de l'homme* (Paris: Ouvrier, 1972); the entire December 1975 issue of *Theological Studies;* entire issue 106 (1972) of *Lumière et vie: Masculin et feminin.*

26. Evdokimov, *La mujer,* p. 159.

27. See Raymond E. Brown, "Roles of Woman in the Fourth Gospel," *Theological Studies* 36 (1975):688–700.

28. Saint Bernard calls Magdalene, who proclaimed the Resurrection to the apostles, an "apostle to the apostles" (*Sermones in Cantica,* 75, 8: *PL* 183:1148). Logion 114 of the Gospel of Thomas has Jesus say of Magdalene, in the language of a male-chauvinist society: "I shall make her male, for she has received the spirit of a male. Every woman who makes herself male will enter the kingdom of heaven."

29. Edward Schillebeeckx, *Mary, Mother of the Redemption,* trans. N. D. Smith (New York: Sheed & Ward, 1964), pp. 109–10; see the important work of Gertrud, Freiin von Le Fort, *The Eternal Woman,* trans. Placid Jordan (Milwaukee: Bruce, 1962), which, instead of encouraging the myth of an eternal feminine (men's fantasy), seeks to represent the reality of woman on the symbolic level and not merely on the level of conceptual rationalism, with special emphasis on the integration of humanity's religiousness in God.

30. Evdokimov, *La mujer,* p. 16.

31. *II Clementis ad 1 Cor.* 12:2, in Alfred Resche, ed., *Agrapha: äusserkanonische Schriftfragmente* (Darmstadt: Wissenschaftliche Buchgesellschaft, 1967), p. 93.

32. See Jean Guitton, *Feminine Fulfillment* (New York: Paulist, 1967), pp. 110–16; Dorothy Dohen, *The Fascinating Female* (New York: Paulist, 1960), pp. 18–31, 239–54.

33. Abel Jeannière, *Antropologia sexual* (São Paulo, 1965), p. 44. Translated by

Julie Kernan under the title *The Anthropology of Sex* (New York: Harper & Row, 1967).

34. See André Manaranche, *O Espirito e a Mulher* (São Paulo, 1976), with its rich bibliography; Gerard Philips, "Fémininité de 'la' Ruach," in "Le Saint-Esprit et Marie dans l'Eglise: Vatican II et prospective du problème," *Bulletin de la Société Française d'Etudes Mariales* 25 (1968):29–33. The Didascalia compares deaconesses to the Holy Spirit: "Honor deaconesses as the antitype of the Holy Spirit . . . ": Franz Xaver von Funk, ed., *Didascalia et Constitutiones Apostolorum* (Paderborn: In Libreria Ferdinandi Schoeningh, 1905), 1:105. The *Constitutiones Apostolicas* (dating from the end of the fourth century), VIII, 9.2 (ibid., p. 525) hand down the following Prayer for Deaconesses: "O God, who didst fill with thy Spirit Mary, Deborah, Anna, and Holda . . . turn thine eyes upon thy handmaid: give her thy Holy Spirit. . . . "

35. "Denis the Areopagite," *De Divinis Nominibus*, 2, 4 (*PG* 3:641); 1, 1 (*PG* 3:588); 1, 6 (*PG* 3:596).

36. Georges H. Tavard, "Sexist Language in Theology?" *Theological Studies* 36 (1975):700–724.

37. See E. Doyle, "God and the Feminine," *The Clergy Review* 56 (1971):866–77; J. Moffit, "Le concept de Dieu comme Mère," *Nouveaux rythmes du monde* 46 (1973/74):296–302; J. Edgar Burns, *God as Woman, Woman as God* (Paramus, NJ: Paulist, 1976); J. Arnold, "María, la maternidad divina y la mujer: Estudio de unas imágenes cambiantes," *Concilium* (Spanish language edition), 111 (1976):54–67; Pieter Aire Hendrik de Boeur, *Fatherhood and Motherhood in Israelite and Judean Piety* (Leiden: Brill, 1974); Lazar Felix Pinkus and C. Valenziano, "Il feminile, Maria e la Chiesa," *Marianum* 34 (1972):386–95, where the authors propose a schema for research; Merlin Stone, *When God Was a Woman* (New York: Harcourt Brace Jovanovich, 1978), a detailed study of the goddesses, but of merely historiographical interest; Andrew M. Greeley, *The Mary Myth: On the Femininity of God* (New York: Seabury, 1977), a disappointing book that constantly and abusively confuses the biographical first person with the epistemological.

38. See Pierre Benoit and M.-E. Boismard, *Sinopsis de los cuatro evangelios* (Bilbao: Desclée de Brouwer, 1975), 1:153. Originally published as *Synopse des Quatre Evangiles en français avec parallels des apocryphes et des Pères* (Paris: Cerf, 1972).

39. Manaranche, *O Espirito*, p. 59.

40. Clement of Alexandria, *Quis Dives Salvetur?* (*PG* 9:641–44).

41. Doyle, "God and the Feminine," p. 875.

42. Ibid., quoting Donald Nicholl, *Recent Thought* Focus (London, 1952), p. 90.

43. Anselm of Canterbury, *Oratio 10* (*PL* 158:40–41); *Oratio 65* (*PL* 158:982).

44. Julian of Norwich, *Revelations of Divine Love*, 2nd ed., ed. Roger Hudleston (London: Burns, Oates & Washbourne, 1935), p. 171; compare Kari Elisabeth Borresen, "¿Cristo nuestra Madre? Dios-Padre y Dios-Madre," *Vida Nueva* 1120 (1978):456–57.

45. Julian of Norwich, *Revelations*, p. 173.

46. Marie Louise von Franz, *Dreams and Visions of St. Nikolaus von der Flüe* (Zurich: C. G. Jung Institute, 1957), Lecture 8.

47. "Deus-Mâe," *Quaternio* (1975):87–103.

48. Victor White, "The Scandal of the Assumption," *Life of the Spirit* 5 (1950):211–12.

49. See Tavard, *Woman in Christian Tradition*, pp. 144–50, 160–63.

50. M. A. Farley, "New Patterns of Relationship: Beginnings of a Moral Revolution," *Theological Studies* 36 (1975):640.

51. D. Spada, "Dio come Madre: Un tema di teologia ecumenica," *Euntes Docete* 29 (1976):472–81.

52. As cited ibid., p. 480.

53. See Leonardo Boff, *A fé na periferia do mundo* (Petrópolis, Brazil: Vozes, 1978), "O que podemos esperar além do céu?" where we develop this argumentation in greater detail.

54. See preceding note 34, and A. Lemmonnyer, "La rôle maternel du Saint-Esprit dans notre vie surnaturelle," *Vie spirituelle* (1921):241–51; Paul Evdokimov, "Panagion et Panagia," *Bulletin de la Societé Française d'Etudes Mariales* 27 (1970):59–71, especially pp. 64–66 on the theandric motherhood as figure of the divine fatherhood. See also following note 56 for abundant material on this subject. See, further, the important work of Salvador Verges, *Imagen del Espíritu de Jesús* (Salamanca: Sígueme, 1977), pp. 289–325.

55. DS 3016.

56. Classic expressions also used in *Lumen Gentium*, 1966, chap. 8, a propos of Mary; see the analysis of each of these expressions in M. G. Bonaño, "El Espíritu Santo y María en el Vaticano II," *Ephemerides Mariologicae* 28 (1978):201–13; along the same lines, see H.-M. Manteau-Bonamy, *La Vierge Marie et le Saint-Esprit: Commentaire doctrinal et spirituel du chapitre huitième de la constitution dogmatique Lumen Gentium, Vie Spirituelle et Vie Intérieur* (Paris: Lethielleux, 1971).

57. Recent literature is most plentiful. See René Laurentin, "Esprit-Saint et la théologie mariale," *Nouvelle revue théologique* 89 (1967):26–42; *Le Saint-Esprit et Marie:* three volumes of the *Bulletin de la Societé Française d'Etudes Mariales* (1968–70) from Lethielleux (Paris), certainly the best collection of current studies; entire issue 28 of *Ephemerides Mariologicae* (1978), *El Espíritu Santo y María;* Heribert Mühlen, "Der Aufbruch einer neuen Verehrung Marias: Der Heilige Geist und Maria: Zur Struktur der charismatischen Grunderfahrung," *Catholica* 29 (1975):145–63; idem, *Una mystica persona,* 3rd ed. (Munich, 1968); J. M. Alonso, "Mariología y pneumatología," I, II, *Ephemerides Mariologicae* 21 (1971):115–25, 22 (1972):395–405.

58. For this entire subject, see Henri Rondet, *La gracia de Cristo* (Barcelona: Herder, 1966), pp. 387–418. Translated by Tad W. Guzie under the title *The Grace of Christ: A Brief History of the Theology of Grace* (Westminster, MD: Newman, 1967).

59. Matthias Joseph Scheeben, *Dogmatik,* vol. 5, par. 276, no. 1612.

60. Mühlen, *Una mystica persona.* In the last century the idea of a substantial union of the Holy Spirit with the Church, analogous to the hypostatic union, was maintained by Henry Edward Cardinal Manning, *The Temporal Mission of the Holy Ghost* (London: Appleton, 1865), p. 58. René Laurentin, in a context of an "incarnation of the Holy Spirit," considers the idea "insane": "Esprit-Saint et théologie mariale," p. 39.

61. Pseudo-Philip of Harvengt, *Moralitates in Canticum* (PL 203:564).

62. See M. Dupuy, "L'Esprit Saint et Marie dans l'Ecole française," *Bulletin de la Societé Française d'Etudes Mariales* 26 (1969):21–39, here pp. 23–24.

63. Evdokimov, *La mujer,* p. 17.

64. Ibid., p. 28.

65. Ibid., pp. 226–42, esp. 235.

66. See H.-M. Manteau-Bonamy, *La doctrine mariale du Père Kolbe: Esprit-Saint et Conception Immaculée* (Paris: Lethielleux, 1975), p. 79, translated by Richard Arnadez under the title *Immaculate Conception and the Holy Spirit: The Marian Teachings of Father Kolbe* (Kenosha, WI: Franciscan Marytown, 1977); D. Fer-

nandez, "El Espíritu Santo y María: Algunos ensayos modernos de explicación," *Ephemerides Mariologicae* 28 (1978):141–43, which lists the existing bibliography on Kolbe.

67. H.-M. Manteau-Bonamy, "Et la Vierge conçut du Saint-Esprit," *Bulletin de la Societé Française d'Etudes Mariales* 27 (1970):7–23, here p. 16; see also the older idem, *Maternité divine et Incarnation: Etude historique et doctrinale de saint Thomas à nos jours* (Paris: Vrin, 1949), esp. pp. 218–24.

68. This expression was popularized by Heribert Mühlen in his *Una mystica persona*, but its roots are patristic. For example, Saint Germanus of Constantinople asserts that the human being was rendered spiritual when the Mother of God was transformed into the dwelling of the Holy Spirit: *Sermo VIII in Dormitionem (PG* 98:350).

69. Saint Athanasius, *Contra Arianos*, 3, 34 (*PG* 26:396).

70. Council of Florence, DS 1330.

71. See Heribert Mühlen, *Person und Appropriation:* "Zum Verständnis des Axioms 'In Deo omnia sunt unum, ubi non obviat relationis oppositio,' " *Münchener Theologische Zeitschrift* 16 (1975):37–57.

72. Karl Rahner, "El Dios trino como principio y fundamento trascendente de la historia de la salvación," in *Mysterium Salutis*, ed. Johannes Feiner and Magnus Löhrer (Madrid: Cristiandad, 1972), 2/1:413 (German original: 4th ed., Einsiedeln: Benziger, 1978).

73. See René Laurentin, *Structure et théologie de Luc I–II* (Paris: Gabalda, 1957), pp. 57–76; Henri Cazelles, "L'Esprit-Saint et l'Incarnation dans le développement de la révélation biblique," *Bulletin de la Societé Française d'Etudes Mariales* 26 (1969):9–21; Marcello Bordoni, "L'evento Cristo ed il ruolo di Maria nel farsi dell'evento," in *Sviluppi teologici postconciliari e mariologia* (Rome: Marianum; Città Nuova, 1977), pp. 31–52; Xabier Pikaza, "El Espíritu Santo y María en la obra de san Lucas," *Ephemerides Mariologicae* 28 (1978):151–68, esp. pp. 162–63.

74. The Greek verb *eperchesthai*, "to come upon, to descend upon," is used in the Greek Bible to denote activity of a mysterious origin that suddenly affects human existence (see, for example, Num. 5:14–30, 2 Chron. 32:26, Bar. 4:24, 2 Chron. 20:9). Luke uses this same expression in the accounts of the Annunciation (1:35) and the coming of the Holy Spirit at the beginning of Acts (1:8). Apart from the cases cited, the word would appear to be used only in Isaiah 32:15, where the sacred writer uses concrete language to denote the transformations, of an eschatological hue, anticipated in nature on the occasion of the coming of the Spirit from on high (the desert will become an orchard, the orchard a forest, the deed of justice will be peace, and so on). Feuillet comments: "Just as sterile land becomes an orchard, so also the sterile woman who engenders offspring (Rebecca, Rachel, the mother of Samson, Anna, Elizabeth) is a frequent sign of God's intervention in the Old [sic] Testament. The virginal character of Mary's motherhood is bound up in similar fashion with the new creation of the age of grace": "L'Esprit-Saint et la Mère du Christ," *Bulletin de la Societé Française d'Etudes Mariales* 25 (1968):39–64, here p. 47; see also the observations on pp. 45–46. In order to be denominated Son of God, it is not enough that Jesus be conceived supernaturally. Any filiation involves the communication of a nature of the same kind. Accordingly, raised to the divine dimension, Mary can have a divine Son—that is, the Son of God. The coming of the Holy Spirit upon her results in a divine motherhood over and beyond the human one. As we know, the Greek Fathers used precisely this Lukan text (1:35, "The Holy

Spirit will come upon you . . .") to prove the divinity of Jesus, conceived *de Spiritu Sancto* who is God; see Maurice Jourjon and Jean-Paul Bouhot, "Lc 1,35 dans la patristique grecque," *Bulletin de la Societé Française d'Etudes Mariales* 25 (1968):65–71, esp. 65–68. The other expression is also profoundly revealing: " . . . the power of the Most High will overshadow you . . . " (*episkiasei*). The Greek term recalls the *skēnē*, the tent or tabernacle of God with human beings. Saint John uses the same word to express the incarnation of the Word (*eskēnōsen*, "he pitched his tent" among us: John 1:14). As we know, in the Old Testament the *skēnē* signified the Covenant, the dwelling, the concrete presence of God in the midst of the people (Exod. 40:34–36; see 25:8–26). In the Book of Revelation (11:19, 12:1) the tabernacle is closely bound up with woman. In the expression *eskēnōsen*, Saint John seeks to reveal the incarnation of the Word who "pitched his tent among us"; it may be that Luke, using the same figure of the *skēnē* (*episkiasei*) apropos of the Holy Spirit and Mary, is suggesting Mary's "spiritualization" by the Spirit: see René Laurentin, *Breve tratado de la teología mariana* (Petrópolis, Brazil: Vozes, 1965), pp. 36–37, esp. n. 14, originally published as *Court traité sur la Vierge Marie*, 5th ed. (Paris: Lethielleux, 1968).

75. Henri Cazelles, in *Bulletin de la Societé Française d'Etudes Mariales* 27 (1970):18.
76. Manteau-Bonamy, "Et la Vierge conçut," p. 16.
77. See Carl Gustav Jung, *Psychology and Religion: West and East*, trans. R. F. C. Hull (Princeton: Princeton University Press, 1969); see also Herbert Unterste, *Die Quaternität bei C. G. Jung* (1972), pp. 137–44, 218–20, 235–41.
78. See this ecumenical objection and the response in the framework of a classical, then a contemporary, Mariology in Laurentin, "Esprit-Saint et théologie mariale," pp. 26–31.

Chapter 6: Mary: The Historical Miriam of Nazareth

1. See Roschini, *La Madre de Dios según la fe y la teología*, 2 vols., 2nd ed. (Madrid: Apostolado de la Prensa, 1958), based on the whole patristic and apocryphal corpus, but pure fantasy in its conclusions; Jaime Falgás, *María, la mujer: Un estudio científico de su personalidad* (Madrid: Coculsa, 1966), which employs the tools of historiography and psychology to sketch a psychological, moral, and physical portrait of Mary, but whose arguments are merely deductive and sometimes reckless.
2. See René Laurentin, "Mythe et dogme dans les apocryphes," in *De Primordiis Cultus Mariani: Acta Congressus Mariologici-Mariani in Lusitania Anno 1967 Celebrati* (Rome, 1970), vol. 4, pp. 13–19.
3. See John McHugh, *The Mother of Jesus in the New Testament* (New York: Doubleday, 1975), considered the best modern study on Mary in the New Testament. McHugh's approach is moderate, but very well informed.
4. See the manuals that have already studied this question: René Laurentin, *Breve tratado de teología mariana* (Petrópolis, Brazil: Vozes, 1965), pp. 19–46, originally published as *Court traité sur la Vierge Marie*, 5th ed. (Paris: Lethielleux, 1968); Edward Schillebeeckx, *Mary, Mother of the Redemption*, trans. N. D. Smith (New York: Sheed & Ward, 1964), pp. 3–34; A. Müller, "¿Un principio mariológico fundamental?" in *Mysterium Salutis*, ed. Johannes Feiner and Magnus Löhrer (Madrid: Cristiandad, 1972), 3/2:471–502 (German original: 4th ed., Einsiedeln: Benziger, 1978).
5. See J. M. Reese, "The Historical Image of Mary in the New Testament," *Marian Studies* 28 (1977):27–43, esp. pp. 32–34.

6. See Leonardo Boff, *Jesus Christ Liberator*, trans. Patrick Hughes (Maryknoll, NY: Orbis, 1978), pp. 171–74.

7. See René Laurentin, *Structure et théologie de Luc 1–2* (Paris: Gabalda, 1957), a classic work on the subject.

8. See René Laurentin, *Jesus au temple; Mystère de Pâques et foi de Marie en Luc 2,48–50* (Paris: Gabalda, 1966).

9. See J. Michaud, *Le signe de Cana* (Montreal, 1963); Albert Vanhoye, "Interrogation johannique et exégèse de Cana (Jn 2,4)," *Biblica* 55 (1974):157–67; B. Lindars, "Two Parables in John," *New Testament Studies* 16 (1969):318–29.

10. See Laurentin, *Breve tratado*, pp. 39–40.

11. See André Feuillet, *Jesus and His Mother: According to the Lucan Infancy Narratives and According to St. John: The Role of the Virgin Mary in Salvation History and the Place of Woman in the Church*, trans. Leonard Maluf (Still River, MA: St. Bede's, 1984); S. Voight, "O discipulo amado recebe a mãe de Jesus 'eis ta ídia': Velada apologia de João em Jo 19,27?" *Revista Eclesiástica Brasileira* 35 (1975):771–823.

12. See Reese, "Historical Image of Mary," pp. 34–42.

13. See Karl Hermann Schelkle, *María, madre del Redentor* (Barcelona: Herder, 1965), pp. 70–78.

14. Schillebeeckx, *Mary, Mother of the Redemption*, p. 25.

15. See Salvatore M. Meo, "Riflessi del rinnovamento della escatologia sul mistero e la missione di Maria," in *Sviluppi teologici, postconciliari e mariologia* (Rome: Marianum; Città Nuova, 1977), pp. 103–28.

Chapter 7: The Immaculate Conception: Culmination of Humanity

1. Pius XI, *Ineffabilis Deus*, 1854.

2. Ibid.

3. See E. O'Connor, "Modern Theories of Original Sin and the Dogma of the Immaculate Conception," *Theological Studies* 20 (1969):112–36; the richest bibliography on this subject has been compiled by J. B. Carroll, "The Blessed Virgin and the 'Debitum Peccati': A Bibliographical Conspectus," *Marian Studies* 28 (1977):181–256.

4. See Karl Rahner, *María, madre del Señor* (Barcelona: Herder, 1967), pp. 60–62. Translated by W. J. O'Hara under the title *Mary, Mother of the Lord: Theological Meditations* (New York: Herder & Herder, 1963).

Chapter 8: Mary's Perpetual Virginity: Seed of a Divinized Humanity

1. The bibliography is immense. Here are a few of the more important works: E. Vallauri, "A exegese moderna diante da virginidade de Maria," *Revista Eclesiástica Brasileira* 34 (1974):375–99; K. Suso Frank, Karl Rahner et al., *Zum Thema Jungfrauenbegurt* (Stuttgart: Katholisches Bibelwerk, 1969); John A. Saliba, "The Virgin-Birth Debate in Anthropological Literature: A Critical Assessment," *Theological Studies* 36 (1975):428–54; Eamon R. Carroll, "Theology on the Virgin Mary, 1965–1975," *Theological Studies* 36 (1975):253–89; L. Scheffczyk et al., *Nato da Maria vergine* (Jaca Book, 1978); John Willoughby Layard, *The Virgin Archetype: Two Papers* (New York: Spring, 1972), pp. 254–307; P. Saintyves, *As virgens mães e os nascimentos miraculosos* (Rio de Janeiro: Livr. Imperio, n.d.); M. O'Carroll, "The Virginal Conception: Some Recent Problems," *Marianum* 37 (1975):429–64.

2. Hans Küng, *On Being a Christian*, trans. Edward Quinn (Garden City, NY: Doubleday, 1976), pp. 450–57.

3. Lucien Legrand, *La virginité dans la Bible* (Paris: Cerf, 1964), pp. 139–45.

4. Meister Eckhart, Sermon 22 in *Deutsche Werke* 1:517; see J. Pintard, "Le principe 'prius mente quam corpore . . .' dans la patristique et la théologie latine," *Bulletin de la Societé Française d'Etudes Mariales* 27 (1970):25–58.

5. DS 427.

6. DS 503.

7. Paul IV, *Cum quorumdam hominum*, 1555.

8. Karl Rahner, "Dogmatische Bemerkungen zur Jungfrauengeburt," in *Zum Thema Jungfrauengeburt*, p. 136.

9. Edward Schillebeeckx, *Mary, Mother of the Redemption*, trans. N. D. Smith (New York: Sheed & Ward, 1964), pp. 55–69.

10. Bernard of Clairvaux, *Homiliae*, 4, 8 (*PL* 183:83–84).

11. Paul IV, *Cum quorumdam hominum*, 1555.

12. Mansi, 3, 665.

13. Karl Rahner, "Virginitas in partu," in *Escritos de teologia* (Madrid, 1967), vol. 4, pp. 177–211; idem, "The Virginity of Mary," in *Theological Investigations*, vol. 19, trans. Edward Quinn (New York: Crossroad, 1983).

14. Michael Schmaus, *El Credo de la Iglesia católica* (Madrid: Rialp, 1970), vol. 2, p. 682; see also idem, *Katholische Dogmatik*, 6th ed. (Munich: Hueber, 1960–63), vol. 5, p. 143, translated by Ann Laeuchli et al. under the title *Dogma* (Westminster, MD: Christian Classics, 1984).

15. Joseph Blinzler, *Die Brüder und Schwestern Jesu* (Stuttgart: Katholisches Bibelwerk, 1967), pp. 145–46.

16. See Marie-Joseph Nicolas, "La doctrine mariale et la théologie chrétienne de la femme," in *Maria*, ed. Julien du Manoir (Paris, 1964), vol. 7, pp. 344–45; Vicenzo Caporale, "Maria e la donna d'oggi," *Rassegna di teologia* 17 (1976):19–36.

Chapter 9: Mary's Human and Divine Motherhood

1. See Edward Schillebeeckx, *Mary, Mother of the Redemption*, trans. N. D. Smith (New York: Sheed & Ward, 1964), pp. 55–69; René Laurentin, *Breve tratado de teología mariana* (Petrópolis, Brazil: Vozes, 1965), pp. 125–50, originally published as *Court traité sur la Vierge Marie*, 5th ed. (Paris: Lethielleux, 1968); A. Müller, "El acontecimiento central: María, Madre de Dios," in *Mysterium Salutis*, ed. Johannes Feiner and Magnus Löhrer (Madrid: Cristiandad, 1972), 3/2:458–70, originally published as 4th ed. (Einsiedeln: Benziger, 1978); Karl Hermann Schelkle, *María, madre del Redentor* (Barcelona: Herder, 1965), pp. 70–78; G. Baraúna, "La santísima Virgen al servicio de la economía de la salvación," in *La Iglesia del Vaticano II* (Barcelona: Flors, 1968), pp. 1165–84; René Laurentin, "Bulletin sur Marie, Mère du Seigneur," *Revue des sciences philosophiques et théologiques* 60 (1976):309–45, 451–500.

2. André Manaranche, *O Espíritu e a mulher* (São Paulo: Loyola, 1976), p. 139. Originally published as *L'Esprit et la Femme*.

3. John Damascene, *De Fide Orthodoxa*, bk. 3, chap. 12: "Non enim hominem nudum genuit Beata Virgo, sed Deum verum, non nudum, sed incarnatum."

4. See H.-M. Manteau-Bonamy, *Maternité divine et incarnation: Etude historique et doctrinale de Saint Thomas à nos jours* (Paris: Vrin, 1949); idem, *La Sainte Vierge et le Saint-Esprit* (Paris, 1971); André Feuillet, "L'Esprit Saint et la Mère du Christ," *Bulletin de la Societé Française d'Etudes Mariales* 25 (1968):39–64; M.

Bordoni, "L'evento Cristo ed il ruolo di Maria nel farsi dell'evento," in *Sviluppi teologici, postconciliari e mariologia* (Rome: Marianum; Città Nuova, 1977), pp. 31–52; L. Melotti, *Maria e la sua missione materna* (Turin, 1976); George A. Maloney, *Mary: The Womb of God* (Denville, NJ: Dimension, 1976).

5. See E. Toniolo, "La santità personale di Maria nel contesto dell'antropologia cristiana, oggi," in *Sviluppi teologici*, pp. 77–102.

Chapter 10: Mary's Resurrection and Assumption

1. See Salvatore M. Meo, "Riflessi del rinnovamento della escatologia sul mistero e la missione di Maria," in *Sviluppi teologici, postconciliari e mariologia* (Rome: Marianum; Città Nuova, 1977), pp. 103–27, with its abundant bibliography; A. Müller, "Transito y glorificación de María," in *Mysterium Salutis*, ed. Johannes Feiner and Magnus Löhrer (Madrid: Cristiandad, 1972), 3/2:503–14 (German original: 4th ed., Einsiedeln: Benziger, 1978); Leonardo Boff, *A ressurreição de Cristo: A nossa ressurreição na morte*, 5th ed. (Petrópolis, Brazil: Vozes, 1978); Karl Rahner, *María, madre del Señor* (Barcelona: Herder, 1967), pp. 113–23, translated by J. O'Hara under the title *Mary, Mother of the Lord: Theological Meditations* (New York: Herder & Herder, 1963).

2. Pius XII, 1950.

3. *Lumen Gentium*, no. 68, in *The Documents of Vatican II*, ed. Walter M. Abbott (New York: America Press, 1966).

4. Donal Flanagan, "Eschatology and the Assumption," in *Concilium* 41 (*The Problem of Eschatology*, ed. Edward Schillebeeckx and Boniface Willems) (1969):144–45.

5. See these works: J. Edgar Bruns, *God as Woman, Woman as God* (Paramus, NJ: Paulist, 1973); Robert Kress, *Whither Womankind? The Humanity of Women* (St. Meinrad, IN: Abbey, 1975); Andrew M. Greeley, *The Mary Myth: On the Femininity of God* (New York: Seabury, 1977), pp. 73–104.

Chapter 11: Mary's Universal Mediation: In Solidarity with the Human Race

1. See René Laurentin, *Le titre de corredemptrice: Etude historique* (Paris and Rome, 1951); G. Baraúna, *De Natura Coredemptionis Marianae in Theologia Hodierna (1921–1958)* (Rome, 1960); idem, "La santísima Virgen al servicio de la economía de la salvación," in *La Iglesia del Vaticano II* (Barcelona: Flors, 1968), pp. 1165–84; A. Müller, "María y la redención," in *Mysterium Salutis*, ed. Johannes Feiner and Magnus Löhrer (Madrid: Cristiandad, 1972), 3/2:515–22, see the entire 1976 issue of *Ephemerides Mariologicae*, entitled *The Meditation of Mary Once More*.

2. Paul Evdokimov, *La mujer y la salvación del mundo* (Barcelona: Ariel, 1970), pp. 159–63.

Chapter 12: Mary, Prophetic Woman of Liberation

1. See the bibliography on the Magnificat in Marie-Joseph Lagrange, *Evangile selon Saint Luc*, 4th ed. (Paris: Lecoffre, 1927), with commentary in great detail; Vincenz Hamp, "Der alttestamentliche Hintergrund des Magnificat," *BK* 2 (1952):L17–18; T. Dehau, "Magnificat," *VS* 79 (1948):5–16; Jacques Guillet, "Le Magnificat," *MD* 38 (1954):60–61; René Laurentin, *Structure et*

théologie de Luc I–II (Paris: Gabalda, 1957); J. Coppens, "La Mère du Sauveur à la lumière de la théologie vétérotestamentaire," *ETL* 31 (1955):16–17; Albert Gelin, "La vocation de Marie d'après le Nouveau Testament," *VS* 91 (1954):115–23; Arthur Gabriel Hébert, "La Vierge Marie, Fille de Sion," *VS* 85 (1951):127–39; G. T. Forestell, "Old Testament Background of the Magnificat," *Marian Studies* 12 (1961):205–44; John McHugh, *The Mother of Jesus in the New Testament* (New York, 1975), pp. 73–79; Jürgen Moltmann, *El lenguaje de la liberación* (Salamanca: Sígueme, 1974), pp. 141–51: "Alegría en la revolución de Dios"; V. Vogels, "Le Magnificat, Marie et Israel," *Eglise et Théologie* 6 (1975):279–96; Alois Grillmeier, "Maria Prophetin: Eine Studie zur patristischen Mariologie," in *Mit ihm in ihm* (Freiburg: Herder, 1975):198–218; Luise Schottroff, "Das Magnificat und die älteste Tradition über Jesus von Nazareth," *Evangelische Theologie* 38 (1978):298–313; Xabier Pikaza, "El Magnificat, canto de liberación: Dios salva a los pequeños," *Mision Abierta* 69 (1976):230–47; P. Schmidt, "Maria in der Sicht des Magnificat," *GuL* 46 (1973):417–30; Rudolf Schnackenburg, "Das Magnificat, seine Spiritualität und Theologie," *GuL* 38 (1965):342–57.

2. There are three current theories on the origin of the Magnificat. The first, the traditional theory, maintains that Mary composed it herself on the occasion of her visit to her cousin Elizabeth as we read in Luke 1:39–56. The second, more modern theory asserts that the Magnificat is a literary composition of the evangelist Luke, placed on Mary's lips to exalt her and proclaim her blessed. The third, most recent theory states that Luke reworked an earlier composition. According to this last explanation, the Magnificat was originally a Judeo-Christian hymn extolling God's liberating deed in behalf of the lowly and poor. Either the primitive community or the third evangelist himself, seeing Mary as special representative of the poor and lowly, and in admiration of the marvels that God had worked in her, simply added verse 48 ("For he has looked upon his servant in her lowliness; all ages to come shall call me blessed") and attributed the whole to Mary. Many Mariologists favor this last opinion.

3. Forestell, "Old Testament Background of the Magnificat," pp. 225–35, "The Piety of the Poor," has meticulously demonstrated that the Magnificat reflected the spirituality of the *anawim*, the poor of Yahweh. The *anawim* did not acquiesce in their poverty, Forestell explains. On the contrary, they longed for the justice that would withdraw them from their inhumane situation. In a word, they looked to their liberation. The prophets, the Psalms, and the post-Exilic literature gave strong encouragement to the conviction that the salvific action of God and the Messiah would consist particularly in the deliverance and exaltation of the poor, and of all who were treated unjustly. See also Jacques Dupont, *Les Beatitudes II* (Paris: Gabalda, 1969), pp. 19–90; A. George, "La pobreza en el Antiguo Testamento," in *La pobreza evangelica hoy*, ed. A. George et al. (Bogota: CLAR, 1971), pp. 11–26; Jacques Dupont, "Los pobres y la pobreza en los evangelios y en los Hechos," pp. 27–44 in the same collection.

4. See a more complete synopsis, with all the Old Testament passages paralleling the Magnificat, in Edward Schillebeeckx, *Mary, Mother of the Redemption*, trans. N. D. Smith (New York: Sheed & Ward, 1964), pp. 7–12.

5. The invitation to praise, joy, and grandeur ("My being proclaims the greatness of the Lord") of the first verse of the Magnificat recalls the frequently recurring Old Testament theme of the salvation of the afflicted and the restoration of Zion. But the restoration of Zion was regarded as the universal

liberation of the afflicted, humiliated remnant of Israel. The expressions "proclaim the greatness" (*megalunein*) and "find joy," or "rejoice," recall, in the Septuagint, motifs of personal and national deliverance (Pss. 9; 30:8, 33:3–4, 56:10–11, 68:30–31, 36–37; 2 Kings 7:22). Mary's Magnificat is sung against this Old Testament background of liberation.

6. Verse 48 ("For he has looked upon his servant in her lowliness") must be interpreted correctly. The reference is liberating and social, not merely spiritual and moralizing as in the usual interpretation. See E. A. Ryan, "Historical Notes on Luke 1,48," *MS* 3 (1952):228–35. The verb for "looked upon" in the Old Testament, when referred to God, denotes the divine compassion for human tribulations, whether individual (Pss. 12:4, 24:16, 68:17–18; 118; 132) or national (Exod. 14:24, Judg. 6:14, Lev. 26:9, 1 Kings 9:16). The expression "lowliness" (in Greek, *tapeinōsis*) means, in the language of the Old Testament, first and foremost the oppressed situation of the poor, their state of disgrace, affliction, and humiliation, either personal, as with Hagar (Gen. 16:11), Leah (Gen. 29:32), Jacob (Gen. 31:42), Joseph (Gen. 41:52), Hannah (1 Kings 1:11), David (2 Kings 16:12), and Esther (Esther 4:8), or national, as in Egypt (Deut. 26:7), in the time of Saul (1 Kings 9:16), upon Jeroboam's accession to the throne of Israel (2 Kings 14:26), or in Nehemiah 9:9, Judith 6:19, 16:13. The expression occurs frequenty in the Psalms, especially in the lamentations or prayers of the poor and oppressed (Pss. 9:14, 21:22, 27; 24:18, 30:6–8, 118:50, 92, 153; 135:23). This depressing situation fosters a hope of liberation, centered on the Messiah and his coming. At the same time, this materially unfavorable situation fosters an attitude of spirit (a "spiritual childhood" or "spiritual poverty"), an attitude of openness, surrender to God, trust, availability for the divine activity, and trusting abandon in the expectation of the liberating act of God. This attitude represents the necessary condition for receiving the Reign of God, and is opposed to pride, self-sufficiency, a closing up of oneself, or confidence in one's own simple strength as capable of achieving liberation. See Albert Gelin, *The Poor of Yahweh*, trans. Kathryn Sullivan (Collegeville, MN: Liturgical Press, 1964): Mary's experience is one of positive lowliness; accordingly, she adopts an attitude of humility (trusting surrender to God), availability, and openness to the reception of God's deed of liberation.

7. Max Thurian, *María, Madre del Señor, figura de la Iglesia* (Zaragoza: Hechos y Dichos, 1966), pp. 138–39. Translated by Neville B. Cryer under the title *Mary, Mother of the Lord, Figure of the Church* (London: Mobray, 1985).

8. See *SEDOC* 7 (1976):784; see also Carlos Mesters, *Maria, Mâe de Deus* (Petrópolis, Brazil: Vozes, 1977); Aleixo Maria Autran, "Mâe do Povo de Deus na América Latina," *Convergência* 11 (1978):538–47; N. Zevallos, "María en la religiosidad popular latino-americana," *CLAR* 15 (1977):1–7; Justo Asiaín, *Maria hoy? Leyendo el Evangelio* (Buenos Aires: Bonum, 1973), pp. 35–42.

Chapter 13: Myth and Its Conflicting Interpretations

1. E. Schwartz, ed., *Acta Oecumenicorum Conciliorum*, 1/1, fasc. 8, p. 104.

2. T. O'Meara, "Marian Theology and the Contemporary Problem of Myth," *Marian Studies* 15 (1964):127–56; René Laurentin, "Foi et mythe en théologie mariale," *Nouvelle revue théologique* 89 (1967):281–307; idem, "Mythe et dogme dans les apocryphes," in *De Primordiis Cultus Mariani: Acta Congressus Mariologici-Mariani in Lusitania Anno 1967 Celebrati* (Rome, 1970), vol. 4, pp. 13–29; Josef Rupert Geiselmann, "Marienmythus und Marienglaube," in

Maria im Glaube und Frommigkeit (Rottenburg, 1954), pp. 39–91; A. Marques dos Santos, "Maria," *Quaternio* (1973):49–60; Nise da Silveira, "Deus-Mâe," *Quarternio* (1975):87–103; Jean Guitton, "Mythe et mystère de Marie," in *De Primordiis Cultus Mariani* (1970):1–12 (the entire issue of 494 pages is devoted to the subject); Jaime Falgás, *María, la Mujer: Un estudio científico de su personalidad* (Madrid: Editorial y Libreria Co. Cul., S.A., 1966); Herbert Unterste, "Der Archetypus des Weiblichen in der christlichen Kultur," in his *Die Quarternität bei C. G. Jung* (Dortmund?: Author, 1972); A. Weiser, "Mythos im Neuen Testament unter Berücksichtigung der Mariologie," in *Mythos und Glaube*, ed. Hermann Josef Brosch and Heinrich M. Köster (Essen: Dreiwer, 1972); Michael Schmaus, "Die dogmatische Wertung des Verhältnisses von Mythos und Mariologie," in *Mythos und Glaube;* Merlin Stone, *When God Was a Woman* (New York: Dial, 1976). Our appraisal of the myth is based particularly on the works of René Laurentin.

3. Mircea Eliade, *Imágenes y símbolos*, 2nd ed. (Madrid: Taurus, 1974), pp. 11, 25. Translated by Philip Mairet under the title *Images and Symbols: Studies in Religious Symbolism* (New York: Sheed & Ward, 1969).

4. Laurentin, "Foi et mythe," pp. 283–85.

5. Michel Foucault, *The Order of Things: An Archaeology of the Human Sciences* (New York: Vintage, 1973).

6. Claude Lévi-Strauss, *Tristes tropiques.*

7. Rudolf Bultmann, *Kerygma und Mythos*, 1:22. English translation: *Kerygma and Myth: A Theological Debate* (New York: Harper & Row, 1966).

8. Claude Lévi-Strauss, *Le cru et le cuit* (Paris, 1964), p. 246. Translated by John and Doreen Weightman under the title *The Raw and the Cooked* (Harmondsworth, PA: Penguin, 1986).

9. Laurentin, "Foi et mythe," p. 287.

10. Gilbert Durand, *Les structures anthropologiques de l'imaginaire: Introduction à l'archétypologie générale* (Paris: Presses Université de France, 1963), p. 31, cited by Laurentin, "Foi et mythe," p. 287.

Chapter 14: Mary in the Language of Myth

1. Later published as the *Summa Aurea* (Tours: J. Bourassé, 1862).

2. See Mircea Eliade, *Patterns in Comparative Religion* (London: Sheed & Ward, 1979), chap. 7: "The Earth, Woman and Fertility."

3. See G. Cardaropoli, "Il culto della B. Vergine in relazione al culto delle dee pagane," in *De Primordiis Cultus Mariani: Acta Congressus Mariologici-Mariani in Lusitania Anno 1967 Celebrati* (Rome, 1970), 4:99–106.

4. *Panagion*, 78, 23, (*PG* 42:736B).

5. Rudolf Bultmann, *Kerygma und Mythos*, 1:21 (English translation: *Kerygma and Myth: A Theological Debate* New York: Harper & Row, 1966); idem, *The History of the Synoptic Tradition*, trans. John Marsh (New York: Harper & Row, 1963), pp. 253–54, 306–7, 346–47, 370–74; idem, *Theology of the New Testament*, trans. Kendrick Grobel (London: SCMP, 1952), pp. 42–53, 164–83.

6. Bultmann, *Kerygma und Mythos*, 1:21.

7. Bultmann, *Theology of the New Testament*, pp. 164–83.

8. Bultmann, *Kerygma und Mythos*, 1:21.

9. See Johann Jakob Bachofen, *Das Mutterrecht: Eine Untersuchung über die Gynaikokratie der alten Welt nach ihrer religiösen und rechtlichen Natur*, 2nd ed. (1897; reprint, Brussels: Culture et Civilisation, 1969) (selections from Bachofen translated by Ralph Mannheim under the title *Myth, Religion, and Mother*

Right: Selected Writings of J. J. Bachofen, Princeton, NJ: Princeton University Press, 1973); Erich Fromm, "Die Bedeutung der Mutterrecht für die Gegenwart," in *Analytische Sozialpsychologie und Gesellschaftstheorie* (Frankfurt: Sührkamp, 1970); Adolf Ellegard Jensen, "Gab es eine mutterrechtliche Kultur?" *Studium Generale* 3 (1950):418–33; Luigi Vannicelli, "La donna nella luce dell'etnologia," in *Problema sociale femminile* (Milan, 1945), pp. 23–58; idem, "Matriarcato," in *Enciclopedia Cattolica*, vol. 8 (Vatican City: Encic. Cat., 1952), pp. 402–7; J. Haeckel, "Mutterrecht," in *Lexicon für Theologie und Kirche* 8:712–14; Mathilde and Matthias Vaerting, *The Dominant Sex: A Study in the Sociology of Sex*, trans. Eden and Cedar Paul (1923; reprint, Westport, CT: Hyperion, 1980). Against the matriarchate: See, for example, F. Heritier, "La femme dans les systèmes de répresentations," in *Le Fait Féminin*, ed. Evelyne Sullerot (Paris: Fayard, 1978), pp. 398–401; Merlin Stone, *When God Was a Woman* (New York: Dial, 1976) is the most complete treatment of the subject, although it develops no heroic perspective.

10. See Haeckel, "Mutterrecht," p. 712.
11. Margaret Mead, *Sex and Temperament in Three Primitive Societies* (New York: Morrow Quill, 1980); see also Vaerting, *The Dominant Sex*.
12. Sonia Mary Cole, *The Neolithic Revolution* (London: British Museum, 1970).
13. Cited by Vannicelli, "Matriarcato," p. 404.
14. Erich Fromm, *Der moderne Mensch und seine Zukunft: Eine Sozialpsychologische Untersuchung* (Frankfurt: Europäische Verlagsanstalt, 1967), p. 43.
15. Neumann, *Die grosse Mutter* (Zürich, 1956). Translated by Ralph Mannheim under the title *The Great Mother: An Analysis of the Archetype* (New York: Pantheon, 1955).
16. Janine Chasseguet-Smirgel, *A sexualidade feminina: Novas perspectivas psicanalíticas* (Petrópolis, Brazil: Vozes, 1975), pp. 11–23: "As opiniões de Freud sobre a sexualidade feminina." Originally published as *La sexualité féminine: Recherches psychanalytiques nouvelles* (Paris: Payot, 1970).
17. Charles Rycroft, *A Critical Dictionary of Psychoanalysis* (Totowa, NJ: Littlefield, Adams, 1973), p. 105.
18. Sigmund Freud, *Totem y Tabú*, in vol. 2 of his collected works. Translated by A. A. Brill under the title *Totem and Taboo: Resemblances Between the Psychic Lives of Savages and Neurotics* (New York: Random House, 1918).
19. Carl Gustav Jung, *Symbole der Wandlung: Analyse des Vorspiels zu einer Schizophrenie*, ed. Lilly Jung-Merker and Elisabeth Ruf, in *Gesammelte Werke* (Olten: Walter, 1985), vol. 5, p. 348. Works of Jung in English: *The Collected Works* (Princeton: Princeton University Press, 1979).
20. For a serious introduction to this problem see Jolande Székács Jacobi, *Die Psychologie von C. G. Jung* (Zurich: Rascher, 1949), pp. 89ff, translated by V. Baillods under the title *The Psychology of C. G. Jung* (London: Routledge & Kegan Paul, 1962); N. da Silveira, "Deus-Mãe," *Quaternio* (1975):87–103, esp. 96–98; Gustav Hans Graber, *Tiefenpsychologie der Frau: Entwicklung vom Mädchen zur Frau und Mutter* (Munich: Goldmann, 1966), pp. 9–17.
21. On this subject see Herbert Unterste, "Das verdrängte Weibliche," in his *Die Quaternität bei C. G. Jung* (1972), pp. 104–8; D. Ferreira da Silva, "Teoria general do feminino," *Cavalo Azul* 3:75–83.
22. Neumann, *Die grosse Mutter*, pp. 19–37.
23. See Erich Neumann, *Ursprungsgeschichte des Bewusstseins* (Munich: Rascher, 1949), pp. 18–160. Translated by R. F. C. Hull under the title *The Origins and History of Consciousness* (Princeton: Princeton University Press, 1970).
24. See Neumann, *Die grosse Mutter*, pp. 147–48.

25. Neumann, *Die grosse Mutter*, p. 51.
26. For this aspect see E. Harding, *Les mystères de la femme: Interprétations psychologiques de l'âme de la femme d'après les mythes, les légendes et les rêves* (Paris, 1976), pp. 180–204; A. Marques dos Santos, "Maria," *Quaternio* (1973):49–60, esp. pp. 57–58; Merlin Stone, *When God Was a Woman* (New York: Harcourt Brace Jovanovich, 1978), pp. 30–62, 163–80; Andrew M. Greeley, *The Mary Myth: On the Femininity of God* (New York: Seabury, 1977), pp. 49–105.
27. See the abundant documentation in Neumann, *Die grosse Mutter*, pp. 229–65.
28. Jung, *Gesammelte Werke*, vol. 11, p. 499; vol. 16, pp. 185–86; Unterste, "Das Bild der vergeistigten Frau in Christentum," in his *Die Quaternität bei C. G. Jung*, pp. 132–37.
29. See Jung, *Gesammelte Werke*, vol. 11, pp. 176, 491.
30. Ibid., vol. 11, p. 150.
31. Ibid., vol. 11, p. 164.
32. See ibid., vol. 11, pp. 498–99.

Chapter 15: The Marian Dogmas: Their Existential and Symbolic Content

1. See G. Vannucci, "I simboli religiosi della femminilità," *Servitium* 11 (1977):335–65, with its rich bibliography; John Willoughby Layard, *The Virgin Archetype: Two Papers* (New York: Spring, 1972), pp. 254–307; Andrew M. Greeley, *The Mary Myth: On the Femininity of God* (New York: Seabury, 1977), pp. 105–223.
2. Paul VI, *Marialis Cultus*, 1974, no. 57, citing *Lumen Gentium*, no. 55.
3. Paul VI, *Marialis Cultus*, 1974, no. 36.

Conclusion: The Radical Feminine

1. See Carl Gustav Jung, *Der archaische Mensch*, in *Gesammelte Werke* (Olten: Walter, 1985), vol. 10, p. 90.
2. Gertrud, Freiin von Le Fort, *La mujer eterna* (Madrid: Rialp, 1965). Translated by Placid Jordan under the title *The Eternal Woman* (Milwaukee: Bruce, 1962).
3. Von Le Fort, *La mujer eterna*, p. 10; see p. 158.
4. See Gabriel Marcel, *Homo Viator* (Paris: Aubier, 1944), p. 32. Translated by Emma Crawford under the title *Homo Viator: Introduction to a Metaphysic of Hope* (Gloucester, MA: Peter Smith, 1978).
5. Jean Guitton, "Mythe et mystère de Marie," in *De Primordiis Cultus Mariani: Acta Congressus Mariologici-Mariani in Lusitania Anno 1967 Celebrati* (Rome, 1970), vol. 4, pp. 1–11; here, p. 9.
6. Jaime Falgás, *María, la Mujer: Un estudio científico de su personalidad* (Madrid: Editorial y Librería Co. Cul., S.A., 1966), p. 226.
7. Pierre Teilhard de Chardin, letter of September 2, 1916. See idem, "The Eternal Feminine," in *Writings in Time of War*, trans. René Hague (New York: Harper & Row, 1968), pp. 191–202, where we read the following (pp. 197–99):

   My charm can still draw men, but towards the light. I can still carry them with me, but into freedom.
       Henceforth my name is Virginity.

The Virgin is still woman and mother: in that we may read the sign of the new age.

... The man who hearkens to Christ's summons is not called upon to exile love from his heart. On the contrary, it is his duty to remain essentially a man.

... Christ has left me all my jewels.

In addition, however, he has sent down upon me from heaven a ray that has boundlessly idealized me.

... I am the unfading beauty of the times to come—the ideal Feminine.

The more, then, I become Feminine, the more immaterial and celestial will my countenance be.